Wellington's Headquarters

Wellington's Headquarters

The Command and Administration of the British Army during the Peninsular War

S.G.P. Ward

Foreword by
Rory Muir

Pen & Sword
MILITARY

First published in Great Britain in 1957 by
Oxford University Press
under the title *Wellington's Headquarters:*
A Study of the Administrative Problems in the Peninsula 1809–1814

This edition published in 2017 by
Pen & Sword Military
an imprint of
Pen & Sword Books Ltd
47 Church Street
Barnsley
South Yorkshire
S70 2AS

ISBN 978 1 47389 682 6

A CIP catalogue record for this book is available from the British
Library

Printed and bound in the UK by CPI Group (UK) Ltd,
Croydon, CR0 4YY

Pen & Sword Books Ltd incorporates the imprints of Pen & Sword
Archaeology, Atlas, Aviation, Battleground, Discovery, Family
History, History, Maritime, Military, Naval, Politics, Railways, Select,
Transport, True Crime, Fiction, Frontline Books, Leo Cooper,
Praetorian Press, Seaforth Publishing and Wharncliffe.

For a complete list of Pen & Sword titles please contact
PEN & SWORD BOOKS LIMITED
47 Church Street, Barnsley, South Yorkshire, S70 2AS, England
E-mail: enquiries@pen-and-sword.co.uk
Website: www.pen-and-sword.co.uk

Contents

List of Figures

Foreword

On a hot summer's day at the beginning of August 1808 an open boat threaded its way through the Atlantic breakers to land at Mondego Bay on the coast of Portugal. On board, getting drenched by the spray and at risk of a ducking, was Major-General Sir Arthur Wellesley, the thirty-nine year old commander of a small British army which had been sent to Portugal to assist a popular uprising against French occupation. Less than six years later Wellesley's army, by then battle hardened and flushed with victory, was advancing through southern France on its way to capturing both Bordeaux and Toulouse. The following summer the Duke of Wellington, as Wellesley had become, won his final victory at Waterloo, bringing to a resounding close the generation of war that had engulfed almost every corner of Europe since the early days of the French Revolution.

Wellington dominated the war in the Peninsula. He did not go home between his return to Portugal in April 1809 and the end of the war five years later, and he spent almost all this time with the troops in the front line. He made a few visits to Lisbon and Cadiz to negotiate with the allied governments, but only when the army was in winter quarters and was unlikely to be involved in any fighting. He was never forced by illness or wounds to relinquish the command, even for a short period, and his authority within the army was never challenged. It was Wellington who took the decisions that shaped British strategy in the Peninsula, and the responsibility for its success or failure fell squarely on his shoulders – never more so than in the long months between the autumn of 1809 and the autumn of 1810 when he persevered in his plans for the defence of Portugal despite the doubts of even the ablest and most trusted of his subordinates.

Nonetheless Wellington did not act alone. He depended on his staff for much of the information he needed in making his plans. Was this side road fit for artillery and wagons? Could that river be forded? Was the spring grass sufficiently advanced to provide forage for the cavalry? Had the French withdrawn their garrison from an outlying position? Were they concentrating troops for an offensive against him, or to assist in operations in other parts of Spain? Big questions, but also little ones: the details that could so easily disrupt grand sweeping plans, as the march of troops was delayed by a bottleneck or brought to a complete halt by a non-existent ford. And when Wellington made his plans, it was the staff who turned them into detailed movement orders that ensured that the different divisions of the army each proceeded along the right road in the right order, and camped in a suitable spot with plenty of water and as much shelter and food as was available. It was the commissariat who collected supplies: some gathered locally, some brought up from the rear, especially when the army was stationary for months in poor country and the local supplies were exhausted. Officers of the Quartermaster-General's department rode far and wide, sketching the country and particularly observing the state of the roads and bridges, and assessing how many troops could be quartered in the towns and villages they passed through. Some were detached far in advance of the army, reconnoitering French positions, liaising with the Spanish patriots, and collecting intelligence of enemy movements and plans. Other staff officers were responsible for the routine administration of the army, dull paperwork at which hot-blooded men of action such as Sir Charles Stewart and Edward Pakenham chafed, but which was essential if the discipline of the army was to be maintained, and if it was to continue to perform efficiently amidst the disruption and difficulties of active service. And it was Wellington's Military Secretary, his ADCs, and sometimes other members of the staff, who made fair copies of his voluminous correspondence, copying page after page in bold, clear writing, while sitting in an ice-cold draughty room in a modest house in the uplands of northern Portugal through the long months of several successive winters.

Early accounts of the war neglected the role of the staff, while even the great histories by Sir Charles Oman and Sir John Fortescue, written a hundred years after the event, took much for granted. This gap was recognized and in time filled by S. G. P. Ward who, in 1944, was a General Staff Officer in the British Army, dealing with problems that bore more than a passing similarity to those faced by Sir George Murray, Wellington's admirably efficient Quartermaster-General. Ward made an intensive study of Murray's unpublished papers and those of the Commissary-General,

Robert Kennedy, and extended his research into the papers in the Public Record Office, other official papers, and the very considerable body of published material relating to the Peninsular War. A dozen years passed before he completed and published his study *Wellington's Headquarters*, and the result is a concentrated distillation of great learning and scholarship, with more original information in its pages than in most works double or even triple its length. This was no quick survey of the subject that skated over the difficult questions, but rather a careful explanation by a scholar who had probed every nook and cranny, and who had taken immense pains to track down as much information as could be found about even the most obscure officers who served on Wellington's staff. At the same time Ward never let the detail obscure the wider picture, and once the necessarily dry material of the first chapter was established, he wrote with wit and colour, bringing little known figures from the past to life with well deployed vignettes and anecdotes.

Later research has confirmed his mastery of the subject, while occasionally supplementing some aspect of the picture he painted. His own later articles in the *Journal of the Society for Army Historical Research* especially 'The Peninsular Commissary', published forty years after *Wellington's Headquarters*, add much further material of great value. Other writers have extended our knowledge of the exploring officers of the Quartermaster-General's department, while the discovery of large collections of letters from two of Wellington's ADCs, Alexander Gordon and John Fremantle, has shed a good deal of new light on Wellington's innermost circle. But the framework Ward established remains intact, and his work provides the essential guide to understanding how Wellington's army was fed for months on end in cantonments in northern Portugal, how it found its way through the mountains of Tras os Montes in the crucial first stage of its extraordinary advance to Vitoria, and how Wellington's orders were turned into effective action.

I never met S. G. P. Ward, but we had an extensive and immensely enjoyable correspondence in the late 1990s and early 2000s when I was working on my early books. He was full of encouragement and immensely generous with his knowledge, and wryly funny in his comments on some of the events of the day. Later he gave several collections of manuscripts, his valuable library of published books relating to the Peninsular War, and his extensive, meticulously organized, notes to the Hartley Library of the University of Southampton, so that they would be available for scholars working on the Wellington Papers, which the library also holds. Many of his books came from Sir Charles Oman's collection which was sold by the bookseller Francis Edwards in the 1940s, so that at Southampton there is, for example, the copy of Andrew Leith Hay's *Narrative of the Peninsular War* (1831) that was used by both Oman and Ward.

Stephen George Peregrine Ward (he was always known by his second Christian name) was born in London in 1917 the son of Stephen Burman Ward and Marion Inez Fox. His mother was a novelist and poet whose father was an influential soldier and advocate of physical training, Malcolm Fox. (Ward later wrote the entry for his grandfather for the *Oxford Dictionary of National Biography*.) Ward saw action firsthand in the Second World War, where he served in the Western Desert and was severely wounded in 1941. He then served as a General Staff Officer, leaving the army in 1946 having been mentioned in despatches. The interest in Wellington's campaigns, inspired then, lasted the rest of his life. He married Hilary Tatam in 1958 and in 1962 they had a daughter Parthenope. Ward's sister Marion worked at the Historical Manuscripts Commission and wrote two biographies on eighteenth century French themes *The Du Barry Inheritance* and *Forth*. And he himself wrote an excellent short life of Wellington published by Batsford in 1963, a history of the Durham Light Infantry, more than a dozen articles on British military history especially the Revolutionary and Napoleonic Wars published in the *Journal of the Society for Army Historical Research*, three entries in the *Oxford Dictionary of National Biography* and edited the letters of Captain R. B. Hawley from the Crimea. He was described to me as 'a really nice man, immensely learned, and completely unassuming.' He died on 24 January 2009.

Rory Muir

The Works of S. G. P. Ward

Wellington's Headquarters. A Study of the Administrative Problems in the Peninsula, 1809–1814 (London, Oxford University Press, 1957)

Wellington (London, B. T. Batsford, 1963)

Faithful. The Story of the Durham Light Infantry (Edinburgh, Nelson for the Regiment, [1963])

The Hawley Letters. The Letters of Captain R. B. Hawley, 89th, from the Crimea, December 1854 to August 1856 edited by S. G. P. Ward (Society for Army Historical Research Special Publication No. 10 1970).

'The Quartermaster-General's Department in the Peninsula, 1809–1814' *J.S.A.H.R.* vol 23 1945 pp 133–154

'Mentions in Despatches' *J.S.A.H.R.* vol 25 1947 p 44

'Defence Works in Britain, 1803–1805' *J.S.A.H.R.* vol 27 1949 pp 18–37

'Some Fresh Light on the Corunna Campaign' *J.S.A.H.R.* vol 28 1950 pp 107–126

'Milgapey, May, 1809 A Peninsular War Puzzle in Geography' *J.S.A.H.R.* vol 30 1952 pp 148–155

'General Sir Willoughby Gordon' *J.S.A.H.R.* vol 31 1953 pp 58–63

'Brenier's Escape from Almeida, 1811' *J.S.A.H.R.* vol 35 1957 pp 23–35

'British Officers in the American Civil War' *J.S.A.H.R.* vol 39 1961 p 53

'Die englische Kriegskunst zur Zeit Napoleons unter besonderer Berücksichtigung Wellingtons' [English Warfare at the time of Napoleon with special reference to Wellington] in *Napoleon I und das Militärwesen seiner Zeit* edited by W. Von Groote and K. J. Müller (Freiburg, 1968)

'The Letters of Private John Bald, 91st Regiment' edited by S. G. P. Ward *J.S.A.H.R.* vol 50 1972 pp 101–106

'The Letters of Captain Nicholas Delacherois, 9th Regiment' edited by S. G. P. Ward *J.S.A.H.R.* vol 51 1973 pp 5–14

'The Scots Guards in Egypt, 1882: the Letters of Lieutenant C. B. Balfour' edited by S. G. P. Ward *J.S.A.H.R.* vol 51 1973 pp 80–104

'The Diary of Lieutenant Robert Woollcombe, R.A. 1812–1813' edited by S. G. P. Ward *J.S.A.H.R.* vol 52 1974 pp 161–180

'Majuba, 1881. The Diary of Colonel W. D. Bond, 58th Regiment' edited by S. G. P. Ward *J.S.A.H.R.* vol 53 1975 pp 87–97

'The Portuguese Infantry Brigades, 1809–1814' *J.S.A.H.R.* vol 53 1975 pp 103–12

'The Letters of Lieutenant Edmund Goodbehere, 18th Madras N.I., 1803–1809' edited by S. G. P. Ward *J.S.A.H.R.* vol 57 1979 pp 3–19

'General Sir George Murray' *J.S.A.H.R.* vol 58 1980 pp 191–208

'"Major Monsoon"' *J.S.A.H.R.* vol 59 1981 pp 65–70

'General the Hon. Sir Alexander Hope' *J.S.A.H.R.* vol 62 1984 pp 1–12

'Obituary. Dr Charles Cruickshank' *J.S.A.H.R.* vol 67 1989 p 105

'Mr Eastlake's Visit to Spain in 1813' edited by S. G. P. Ward *J.S.A.H.R.* vol 70 1992 pp 71–86

'The Author of the "Accurate and Impartial Narrative"' *J.S.A.H.R.* vol 70 1992 pp 211–223

'The Peninsular Commissary' *J.S.A.H.R.* vol 75 1997 pp 230–39

Entries in the *Oxford Dictionary of National Biography* on Sir George Murray, Sir William Howe De Lancey and Sir (George) Malcolm Fox.

Acknowledgements

I am very glad to have this chance to thank all those who have made the reprinting of my father's book possible, sixty years since it was first published, and it is hoped the reprint will interest readers, both new and familiar.

First of all, I am very grateful to Pen & Sword, who initiated the reprint, for the planning and preparation of the book. I am particularly indebted to Rupert Harding, for his unfailing guidance, encouragement and dedication in all stages of the production.

In addition, I would like to express my thanks to Oxford University Press, who first published the book, for their valuable assistance.

I would also like to thank those who have kindly provided the illustrations: the National Portrait Gallery and the National Army Museum and Philip Haythornthwaite, who has been very generous in supplying illustrations from his collection.

To Dr Rory Muir this book owes a special debt of gratitude, following his suggestion which led to its reprinting. Since then, he has been exceptionally generous in his advice and enthusiasm and in writing the foreword and the author's list of works. My father enjoyed and valued greatly the correspondence he had with Rory; he would have admired so much his definitive and superb new biography of the Duke of Wellington, and would also have been deeply honoured by his foreword. My mother and I likewise feel very honoured by Rory's involvement, and profoundly grateful.

Parthenope Ward

Preface

The following study of the organization of Wellington's Headquarters and the administration of the Peninsular Army is based upon the papers of General Sir George Murray, the Quartermaster-General, to which I was introduced in 1944, at a time when, as a General Staff Officer, I was immersed in problems very similar to, though less august and imposing than, those which formed Murray's principal daily occupation. It was possible to expand the scope of the study when the papers of the Commissary-General, Kennedy, came into my hands a year or two ago. These two sets of correspondence have tended perhaps to throw the emphasis too heavily upon the two departments, but since they were the most active and important and little attention has been paid to them up to now, there can be no harm in stressing, even unduly, what is novel and significant. In the spelling of Spanish and Portuguese place-names it is mistaken to be pedantic, as even now it is permissible to spell them in more than one way. My rule of thumb has been to use the form now current in the country (a method which leads to consistency and accuracy) unless there is already a well-recognized English variant. This method condemns unfortunately many proud and resounding names that are borne on our regimental colours, such as Vimiera, Busaco, Fuentes d'Onor, Orthes, and others; but they are hardly so well known as Blenheim, and there seems no just reason for perpetuating such mere clerical errors as Roleia and Foz d'Aronce, particularly when there is every reason for spelling correctly adjacent village names that have no such claim to immortality. I have received the greatest assistance from three generations of Librarians of the National Library of Scotland, Dr. H. W. Meikle, C.B.E., D.Litt., Mr. M. R. Dobie, C.B.E., and Mr. W. Beattie, M.A.; and Mr. W. Park, M.A., Keeper of Manuscripts, and my other good friends on the staff there; from Sir James Fergusson of Kilkerran, Bart., Keeper of the Records, and Mr. C. T. McInnes, Curator of Historical Records at the Scottish Record Office; from the staff of the Public Record Office; of the London Library; from the Secretary, the Librarian, and Mr. Holland, of the Royal United Service Institution;

from Mr. A. S. White, I.S.O., Librarian of the War Office Library; from Mr. Webb of the Codrington Library, All Souls College, Oxford; Miss W. D. Coates, Registrar of the National Register of Archives; and the Trustees of the Linlithgow Trust. I have also to thank Lieutenant-Colonel A. H. Burne, D.S.O., for permission to quote from his work. I have received from my family and many friends (who shall be nameless) great encouragement. But I cannot, whatever he may say, fail to mention that given me by Mr. C. T. Atkinson. The most self-confident researcher, the most inveterate corrector of faults in other authors, can only have some misgivings when he submits the corpus of his knowledge to the scrutiny of the public; and he can only be gratified and reassured when he receives help and encouragement from the acknowledged authority on his subject. I wish also to thank Miss D. R. Searle, who has now struggled manfully with my handwriting for many years and has succeeded in deciphering it on this occasion as well.

S. G. P. W.
January 1956

I

THE ADMINISTRATION OF THE ARMY
IN PEACE AND WAR

THERE seems to be nowadays a more general just appreciation of Wellington's extraordinary gifts. But there used to be a reluctance to believe that they all could belong to a single person, and various claims were put forward in favour of others who were said to have advised and suggested and whose credit for this advice and these suggestions have consequently become merged in his own. A great deal of this credit has been given to various members of his Staff and to others who visited him casually and out of the course of duty. This was a comfortable explanation of his success, as it implied that a second-rate commander had only to be surrounded by first-class Staff Officers for the most resounding victories to be won. It was a line of thought that during the last century was particularly favoured on the continent, where Chiefs of Staff were given both an authority and an independence which their commanders were not.

It is certainly not an explanation that will account for Wellington's success. No one who served in the Peninsula during those years ever doubted who commanded and decided there, or who dominated at Headquarters. A newly joined general might in his rashness hazard a suggestion over the dinner table, but he would quickly discover that his commander had no need of advice and looked to him only to obey his orders. At other generals' Headquarters proposals and counter-proposals might be tolerated and even encouraged, but the Headquarters of the British Army in the Peninsula belonged to one man. It was not merely the Headquarters of an Army abroad; it was Wellington's Headquarters.

The individuality which Wellington impressed upon his administration does not become apparent until the ordinary administration of the army at that period is examined in some detail. Some of the peculiarities of the former are no doubt due to the circumstances of the theatre of war. Some were imposed upon him by the government at home, some were devised by him, others were habits that grew out of the common intercourse between Wellington and his staff officers. But he inherited the staff and the administrative apparatus with which any other general would have been sent abroad, and it is important to carry an idea of what this consisted in, or Wellington's personal contribution towards it will be lost. No one would suggest it was ideal, even with the improvements effected with time and ingenuity, or that it would serve as a pattern for the future. But it was the administration that, laying the foundation for Wellington's victories, drove the French armies out of Spain, and ultimately defeated Napoleon; and it is worth study on that ground alone.

In understanding the complicated manner in which military affairs in this country were managed at the end of the eighteenth century it will help the modern critic if he remembers two considerations. The first is the deep-seated prejudice against the army throughout society. It is a jealousy which has, perhaps, persisted to our own day and evaporates only at moments of intense emotion. But at the period of which we are speaking there were other reasons besides latent prejudice. The pay in the army was low, particularly by the end of the century, and the man who enlisted was usually one who could make his livelihood in no other way. There being few barracks, the soldiers were usually billeted in the midst of the public, which had before it the spectacle of the redcoats as they staggered back and forth from one pothouse to another. They were sons no mother could be proud of. Yet in the absence of a police force these men, drawn up in ranks, personified authority; and authority in whatever form it may come is never welcome. Moreover, until late in the century a considerable proportion of the officers came from families of little consideration, or, like Ensign Northerton in Fielding's *Tom Jones*, were young men who had deliberately avoided their schooling. It followed that the army lacked that backing from the propertied classes that it would have had if these classes had contributed the flower of their manhood more largely to its ranks.

But there was more in this jealousy than social prejudice. There was a constitutional jealousy which, dating from the Civil War, Pride's Purge and the Major-Generals of the Protectorate, was inextricably confused with the struggle between Parliament and the Crown. Whether as an instrument of the Crown, of a Protector, or as an independent body, the army was feared, and for 200 years after these events the efforts of Parliament were directed at ensuring that the army in peacetime had no power. This constitutional antipathy was as strong during the Napoleonic wars as it ever was throughout the eighteenth century. It was less than one year after Waterloo that objections were raised against the foundation of the United Service Club on the ground that 'such a vast extension of military association in this free country, coupled with other signs of the times, wears an unconstitutional aspect, and cannot fail to attract the attention of Parliament'.[1]

A contemporary would have been aware of the foregoing consideration; but of the second, the weakness of the central government, he would have no conception. It is only now, when the funds at the command of Parliament and the number and variety of enterprises in which the central government concerns itself have become almost boundless, that we can see on what a limited scale and with what a limited revenue the government of the eighteenth century operated. Even in 1830 the national expenditure was but £50-million, of which the Debt absorbed £29-million, defence £15-million, leaving £6-million only for collection, for the Crown and the whole civil administration.[2] The government concerned itself with little more than the guarding of rights and the restriction of abuses. Enterprises outside this range were

[1] Lord St. Vincent to Lynedoch, Rochetts, 25 Jan. 1816 (Alex. M. Delavoye, *Life of Thomas Graham, Lord Lynedoch* (London, 1880), p. 752). 'A general military club with the Commander-in-Chief at the head of it is a most ill-advised measure, and so far from its being serviceable to the army it will inevitably create a prejudice against that branch of our military establishment, and we shall feel the effects of it even in Parliament. . . .' Lord Liverpool to Huskisson, cit. in Maj.-Gen. Sir Louis C. Jackson, *History of the United Service Club* (published by the Committee, London, 1937).
[2] G. M. Young, *Victorian England* (Oxford, 1934), ii. 446.

undertaken by private individuals who, having risked their resources in the service of the Crown, could look to the profit which their own endeavours brought in. This explains the curious position of the regiments of the army, which, though progressively losing their character of proprietary forces, nevertheless in 1795 still retained some of the characteristics of an investment by private individuals in a concern of the state of which the state could not afford the outlay or the risks. It accounts also for the complicated machinery of controls and checks, which alone were the outward and visible signs of administration by a central authority. The individual could be looked to to do all in his power to improve his property, and while his endeavours corresponded with the public interest the government did not interfere and itself subsisted on his energies; beyond that point the government intervened and trimmed the individual's interests to its own.

Together, these two considerations, the deeply rooted antipathy to an army and the government's lack of resources, explain almost all of the peculiarities and some of what to us may appear absurdities in the military administration on the outbreak of war with France in 1793. They are the ultimate explanation of the reluctance to keep an army prepared for war; of the unpreparedness when war comes; the eagerness to reduce the army to the barest necessities when the war is over; of the existence of the multitude of small offices and boards scattered over London which anyone who takes up an almanack of the day will be astonished to find constituted the government of the military force of this country.

By the end of the eighteenth century the conditions under which the army existed, after having been subjected for over a hundred years to pressure from Parliament, were broadly as follows. The Crown held both the army's command and allegiance; this had been conceded after the Restoration in preference to the evil of an army commanded by Parliament. But pay and supply were placed in the hands of the Treasury, and the maintenance of the army was only on sufferance, being renewable from year to year by the Mutiny Acts. For the size of the army the Secretary of State, a minister responsible to Parliament, answered, and parts of it could be moved and billeted only with the sanction of a responsible minister, usually the Secretary-at-War. 'The Commander-in-Chief', said Wellington, giving evidence before a Commission, 'cannot at this moment move a corporal's guard from London to Windsor without going to the civil department for authority.'[1] The administration of the army, apart from its internal arrangements, was thus deliberately denied to military officers and kept firmly in the hands of the civil power. The reasons are illustrated by the following statement by Fox:

I have as high an opinion of the integrity, the honour and principles of the officers of the British army as any man, but I will not pay them the compliment at the expense of the Constitution. I will not sacrifice to them that jealousy which it is the duty of the House of Commons to entertain of every set of men so immediately connected with the Crown. To the Crown they must look for promotion; by the Crown they may be dismissed from their profession without any cause assigned; and to the Crown they must be attached in different degrees from men on whom similar motives do not operate. This attachment arises from the situation in which they are placed; it applies to them collectively as a body, and is no disparagement to them as individuals. ... Such being the situation of all military officers, they are fit and necessary objects of the jealousy and vigilance of the House of Commons....[2]

All the parliamentary struggles over the army had led to this end: that in peace the control and administration of the army should be in civil hands, while military officers confined themselves to purely professional matters.

The diagram overleaf shows the most important of the various offices and boards which constituted the military administration at the beginning of the last century. As with all other state activities it was the Treasury which played the dominant part. It released the money on which the army subsisted in normal circumstances, the 'Ordinaries' which Parliament had voted to it according to the approved Establishments, and in wartime it disbursed the 'Extraordinary' sums which enabled the army to meet the unusual circumstances of war. The Ordinaries, being for the most

[1] Evidence on the civil administration of the army, 1837, cit. in Clode, *The Military Forces of the Crown* (London, 1869), i. 219 (cit. hereafter as 'Clode').
[2] 30. *Parl. Hist.*, p. 488, cit. in *Clode*, ii. 271.

part pay and allowances, were handed over to the Paymaster-General, a political office held jointly by two persons, who for a fee distributed the sums between the various regiments. The Extraordinaries on the other hand remained in the hands of a Treasury official, the Commissary-in-Chief, whose subordinates kept the field with the army and made the payments as they were called for.

In peace, the most important executive office was that of the Secretary-at-War. Nothing can illustrate better the peculiar hazards to which a military appointment was exposed than his history during that century. He had started as the Secretary to the King in his capacity as Commander-in-Chief of the army, a private individual with no political affiliation. Subjected to the various parliamentary pressures of the kind described earlier, he emerged at the end of the century a political man responsible to Parliament. At a subsequent period he acquired Cabinet status. He was the chief administrator of the army, so far as any one man was allowed this jealously guarded situation. He approved the Establishments (the authorized strengths of the various regiments), which were the instrument by which the civil power measured and checked the expense and extent of the military power at the disposal of the Crown. He approved rates of pay and allowances for various contingencies, and he answered in all questions in which the interests of the public and the army were opposed. His functions are often described as being mainly financial. This would underestimate the importance of his office. He was the hub of the military government. The smaller subordinate departments were at his command, and even in war it was usually impossible for the military departments to get these sub-departments to act unless the Secretary-at-War had given the word. Though he took no part in the Peninsular War it is essential to appreciate the vital position of his office, the War Office, in the hierarchy.

He carried on a continuous rivalry with another Department of State which has hitherto remained unmentioned, the Board of Ordnance. The head of the Board, the Master-General, was a distinguished soldier holding a seat in Parliament and occasionally a place in the Cabinet, but the Board itself was civil. It had existed long before the standing army

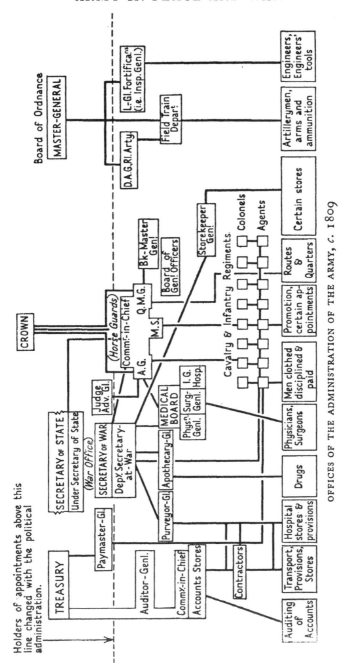

OFFICES OF THE ADMINISTRATION OF THE ARMY, c. 1809

and it still retained traces of its medieval foundation. It was the custodian of the public treasure in lands and stores and it was responsible for supplying both the army and the navy with warlike munitions and equipments. Though the intricacies of the organization of this ancient institution do not, fortunately, concern us, in passing it may be said they were so complex that in the reforming age of the mid-nineteenth century it was found easier to abolish the Board despite its many good qualities than to reform it. But the Ordnance as a storekeeper and in other capacities played an important part in all wars, and there are these points to be observed. It was an expending department maintained by a separate vote from Parliament, and it had the power of making disbursements not previously sanctioned by Parliament in the case of unforeseen emergencies. Moreover, it paid, maintained, and organized a separate force of its own, consisting of the artillery, the body of officers known as the Royal Engineers, and the Royal Military Artificers, who were officered by the Engineers. Together, these were known as the two Ordnance corps. The word 'army' did not include them. Being maintained by a separate vote they were reckoned separately from the infantry and cavalry both as to numbers and cost. The army and the Ordnance corps were as far apart as the three services are from each other today. The army was clothed by the colonels of the regiments by private contract: the Ordnance clothed its men by large-scale contracts. The army gave no instruction to its officers at all: the Ordnance educated its own. Commissions in the army were for the most part open for purchase: promotion in the Artillery and Engineers was by seniority. The ranks were different: the pay was different. The Ordnance had its own commissaries, its own stores, its own physicians, its own surgeons. In fact, the only points the red-coated and the blue-coated forces had in common (though much of the correspondence between them would appear to belie this statement) were that they both owed allegiance to the King and both, at the time we are speaking of, were engaged in the war against France.

Under the supervision of the Master-General but at the head of the military branch of the Ordnance were the two heads of the respective corps, the Deputy-Adjutant-General of the Royal Artillery (a major-general), and the Inspector-General of Fortifications (a general or lieutenant-general). The latter acted as adviser on the construction of permanent fortifications but he was also the principal Engineer officer acting in an executive capacity. Owing, probably, to the common bond of their education the senior officers of these two corps exercised an almost paternal watch over the younger members of their craft. They knew each other and corresponded with each other. General Macleod, who was D.A.G. Royal Artillery during the Peninsular War, kept up an unofficial correspondence with several officers serving in the field, in particular with Colonel Alexander Dickson, on all kinds of subjects, guns, carriages, limbers, even on Dickson's superior officers. Other correspondence shows that this family sentiment was shared by the juniors and passed on to succeeding generations. Scarcely existing outside the Ordnance corps, it emphasizes what they were: exclusive technical societies. Just as they admitted no profane officers to their secrets, so the army admitted none of them—not that they asked—to commands or staff appointments. Gunners and Engineers rarely held and did not compete with infantrymen and cavalrymen for such situations until several years after the Crimean War.

The Master-General suffered no interference with his two corps from the Secretary-at-War or any other civil department administering the army, and in peace he answered only to Parliament. However, even in peace he must have recognized the supreme authority of the Secretary of State as to the employment of his force; and in war, as a supplier of military stores and men (although, as will appear later, neither his stores nor his men were at the unlimited disposal of a commander in the field), there should have been no doubt of his subordination to the Secretary of State also.

The Secretaryship of State, which has been since 1540 and still is a single office but held by more than one man, had been held throughout the eighteenth century by two secretaries, except for the period 1762–82 when a third had been introduced to conduct colonial business. In 1794 a third secretary was again appointed to be in charge of 'certain

military business', and he in his turn in 1801 was given the
care of all colonial business besides; largely because the military operations of this period were mainly conducted outside
Europe. He had already, as has been previously mentioned,
had a general responsibility for the size of the armed force.
He was responsible too for the appointment of officers to
command. In peace the powers of the Secretary of State for
War and Colonies, as he became after 1801, were not much
felt in the daily administration of the army. In war, however,
they were the powers that actuated the whole military effort
of the nation in every theatre of war.

We turn now to the Horse Guards, which was, strictly
speaking, the office of the King in his capacity of Commander-
in-Chief of the army. Since the reorganization that took
place in James II's reign and the immediately succeeding
years, the King had two assistants, the Adjutant-General and
the Quartermaster-General, who took over between them
the functions of the numerous staff officers who had surrounded a commander in previous generations, the Scoutmaster-General, the High Harbinger, and others.[1] The new
appointments were in accord with recent developments in
all European armies and were by no means an English
invention. Most armies had or claimed to have an adjutant-
general and a quartermaster-general, and staff officers of all
armies would have readily understood their duties if, as they
often did, they took service under another sovereign. Louis
XIV, 'quelquefois trop fastueux', as an acute observer many
years later remarked,[2] had divided his staff not into two but
four, having a *major-général*, equivalent to an adjutant-
general, each for the infantry and cavalry, and a *maréchal-
des-logis*, or quartermaster-general, one for the whole army
except the dragoons and one for the dragoons. But the
principle was the same in all armies, and it persisted without
much change until the wars of the French Revolution.

---

[1] To be strictly accurate there was a Scoutmaster-General on the establishment
until after the institution of the Quartermaster-General (Col. Clifford Walton,
History of the British Standing Army, 1680–1700 (London, 1894), pp. 622–4, cit.
hereafter as 'Walton').

[2] Gen. P. H. de Grimoard, *Traité sur le Service de l'État-Major Général des
Armées* . . . , p. 6. (This treatise was published in Paris in 1809 but much of it was
written in 1778.) Cit. hereafter as 'Grimoard'.

By far the more important of these two staff officers at this time was the Adjutant-General. Since his main duty was to ensure that the commander's orders were carried out, even those which had been issued through the quarter-master-general, he so flourished on this overriding authority that the latter was reduced to less than the barest exercise of his functions, which were the arrangement of camps and quarters and of marches. Even in active war the Adjutant-General played the leading part. That he usurped the duties properly belonging to his colleague may be seen in the testimony of Lieut.-Col. Charles Hotham, Adjutant-General to the British contingent in the Minden campaign, who deposed[1] that the Adjutant-General of the Army gave out the Duke of Brunswick's movement orders in German to the majors of brigade and aides-de-camp, and in French to himself as Adjutant-General of the British contingent, and that he passed them on in English to the British majors of brigade and aides-de-camp. As late as 1801 the adjutant-general in the British service was transmitting the commander's operation orders. In this respect it seems as though British practice was merely conforming to practice on the continent where the *Adjutantur* had come to usurp many of the duties of the *Quartiermeisterstab*.[2] But if the adjutant-general could do all this in war it can only be imagined what his position was in peace, when the quartermaster-general had no camps to lay out and no armies to march.

The Adjutant-General was responsible for issuing all orders and for making up returns and states and rosters of duty. His principal care as an officer on the King's staff was the maintenance of discipline and the ensuring that offenders were punished. In a general fashion he was also responsible for the drill of the regiments, but as half the regiments were scattered singly over the globe, it cannot be said that this general responsibility amounted to anything very effective. He was responsible for seeing the infantry and cavalry were armed, but the arms themselves were supplied by the

---

[1] *Proceedings of a General Court Martial ... upon the trial of Lord George Sackville* (1760), p. 165 (cit. hereafter as 'Sackville's Trial').

[2] See, for instance, Walter Görlitz, *Der Deutsche Generalstab : Geschichte und Gestalt* (Frankfort, 1953), pp. 13–14, 17.

Ordnance Board. He had besides a duty in ensuring that the army was properly clothed. But again, since each colonel provided the clothing for his regiment by contract (subject to the satisfaction of the Board of General Officers) against an allowance made to him for the purpose from the Paymaster-General, and had it packed and forwarded to the regiment by his packers, the Adjutant-General's concern was little more than supervisory. In practice, the greater part of the administration was conducted by the Secretary-at-War in correspondence with the regimental colonel's secretary, that is to say, his agent, and scarcely touched the Adjutant-General at all.

The Quartermaster-General had, as we have seen, surrendered much of his proper functions in active warfare, and inasmuch as none of them could be practised to any great extent in peace for an army which was distributed over the pothouses of the Kingdom, his life at the Horse Guards was untroubled with many cares.[1] In 1792, before the war broke out and at a time when the whole of the cavalry and infantry numbered no more than 42,668 men, his office appears to have comprised three officers: the Q.M.G. himself, his Deputy, and an Assistant Q.M.G., an elderly lieutenant-colonel of the name of Paterson. Their duties were almost entirely confined to the supply of routes for the march of detachments from one station to another. The order for such a move

was made out in the quartermaster-general's office in the form of a Memorandum accompanied with the particular routes and days of march which such regiments (or its divisions) were to take. In this Memorandum were also comprehended the several notices to be given as follows: to the general of the District . . .; to the Barrack Office, if the troops were moved into or out of barracks; to the Commissary-General in all cases. The Memorandum so made out was sent to the War Office, and not only the orders and routes, but all the above notices were dispatched by that Department.

If a regiment were to be sent abroad to relieve in the colonies,

[1] The appointment of Quartermaster-General in Ireland appears to have been open to purchase in the 1760's. Whether or not it ever had been in England, such a procedure was thought objectionable in 1769. Maj.-Gen. Harvey, the A.G., to Lieut.-Col. Burton, 16 Nov. 1769 (W.O. 3/2, pp. 33–34).

it would be designated by the Adjutant-General, and the Quartermaster-General would supply the route to the port and notify the Military Secretary that he might apply for transport from the Admiralty, but the War Office would similarly issue the routes.[1] That the civil department should interfere in such matters is not so strange as it might seem. If, as often happened, the troops misbehaved in their quarters, to whom should the chief magistrate of the town appeal for redress? Not to a military office beyond the control of Parliament, but to the Secretary-at-War, a responsible minister, who was the proper authority therefore for issuing the orders.[2] Nevertheless, this procedure deprived the Q.M.G. of almost the last of his functions that he could exercise in peace.[3] As the Q.M.G. of ten years later testified, 'all those duties which naturally belong to the Quartermaster-General were transacted by other departments'.[4] Like the Adjutant-General's, his business was done for him.

Besides the great departments of state and the military office at the Horse Guards there were a number of smaller civil offices which concerned themselves with other branches of the administration of the army. The medical business was conducted by three such offices. The Apothecary-General, who had been appointed in the reign of George II by Royal Warrant as the 'perpetual furnisher, with remainder to his heirs, of all the medicines necessary for the general service of the land forces of Great Britain', exercised a monopoly in the supply of drugs, surgical materials, and surgical instruments.[5] The Purveyor-General supplied hospital clothing and bedding, wines, articles of comfort for the sick, hospital tents and marquees. The Medical Board, as constituted in

[1] *Commission of Military Inquiry, 11th Report*, appx. no. 11, pp. 73–75 (cit. hereafter as '11th Report').

[2] See, for instance, correspondence in W.O. 4/188, p. 39: Secretary-at-War to the Clerk to the Magistrates, Romford, War Office, 17 Nov. 1802; and pp. 279–80, Charles Yorke to the Mayor of Stafford, War Office, 10 Jan. 1803.

[3] Lieut.-Col. Paterson used his leisure to compile the useful *New and Accurate Description of all the Direct and Principal Cross-Roads in Great Britain*, to which his name is given and which went through many editions between its first publication in 1771 and 1828.

[4] *11th Report*, loc. cit. *sup.*

[5] *The Autobiography and Services of Sir James McGrigor, Bart.* (London, 1861), pp. xvii–xviii, 266 (cit. hereafter as 'McGrigor').

1798, was composed of three members: the Physician-General, the Surgeon-General, and the Inspector of Hospitals, who, being subject to the jealousies that subsisted between the College of Surgeons and the College of Physicians, each exercised an exclusive and independent patronage over one branch of nominations and promotions.[1] The Physician-General nominated all the physicians of his department and inspected the medicines furnished by the Apothecary-General, whose accounts he controlled jointly with the Surgeon-General. He also examined all candidates for the Medical Department and the military hospitals. The Surgeon-General had the appointment of all surgeons to his department, and the discretion of attaching all surgeons that were disposable to the hospitals and military stations. The Inspector of Hospitals was given the appointment and promotion of the apothecaries, purveyors, and their deputies and assistants, and he was responsible for the transport of medical supplies to the army and the hospitals. The responsibilities of these three members were not, however, very satisfactorily distributed, since, though the Surgeon-General answered for the efficiency of the physicians, the inspectors, apothecaries, and purveyors in the army, because he possessed the disposal of them in the different stations, he was denied all right to promote them. And similarly, the Inspector of Hospitals selected the medical officers for the hospitals under his charge from among men who were nominated and promoted on other recommendations than his own.

We are hardly concerned with the Barrackmaster-General's Department, a new department set up by the Secretary-at-War shortly after the beginning of the Revolutionary War to build barracks and the hutted camps such as Weeley, Silverhill, Brabourne Lees which figure so frequently in military reminiscences. It had no jurisdiction outside Britain and plays no part in the Peninsula.

The Storekeeper-General's Department, however, deserves mention. It originated in the firm of Trotter, which, having had experience during the American War and anticipating the needs of the army on the outbreak of war with France, had bought wisely and was in a position to supply a

[1] *McGrigor*, pp. xviii–xxi.

great variety of articles, especially articles of camp equipment, at a low price. These were normally furnished by the regiments themselves and the cost charged to the Extraordinaries; but Messrs. Trotter's prices were so favourable that from 1794 they practically supplied all the regiments and even provided tentage for the Ordnance corps.[1] In the same year they were requested to open a depot at Portsmouth, to which during the following years there were added successive depots throughout the country, so that by 1807 there were no less than 109 in existence, containing not only articles of Trotter's own manufacture but barrack stores, medical equipment, saddlery, and, in fact, anything that might have to be distributed suddenly in an emergency. The expansion of their business was due as much to Trotter's enterprising activity as to the ponderous arrangements of the storekeeping department of the Ordnance and the Secretary-at-War's jealousy of the Board, which induced him to encourage the establishment of rival depots under his own control. In 1808, although Trotter's account ran into millions, the Secretary-at-War had no definite agreement with him; and without any aspersion upon Trotter's integrity objections were raised to the faulty principle of combining the duties of provider and storekeeper in the hands of one private individual. Accordingly a new department was created by Royal Warrant, the Storekeeper-General's, and Trotter's nephew appointed to the new post. Thenceforth, the Storekeeper-General had charge of the safekeeping and issue of all stores for the army apart from munitions and regimental clothing. Since, however, he sent no representatives abroad the stores forwarded to foreign stations were placed in the hands of the Commissariat. Throughout the Peninsular War the demands of the Quartermaster-General for camp equipment (which was generally but inaccurately known to the army as Quartermaster-General's Stores) were made upon the Commissary-General. But the Storekeeper-General made

---

[1] Trotter introduced the bell-tent to replace the inferior ridge-pole tents formerly used. See the anonymous *Accurate and impartial Narrative of the War* (London, 1795), i. 81, under date Menin, 19 Aug. 1793:

> 'But 'tis easier by far to compose and invent
> By an English fireside than in Trotter's bell-tent.'

an appearance in Flanders in 1815 and he maintained depots in France throughout the Occupation until 1818.[1]

The final chapter of the history of his department is ironical. Created by the Secretary-at-War to avoid the slow processes of Ordnance machinery, it was transferred first to the Commissary-in-Chief acting under the Treasury and later, in 1822, to none other than the Board of Ordnance.

That this peace administration of the army, with the sub-ordination of the military to the civil, the tensions between Secretary-at-War and Ordnance, the checks, the controls, and the exclusion of the military staff from the management of its own affairs, should have any relation with Wellington's strictly controlled staff in the Peninsula comes as something of a surprise. Yet it is not that the business of these depart-ments was altered in time of war: only that another emphasis was laid on each department. In war, the Secretary of State exercised the directing influence. He spoke for the Cabinet in military affairs and became the ultimate arbiter both as to the employment of the Army and the Ordnance Corps and to the manner in which it should be equipped, supplied, and maintained. Moreover, to improve the connexion with the military departments, a second Under-Secretary, a military officer, was added to the already existing political Under-Secretary in 1809. To some extent therefore all departments, civil and military, became supplying departments in respect of what they could offer to the Secretary of State.

However, circumstances peculiar to the war which broke out in 1803 combined to lend an importance to the military office which it had not had in previous wars.

The first was the presence of a Commander-in-Chief. There had been a commander-in-chief acting under various titles during the previous century, and indeed Amherst was acting in this capacity at the beginning of the Revolutionary War in 1793. But the Duke of York, who was appointed to this position in 1795, was the King's favourite son and a very capable administrator, and carried an influence such as no commander-in-chief had had since the King commanded the

---

[1] *Clode*, ii. 212–13; Maj.-Gen. A. Forbes, *A History of the Army Ordnance Services* (London, 1929), i. 177–81; *Murray Papers*, 123, fos. 67–69 *et al.*

army in person. With the assistance of a strong staff at the Horse Guards he had reduced the chaos he inherited from Amherst and laid the foundation of a uniform system throughout the enormous new army. The Horse Guards was no longer the quiet residence of the Adjutant- and Quartermaster-General. The original building dates back to the reign of Charles II but as an institution it starts in 1795. It contained now a third office, that of the Military or Public Secretary, who acted for the Commander-in-Chief in all classes of business not already in the competence of the Adjutant- and Quartermaster-General, in particular the vast patronage in the appointment and promotion of officers.[1] These three men under the leadership of their commander were out to assert themselves, extend the boundaries of their duties at the expense of the civil departments, and repair the encroachments of the previous decades.

Secondly, the fact that the war in 1803 started not with a campaign on the continent but with an immediate threat of invasion by a powerful and very formidable enemy gave to all military measures an urgency which brought the Horse Guards into an unwonted prominence. The raising and organization of the new levies, the preparation of the militia, the volunteers and the yeomanry, the stationing of all these troops fell squarely upon the shoulders of the Commander-in-Chief and his staff. The theatre of war was no longer the concern of a commander abroad whom each department might plague with correspondence, but the concern of those very departments themselves. The Secretary-at-War had never been required to exercise any military judgement and could not. The Secretary of State, who previously had no professional body to consult, could now look to the Horse Guards for advice in such matters. He looked also to the Ordnance Board for advice in matters of fortification; but in the years 1803–5 he looked vainly to the Master-General, Lord Chatham, an able man but an idle one at the head of an unenterprising department, which had, admittedly, few

---

[1] The extent of the Military Secretary's business may be appreciated from the Memoranda drawn up by a subsequent holder of the post, Col. Willoughby Gordon, which are printed in *Clode*, appx. cxl, ii. 732–8. The Duke also had a private secretary.

officers to spare to undertake new commitments. Thus the brunt of the arrangements for meeting the invasion was borne by the Duke of York, and it must be admitted that he and his staff were fully prepared for it and relished the opportunity.

Much of the new work was delegated. The recruiting was in the hands of the Inspecting Field Officers of the twenty-six Recruiting Districts of Britain and Ireland, under the supervision of the Inspector-General of the Recruiting Service. The command of the troops was delegated to the commanders of the Military Districts, the number of which had been raised in England to eleven. These were officers of varying merit: from Dundas and Craig in the South-East and East, where the danger was most imminent, to 'Silly Billy', afterwards the Duke of Gloucester, the King's nephew, who commanded the North-West, where the blow was least likely to fall. But the policy and the manner in which each commander occupied his District was firmly controlled from the Horse Guards. The Quartermaster-General had made his appreciation of the enemy's intentions, and that remained the basis of subsequent preparations.[1]

As a result the military departments enjoyed a status to which they had never before attained. The Adjutant-General's Department became greatly enlarged. In 1799 the responsibility of raising troops had been taken over by the Crown and placed under the superintendence of an Inspector-General of the Recruiting Service, whose office was in Great George Street. In 1807 the appointment of Inspector-General was abolished and his office was placed under the immediate control of the Adjutant-General. Moreover, under the new Adjutant-General, Sir Harry Calvert, who was appointed in 1799, the Departments strenuously enforced the regulations of the service. 'Quietly and unostentatiously', Calvert's biographer writes,[2] 'but with the utmost steadiness and perseverance he cast a searching eye into all the details of the service, probed the latent sources of mischief, destroyed by anticipation the germs of nascent

---

[1] For this and the performance of the Board of Ordnance at the time I must refer to my article on 'Defence Works in Britain', in *Journal of the Society for Army Historical Research*, xxvii (1949), 18–37 (cit. hereafter as 'J.S.A.H.R.').

[2] Obituary in *Colburn's United Service Magazine* (1829, Part I), pp. 27–28 (cit. hereafter as 'Colburn').

disorder and tightened with a firm but temperate hand the reins of discipline which had been so greatly relaxed.' Calvert's system was not new: the novelty lay in the 'uniformity of regulations established in and extended to "every description of the military force of the empire [i.e. Great Britain] as applicable to clothing and arming the troops, to their field exercise and discipline and to the interior economy of the several corps"'.[1] The increased business that resulted from his reforms brought with it a sensible increase in the establishment of the Department; and whereas in 1792 it apparently consisted of no more than himself and his Deputy, in 1808 there were, besides an Assistant-A.G., two Assistants in the Recruiting Branch and fourteen clerks.

The Quartermaster-General's Department at the same time grew out of all recognition. The experiences of the late disastrous campaign in Flanders and Holland had impressed on the more thoughtful officers the need for a trained staff, and while the Adjutant-General's business could be conducted by any good officer who had done duty as an adjutant in a regiment it was plain that a quartermaster-general could not be extemporized without a previous education. The old days were over when an army moved in a leisurely fashion across Flanders, camping here one week and a league or two away the next,[2] with each regiment in its correct order of precedence, every tent at a stated interval apart according to the approved rules of the science of 'castrametation'. A new and more hurried style of warfare was coming in.[3]

[1] Maj. Charles James, *The Regimental Companion* . . . (London, 1811), iii. 109-11.
[2] In the manner described in the anonymous *Relation des Campagnes, 1745, 1746, 1747*; and in J. de Beaurain, *Histoire militaire de Flandres* (Paris, 1755), *pass.*
[3] A favourite story of Napoleon was of the old officer who had served under Marshal Saxe and who maintained: 'Voilà qui étaient vraiment des prodiges de guerre. . . . Alors la guerre était sans doute un art. . . . De notre temps nous la faisions en toute décence, nous avions nos mulets, nous étions suivis de nos cantines, nous avions notre tente, nous faisions bonne chère, nous avions même la comédie au quartier-général; les armées s'approchaient, on prenait de belles positions, on donnait une bataille, quelquefois on faisait une siège, et puis on prenait ses quartiers d'hiver pour recommencer au printemps. Voilà ce qui s'appelle . . . faire la guerre. Mais aujourd'hui, une armée toute entière disparaît devant une autre dans une seule bataille et une monarchie est renversée; on parcourt cent lieues de pays en dix jours; dort qui peut, mange qui en trouve. Ma foi, si vous appelez cela du génie, moi je suis forcé alors d'avouer que je n'y entends plus rien. . . .' Las Cases, *Mémorial de Sainte-Hélène*, v. 323-4 (Wednesday, 20 Aug. 1816).

The army, as opposed to the Ordnance, gave its officers no military education. The eighteenth century was in any case not an age in which abstract qualifications counted for much, and appointments to the head of the department were handed out by commanders either to officers who showed an aptitude, as Sir John Mordaunt did to young Wolfe in 1757, or to relations whom they wished to bring on. Once appointed these officers picked up the rudiments of their new duties as they best could. Lord Adam Gordon, Commander-in-Chief North Britain, made his aide-de-camp, Captain Sir James Cockburn, Bart., his Deputy Q.M.G., for whom he requested the rank of major and permission to go to Town to 'inform himself of such parts of his duty as he may wish to know from General Morrison and the Office'.[1]

During the latter part of the Seven Years War a fairly competent Q.M.G.'s Department had grown up, and two of those who composed it, Roy and Dundas, lived long enough to influence it in the Revolutionary War. But it had been reduced at the Peace, and so little had the experience of the campaigns in Germany and even of those in America been absorbed that the Duke of York, on taking command of the British contingent in 1793, appointed an Engineer officer, Colonel Moncrieff, to take charge of the Department.[2] Moncrieff was killed at Dunkirk a few months after the campaign had begun; and there was no military science in his successor, General Henry Fox, brother of Charles James, who seems to have left the duties of the department to his Deputy or his secretary to carry out while he commanded detachments in enterprises quite unconnected with his staff appointment. Fox, however, received valuable technical assistance from the officers of other services who joined it: Major Sontag and Captain Offeney from the Hanoverian service, Major Lindenthal from the Austrian, and Lieutenant van Zulikom, who were brought in to instil into the department that knowledge of staff work which continental armies were reputed to give to their officers. But they were not enough, nor did even

[1] Lord Adam Gordon to the Commander-in-Chief, Mar. 1795 (W.O. 1/617, p. 315). Gen. Morrison (1730–99) was Quartermaster-General of the Forces, 1762–96.

[2] One of the very few examples of an Ordnance officer holding a command or a staff appointment at this date.

the continental armies pay sufficient attention to work which was essential then and which in the Peninsula became commonplace. Scharnhorst, who afterwards reorganized the Prussian General-Quartiermeister-Stab and was at this time serving as an artillery captain in the Hanoverian contingent, thought little of the Hanoverian staff, which, he said, consisted in peacetime only of a quartermaster-general to whom in war a few engineer officers were attached as assistants. 'Posterity', he wrote subsequently, 'will hardly believe that we campaigned in the neighbourhood of Mouscron, Menin, Werwicq and Courtrai without possessing a plan of the country, and that we fought over it without making any reconnaissance, although a couple of engineers could have made a sketch in five or six days. . . . We can almost say that the Duke of York and General Wallmoden possessed no General Staff.'[1]

On the shortcomings of the staff of the British Army in the Flanders campaigns, which were even more apparent, views similar to Scharnhorst's were being entertained in this country by British officers. Among them was Colonel Charles Craufurd (brother of the better-known Robert Craufurd of the Light Division). He had spent part of the war on the Duke of York's personal staff and part attached to the headquarters of an Austrian army, whose staff officers had a very high reputation. 'As we stand at present', he wrote, either in December 1795 or January 1796, 'when an [English] Army goes upon service we are so destitute of officers qualified to form the Quartermaster-General's Department and an efficient corps of aides-de-camp, and our officers in general have so little knowledge of the most essential parts of their profession that we are obliged to have recourse to foreigners for assistance or our operations are constantly liable to failure in their execution. . . . That we might have as good a Quartermaster-General's Department and as good a staff in every respect as other nations I am quite convinced.'[2]

[1] Max Lehmann, *Scharnhorst* (Leipzig, 1886–7), i. 240–1, quoting Scharnhorst's 'Von dem Dienst der Offiziere des Generalquartiermeister-Stabes', his 'Über die Einrichtung des Generalstabes einer Armee', and his 'Notwendigkeit eines Generalquartiermeister-Stabes für die hannoverschen Truppen in Friedenszeiten', written between 1797 and 1800.
[2] Undated letter Craufurd to Le Marchant, cit. in Sir Denis Le Marchant,

For a model Craufurd and those who thought like him very naturally turned to the enemy who had defeated them. It was plain to them that in spite of the havoc wrought in the French army by the Revolution there was nevertheless sufficient cohesion in the higher branches of its military administration to enable the French to form competent staffs for their armies. 'The vulgar idea of their having been often conducted by men of no knowledge or experience in the profession', Craufurd wrote,[1] 'is perfectly erroneous. Go back to the commencement of the war and you will find a most able military committee established, whose first care was to select from the Engineers, Artillery and Staff of the old army (few of those emigrated) numbers of excellent officers, men of very extensive science and great abilities, of whom they composed the Quartermaster-General's Departments, corps of aides-de-camp and other staff officers for all their armies.'

In this respect Craufurd was strictly speaking misinformed. The whole staff of the French army had been remodelled and placed under one head in 1790,[2] and there was no Quartermaster-General's Department nor any one branch of the staff that exactly corresponded with it. In his appreciation of the influence of the committee he mentions it is difficult to say whether he was right or wrong. Count Langeron, a French officer who took service with the Russians early in the Revolution, speaks of a *comité dirigeant*, composed of artillery and engineer officers who added to their knowledge of the theatre of war all the information that was to be gained from the memoranda drawn up by the officers of Louis XIV and Louis XV. 'This committee being responsible for nothing,' he says, 'directed the operations of the generals, thrown up or cast down according to the pleasure of the anarchists: while the generals, so long as they followed the plans of the committee, could always carry on an intelligent plan of campaign even if the composition of their army did not allow of its being brilliant.'[3] The existence of such a committee, annexed to the Committee of Public Safety, and consisting of

Memoirs of the late Major-General Le Marchant (London, 1841), pp. 83–85, hereafter as 'Le Marchant'.

[1] Ibid., loc. cit.   [2] *Grimoard*, pp. 143, 156.

[3] Comte de Langeron, *Mémoires sur les Guerres de la Première Coalition* (1792–4), ed. Léonce Pingaud (Paris, 1895), p. 41.

fifteen officers of the old army, is sufficiently attested.[1] But the importance of this *état-major occulte*, its power to interfere and the extent to which it was consulted by the Revolutionary Government, is not so certain. Bouchotte, as Minister of War, does not seem to have made much use of it;[2] while Carnot, on the other hand, availing himself of its plans assumed their authorship for himself. What the French did have, however, and had maintained for several generations, were the Ingénieurs-Géographes, a branch of the engineers entrusted with the task of sketching the country and drawing up memoranda upon military operations that could take place both in the frontier provinces and in the states immediately adjoining.[3] These memoranda were deposited in the Dépôt de la Guerre at Versailles, where they were stored for reference and brought up to date from time to time.[4] The Dépôt was untouched by the Revolution, and there is little doubt that it was to this great storehouse of knowledge to which Langeron was referring. Though the Ingénieurs-Géographes were suppressed at the Revolution they appear to have been reconstituted shortly after. It is said that the standing instructions for officers of this department, drawn up by Vauban a hundred years previously, remained unchanged even after 1793. The continuity of the tradition is revealed in the careers of Berthier and Bacler d'Albe, the closest associates of Napoleon in his campaigns: the former (like his father) an Ingénieur-Géographe and aide-maréchal-des-logis under the old régime, the latter an Ingénieur-

---

[1] Gen. Herlaut, *Le Colonel Bouchotte, ministre de la guerre en l'An II* (Paris, 1946), i. 275 n., ii. 372.

[2] One instance is quoted in Herlaut, ii. 239, on 9 June 1793, when Custine's plan of campaign was compared with the Committee's and found to agree with it.

[3] They were first organized by Vauban as *géographes* or *topographes militaires*. In 1696 they were renamed *ingénieurs des camps et armées*; in 1726 *ingénieurs-géographes des camps et armées*, and in 1777 *ingénieurs-géographes militaires*. They were reduced in Aug. 1791 but appear to have been reconstituted in 1793 (*Grimoard*, cap. 3, art. 1, sec. iii).

[4] Curiously enough, a copy of parts of these memoranda came into Murray's hands after the war, having been sent to him by William Hamilton from the Foreign Office. It is headed 'Extrait des différens mémoires que le gouvernement françois puisoit dans les Dépôts de la Guerre pour remettre aux Généraux qui commandoient sur le Rhin. Le Général Pichegru, sous les yeux duquel cet extrait a été fait, a ajouté et rectifié beaucoup de choses à l'article des positions.' (*Murray Papers*, 125, fos. 103–56.)

Géographe in the new army. It is not often appreciated that the staffs of the Revolutionary and Napoleonic armies were brought up on traditions initiated by such hazy figures from the past as Vauban.

However, whether Craufurd and men of his way of thinking were right or wrong is of less importance than the fact that they knew of the Dépôt de la Guerre, believed in the existence of the mysterious standing committee, and wished to see some such permanent body of military knowledge established in the British army. One of these men, who perhaps deserves to be remembered more than Craufurd (whose part in the regeneration of the Quartermaster-General's Department is, as a matter of fact, not at all clear), was Lieut.-Col. J. G. Le Marchant, a cavalryman who, having served both as a regimental officer and as a brigade-major in the late campaign, had brought back vivid recollections of the results of the defective military administration. On his return he had at first devoted most of his attention to improving the sword exercise of the cavalry. But to judge from the letter quoted above which he received from Craufurd, it must have been at about the same time that he turned his mind to what the army has best reason to thank him for, the project of a school for training staff officers. Though coming of a modest Jersey family without influence or interest, Le Marchant was well known to the King and had the patronage of the Duke of York. His project won the approval not only of Craufurd, who was strongly in favour of the establishment of a school which would train *British* quartermasters-general, but of Dundas, now Quartermaster-General, and Brownrigg, the Military Secretary, later Dundas's successor. His plan was presented in January 1799, and the school was opened in the May following.

The plan proposed, says Le Marchant, 'the establishment of a Military College for the education of persons intended for the land service, which also comprised a course of instruction for officers intended to serve on the General Staff'.[1] The school was divided into two, a Senior and a Junior Department, and as no accommodation offered to house the two

---

[1] Le Marchant's Record of Service in his own hand, 1 Jan. 1810 (W.O. 25/747, M(i), N. 24).

under one roof, the Senior Department was placed at High Wycombe, the Junior at Marlow.[1] The chief instructor at the former, which those intending to serve on the staff attended, was a French émigré officer, General Jarry, who had been, with Berthier, the most valued staff officer in the French Northern Army in the old days of 1792.[2] He spoke nothing but French, and his age and his eccentricities disqualified him from being an ideal professor. There was a moment in 1803 when it was proposed to ask Scharnhorst, then enjoying the favour of the King of Prussia, to take his place.[3] But Jarry continued until his death in 1807, and his eight lectures on 'La manière de lever à vue, de dessiner et représenter le relief et les autres accidents du terrain pour les opérations de la guerre' were the foundation of the work carried out under Murray in the Peninsula.[4] It is a curious reflection that both French and British military topographers in Spain and Portugal and both Murray and Berthier, the most distinguished staff officers of their time, were thus brought up in the same tradition.[5] Both strains could trace their ancestry to Vauban.

The total number of students at any one time never exceeded thirty-four, and although a small party of both instructors and students performed some useful services in Egypt in 1801,[6] the effects of a staff education did not begin to make themselves felt until the Baltic Expedition of 1807, or even the Peninsular War. The army on the whole found

---

[1] The Junior Department, which gave instruction to cadets before they received their commissions, was not opened till 1801. The instruction was by no means compulsory, and most infantry and cavalry officers continued to enter the army without any previous military education until late in the century. The two departments later moved to Sandhurst, the Senior becoming the Staff College, the Junior becoming the Royal Military College.

[2] Col. R. W. Phipps, *The Armies of the First French Republic* (Oxford, 1926), i. 85.

[3] Col. W. H. Clinton, Military Secretary, to Lord Harcourt, Governor of the College, Horse Guards, 29 Dec. 1803 (W.O. 3/592, p. 329). As the fact is not mentioned by Scharnhorst's biographers it may be that the proposal was never actually made to him. See Lieut.-Gen. Sir A. R. Godwin-Austen, *The Staff and the Staff College* (London, 1927), p. 45.

[4] Anon. (probably the 2nd Earl Cathcart—see Appx. I) in *Colburn*, 1830 (pt. ii), p. 487.

[5] It is to be observed that the staff of the British army, throughout the Napoleonic period, owed nothing to Prussian influence.

[6] Sir Robert Wilson, *History of the British Expedition to Egypt* (1803), i. xxi.

the graduates inclined to be pedantic. One young man straight from Wycombe who came up to an officer's party constructing a battery at Copenhagen, asking a way to the advanced posts, said in passing, 'I perceive, Sir, that you are raising an epaulement; let it be a special observance of yours to make your base equal to your perpendicular.'[1] It was behaviour of this kind that prejudiced Wellington against the College. But its establishment had transformed the old methods of selecting officers for the Department. 'As to Moore's putting me on the Quartermaster-General's Staff', wrote a young major under Sir John Moore's protection to his mother, 'he cannot. His interest would of course be great, but I have no right to ask for it, nor would that be a proper way. As to being placed as Father was it is as impossible as to be made Commander-in-Chief. The system of the Department is now different; and so many are fit, and so many more think themselves fit, and so many are employed that the situation is in fact become a very extensive command and is generally given to lieutenant-colonels who are favourites at the Horse Guards.'[2] The old days of casual patronage had gone. Selection rested firmly in the hands of the Quartermaster-General, and a young man who had distinguished himself at High Wycombe, whatever his connexions, was certain of a recommendation for employment.

Had the organization of the Ordnance Department been more supple it is quite possible that the training of these officers and their duties would have been supervised by the Engineers as they were in other armies. Certainly Engineer officers would have taken a share of the staff's duties. But they were kept out, and the establishment of the Royal Military College under the aegis of the Secretary-at-War and the Horse Guards set up a friction between the two branches which excluded the possibility of their assisting each other. As it was, the Adjutant- and Quartermaster-General ruled

[1] [Maj. H. Ross-Lewin], *Life of a Soldier, a narrative of 27 years' service in various parts of the world* (London, 1834), p. 73. (Cit. hereafter as 'Ross-Lewin'.)

[2] Maj. Charles (afterwards Gen. Sir Charles) Napier, to his mother, Ashford, Feb. 1808 (Lieut.-Gen. Sir W. Napier, *The Life and Opinions of Gen. Sir C. Napier* (London, 1857), pp. 82–83). His father, Col. Hon. G. Napier, had been Q.M.G. to 'Lord Moira's Army', the expeditionary force that was to have landed in France, 1793–4.

unchallenged over the staff, each over his own department.

In the past, the Quartermaster-General and his assistants had borne the responsibility of hiring transport and labour for road making when on active service. Braddock's Q.M.G. had undertaken these duties in the unfortunate Monongahela campaign in 1755;[1] and Erskine and Cathcart, Howe's Q.M.G.s in America, had agreed the prices for the hire of drivers, horses, wagons, and vessels during the years 1777 to 1781.[2] The conduct of the Department had been subjected to the scrutiny of a Commission in 1782, which exposed the fact that by these transactions the public had lost and that the officers of the Department had gained a total of £417,592.[3] However, even this unpleasant disclosure did not prevent General Fox, the Duke of York's Q.M.G. in Flanders, from being a public accountant,[4] to whom the Commissary-General at least on one occasion disbursed so large a sum as £22,000, which remained unaccounted for.[5] This state of affairs could be satisfactory neither to the Q.M.G. nor to the Treasury. The new Quartermaster-General, in his desire to give advice on purely military grounds, neither fettered nor degraded by such responsibilities, willingly surrendered his functions as a public accountant during the succeeding years, and by the outbreak of war in 1803 a procedure, long since devised, by which the Commissary-General made all disbursements for such purposes on the authority of the military commander, was now strictly enforced. The Q.M.G.'s authority was accepted only in certain and very few instances.[6] In 1805 Brownrigg, the Quartermaster-General, could say that he had no power over public money and none in his hands.[7] And, as Murray wrote later: 'it is a general principle in the Quartermaster-General's Department that no officer of it is to become a public accountant. This principle is observed by

[1] D. S. Freeman, *George Washington* (New York, 1948–51), ii. 10, 22, 52, 53, 62.
[2] Edward E. Curtis, *The Organisation of the British Army in the American Revolution* (New Haven, Conn., 1926), pp. 134, n. 57, 189.
[3] *Clode*, i. 136.   [4] *Murray Papers*, vol. 118.
[5] W.O. 1/173, pp. 743 et seqq.
[6] Such as the issue of Bât and Forage Money, and the settlement of the contingent accounts of officers employed by the Quartermaster-General.
[7] Brownrigg to Cook, Deputy Secretary-at-War, Horse Guards, 4 July 1805 (W.O. 1/630, pp. 381–2).

the Quartermaster-General in England and I have always endeavoured to adhere closely to it.'[1]

The Q.M.G.'s dissociation from financial concerns not only left him in a more independent position in undertaking his military duties but brought him closer to the ideal that Craufurd had detected in the French service, where there existed an undisturbed tradition of military science. In this Dundas and his successor as Q.M.G. to the Forces, Brownrigg, were evidently in agreement, since there can be observed during the early years of the century a continuous movement towards the foundation of a similar tradition here. Dundas himself[2] was anxious that a corps of Permanent Assistants to the Q.M.G. should be formed, a corps of staff officers who had vacated their regimental commissions.[3] This corps, which made its first appearance in the Army List of 1805, owed its origin to the Establishment of 1803–4.[4] The manner in which it was inserted is interesting, for it seems to have been presented in such a way as to be easily overlooked. The Establishment of 1803–4 lists eleven assistant-adjutants-general and five assistant Q.M.G.s, but it also inserts five 'district assistants to the Quartermaster-General' at a higher rate of pay. The latter are the Permanent Assistants. They are Dundas's staff corps, which later numbered ten.[5] However, if the intention was to form a staff similar to the Ingénieurs-Géographes or even something similar to what the Prussian General Staff became, it must be considered a failure. Its numbers were never sufficient to avoid employing regimental officers on the Q.M.G.'s staff, and it disappeared after the Peace.

It is not to be confused with the Royal Staff Corps, a body of officers and men raised by the Quartermaster-General to assist in what the French staff called the *ouverture des marches*,

[1] Murray to Maj. Hon. C. M. Cathcart, A.Q.M.G. at Cadiz, Celorico, 16 June 1810 (*Murray Papers*, 60, pp. 45–47).

[2] Dundas is named as the author of this project in Torrens to Gen. Gower, Horse Guards, 29 Oct. 1811 (*Murray Papers*, 38, fos. 37–38).

[3] *11th Report*, appx. no. 14A; James's *Companion*, iii. 115–18.

[4] W.O. 24/609, Part I.

[5] One of the first officers to be nominated was Maj. Birch, who was assigned to the Eastern District (*11th Report*, appx. no. 16). The number of Permanent Assistants who served in the Peninsula will be seen on reference to Appx. I below to have been very small.

rapid bridge-building, roadmaking, sketching. Many of the officers had started their careers in the Ordnance corps but, far from being an Ordnance corps, the Royal Staff Corps was a Horse Guards organization exclusively under the control of the Q.M.G. and raised because the Board could not furnish such assistance. Its relationship with the Engineers was never cordial. The practice in the Peninsula was to leave siege-works and defence-works to the Engineers while the Staff Corps confined themselves to temporary works.[1] But the distinction became very fine when temporary field-works had to be constructed, and in the Peninsula it needed all Murray's tact to allay the professional jealousy of the Engineers.[2]

Besides instituting a school to train his officers, establishing a permanent nucleus of staff officers, and forming a body of field engineers to assist them on active service, the Quartermaster-General also enlarged the competence of his own office at the Horse Guards. The proposal for an increase was put forward in March 1803, soon after Brownrigg succeeded Dundas. It not only consisted of the addition of two Assistants and three Deputy-Assistants but, in conformity, as it appears, with the wish to copy the French Dépôt de la Guerre, it included the establishment of a 'Deposit' or 'Repository for Military Knowledge', as it is described.[3] Part of the Military Depot was devoted to a drawing office, in which the maps and plans could be stored and copies of them prepared 'to be given out to officers destined for particular service', and part to a collection of manuscript memoranda and printed books.[4] Though agreed to by the Treasury in April these proposals were not put into execution until some years

[1] Murray to Graham, Lesaca, 12 Aug. 1813 (*Murray Papers*, 45, fos. 86–89).

[2] A good instance of this professional jealousy is to be found in the diary of Burgoyne, the Engineer, in his remarks on the way Sturgeon, the most ingenious of the Staff Corps officers, proposed blowing the bridge of Cabezón on 26 Oct. 1812 (*Life and Correspondence of Sir John Burgoyne, ed. Lieut. Col. Hon. G. Wrottesley* (London, 1873), I, 242, cit. hereafter as 'Burgoyne').

[3] Brownrigg to the Commander-in-Chief, Horse Guards, 26 Mar. 1803 (W.O. 1/630, pp. 457–79). Duke of York to Pitt, Horse Guards, 28 June 1804 (Quartermaster-General's Letter-book in the War Office Library, p. 151).

[4] The library was placed under Lieut.-Col. Lindenthal, and the drawing office under Lieut.-Col. John Brown, the 'inventor' of the Hythe Military Canal. Mr. A. S. White, Librarian of the War Office Library, informs me that many of the books there still bear the bookplate of the Military Depot.

later owing to lack of space. They involved the addition of a story to part of the Horse Guards, which was not completed until 1805,[1] and the ejection of one of the Joint Paymasters-General, Mr. Hiley Addington, who occupied one of the pavilions of the Horse Guards, and whom it was not thought advisable to disturb until he should lose his appointment with a change of government.[2] By the time of the Peninsular War, however, the Military Depot was in working order. From 1808 the drawing office was producing plans of Wellington's actions in Portugal by what must be some early lithographic process.[3] Memoranda on operations in the Peninsula and elsewhere, drawn up by Lindenthal from letters of officers of the Department, were being prepared which, written up from time to time, were conveyed to Windsor and read to the old King.[4]

By 1809 the Quartermaster-General's Department at the Horse Guards consisted of the Q.M.G. himself, his Deputy, five Assistants and three Deputy-Assistants, a draughtsman and seven clerks.[5] Old Colonel Paterson continued to make out the routes, and the routes continued to receive the Secretary-at-War's signature, but the status of the Department had risen appreciably since the old days before the war. It was designed with a view, as Brownrigg said, 'towards its performing the higher duties of the army in the various operations of offensive and defensive war'.[6] It was allowed to correspond directly with the Secretary of State.[7] It provided the government with what it had scarcely had previously, namely a body of expert military opinion which could be consulted on questions beyond those purely departmental ones

[1] Sir Charles Yorke to the Commander-in-Chief, War Office, 6 Apr. 1803 (W.O. 4/189, p. 155); A. C. Pugin and J. Britton, *The Public Buildings of London* (London, 1825–8), ii. 148–50.

[2] Duke of York to Pitt, cit. *sup.*

[3] Specimens are contained in Murray's collection of maps (*Murray Papers*, Maps, vol. i). [4] *Murray Papers*, vol. 110.

[5] *11th Report*, pp. 82–85, appx. no. 11B. It should be explained here that Assistants were either lieutenant-colonels or majors, and that Deputy-Assistants were either captains or lieutenants (in the few instances in which lieutenants were admitted to the staff). This applies both to the A.G.'s and the Q.M.G.'s Departments. For the sake of brevity these appointments will be written as: A.A.G., A.Q.M.G., D.A.A.G., and D.A.Q.M.G.

[6] Ibid., pp. 74–75.

[7] Duke of York to Lord Hobart, Horse Guards, 6 July 1803 (W.O. 1/625, p. 439).

on which the Master-General could speak. It was in all essentials what the Prussian *Generalstab* ultimately became for the German Empire.

Yet it is to be observed it had grown independently of any developments taking place concurrently in Prussia. On the contrary 'the German school', whatever reputation it may have had before 1792, was synonymous in this country with a pedantry of an antiquated brand, particularly after 1806, and was deliberately shunned. The British Quartermaster-General's Department and its representatives were in 1815 regarded on the continent as a model, and foreign observers were at pains to discover the workings of its machinery. But even as they studied it the vision was fading. After 1815 no money and no efforts were devoted to the continuance of the tradition. While in Prussia and most countries abroad there always remained a small body within the military government to keep alive a similar tradition, the British army lost what it had, by negligence as much as suppression, and possessed nothing of the kind until the establishment of the Intelligence Branch of the Q.M.G.'s Department in the 1870's. There was nothing of equal power and influence until the formation of the General Staff in 1904.

Such was the aspect of the military administration in time of war: the Secretary of State directing, the Treasury financing, and a military staff devising the operations. The Secretary-at-War has become merely a regulator of the army's affairs for economy's sake, and the civil boards no more than suppliers. Perhaps this broad statement of the constitutional or hypothetical position of the various departments needs some qualification, for it must be admitted that from other circumstances the limits of the Secretary of State's influence were not always nicely drawn. It appears, for instance, that the amphibious expedition to Ostend of 1798 was promoted and managed by others not normally responsible for military operations.[1]

Nevertheless at the time of the war in the Peninsula the positions of the various departments were very much as

---

[1] Sir John Fortescue, *History of the British Army,* iv (Part II), 874, where Huskisson, who had a post at the Admiralty, is said to have been responsible.

described. When it came to dispatching expeditionary forces abroad there can be no question of the Secretary of State's responsibility for their employment and maintenance, and for the selection of competent officers to command. The Letter of Service which he addressed to the Commander, delegating to him the power of holding courts-martial and issuing warrants for the settlement of the expenses he incurred, and the detailed instructions which accompanied it virtually made of the Commander a representative of the Secretary of State abroad; and to this Commander all the representatives that the other departments sent with the expedition looked for their orders. Thus a Commander abroad, surrounded by a military staff which he could make a channel of communication or not as he thought fit, was supreme. In fact the Commander and his staff abroad occupied precisely the situation which all the parliamentary struggles of 150 years had been aimed at denying him at home.

However, there were limitations. Each civil department that sent a representative to the army gave him its own departmental instructions. The Treasury, for instance, had its own standing orders for the acceptance of contracts, the discharge of accounts, and so on, to which it strictly held the Commissary-General in the field: in cases where the instructions and the Commander's will conflicted, the Commissary made a reference to his chief in London. Other examples will appear subsequently. The Commander's departmental heads owed, therefore, a divided loyalty. How each resolved it depended on the personal qualities of the man and the Commander. But it is clear that the Commander's plan could be at the mercy of a Commissary-General's timidity.

Moreover, the Commander abroad was limited in his powers of selecting his own officers. He himself had been chosen not by the military but by the civil department, which extended its interference into subordinate commands as well. In this respect successive governments appear to have followed no fixed principle, though the elder Pitt's had been clearly expressed fifty years earlier: 'that in order to render any general completely responsible for his conduct he should be made as far as possible inexcusable if he should fail, and that, consequently, whatever an officer entrusted with a service of confidence requests should be complied with'.[1] It was certainly not acted upon at the time of the Peninsular War. Wellington and his contemporaries had to accept generals and heads of departments not of their own choosing but those who had been approved by the Cabinet. That occasionally there was a danger of having officers appointed for quite other than military reasons is shown by the following account of General Ferguson's appointment to Cadiz.

Some time ago Lord Liverpool proposed to Sir David Dundas . . . that General Ferguson should be employed, to which he replied that 'while there were other people to choose he did not think that officer the person to select or appoint to an active situation. . . .' Lord Liverpool did not press the matter until the receipt of dispatches from General Graham, stating that General Stewart has left him to join the Army in Portugal and requesting that either Lord Dalhousie or Charles Hope should be sent out to him. . . . The former was immediately written to but (very improperly, in my opinion) he declined the service—respecting which no option had been given him!—and in considering Charles Hope, Sir David Dundas could not but feel that he was not a man of sufficient talent to place in a situation that might become ostensible should anything happen to Graham; and besides, had he been sent to Cadiz, SirDavid must have urged the appointment on his own responsibility as it was known that Lord Liverpool would not have approved of Charles Hope. In looking over the Army List, after it was decided that neither Dalhousie nor Hope should go, Sir David (I confess to my great astonishment) fixed upon ordering Ferguson, with the *intention of forcing* him to go; and I am persuaded from his manner and from the way in which he spoke of Ferguson that, so far from meaning him a kindness, Sir David really thought that he would not like the service and that he would object to it as Dalhousie had done.[2]

Within these limitations, however, and any others which the Secretary of State may have imposed, the Commander of an army abroad had the control of all the supporting departments; and his headquarters comprised the following officers:

[1] Beckles Willson, *The Life and Letters of James Wolfe* (London, 1909), pp. 410–11 (cit. as 'Beckles Willson').

[2] Secret letter Torrens, M.S., to the Duke of York, Upper Spring Street, ½ past 5 o'clock, Tuesday morning, 29 May 1810 (W.O. 3/597, pp. 10–13). Sir David Dundas was Commander-in-Chief during the years 1809–11.

(i)   his Adjutant-General and

(ii)   his Quartermaster-General, who were the channels through which he issued his orders to the Army:

(iii) his Military Secretary cared for his financial business and all business respecting officers' appointments;

(iv)   the Commissary-General, representing the Treasury, provided the transport, the food, and forage, kept the stores and, with the Deputy-Paymaster-General, acted as the Army's banker;

(v)   the Officer Commanding the Royal Artillery provided all ammunition and arms as well as acting as the Commander's artillery adviser, and together with with his civil subordinate, the Inspector of the Train, represented in general the interests of the Ordnance Department:

(vi)   the Commanding Royal Engineer was a storekeeper for engineering tools and pontoons besides being the expert consultant in siegecraft and defences;

(vii) the Inspector-General of Hospitals, representing the Medical Board, the Purveyor's Department, and the Apothecary-General, had charge of all the medical arrangements.

It was on these seven men that the Commander relied for the movement, the maintenance, and the efficiency of his Army. And it is with them that we shall henceforth be concerned.

II

THE PERSONAL AND OFFICIAL
RELATIONSHIP AT HEADQUARTERS

HITHERTO the word 'staff' has been used in a loose sense corresponding neither with the restricted use made of it nowadays nor the very much more extended use that was current in Wellington's time. The staff since 1904 has been divided into three parts: the General Staff, the Adjutant-General's, and the Quartermaster-General's; and only those serving in these three branches may properly describe themselves as staff officers. At the beginning of the last century there were but two branches, the A.G.'s and the Q.M.G.'s, and it was customary by speaking of the 'General Staff' to include all officers, civil as well as military, receiving pay for being employed outside the regiments. The word 'general' implied this extra-regimental employment, as opposed to a 'particular' or regimental one.[1] The yearly Establishments invariably began with a list of the 'General and Staff Officers of the Hospitals serving with the forces in Great Britain', which included: the Commander-in-Chief, his secretary and aides-de-camp, the generals, the lieutenant-generals, the major-generals and their aides-de-camp, the A.G., the Q.M.G., and their assistants, the Barrackmaster-General, the Chaplain-General, the brigadier-generals, the majors of brigade, the Physician-General, Apothecary-General, and so on. All these were staff officers, and all could properly describe themselves as having served on the staff. It was possible, until 1812, say, for an officer to be a major-general and yet not to be employed on the staff, whether of this country or of an Army 'sent on particular service', as there were many general officers who at any one time, being unemployed, received nothing but their regimental emoluments. Yet whatever the reservations, it is important to appreciate this extended meaning of the word. When Wellington wrote 'I have got an infamous Army . . . and an inexperienced

[1] *Walton*, p. 618.

staff', he was referring not only to those who would nowadays be called staff officers but to his divisional and brigade commanders as well as the officers of the Ordnance and civil departments.[1]

Though confining our attention in this chapter mostly to the military staff, we are concerned more with this extended meaning than with the modern one. The staff in this sense may be divided into three: the personal staff; the officers of the Adjutant- and Quartermaster-General's Departments; and the staff of the civil departments.

'Personal staff' is used to include aides-de-camp and brigade-majors. Every general officer was allowed to be accompanied by at least one aide-de-camp; lieutenant-generals were allowed two, and the Commander of the Forces was allowed almost as many as he chose. The general, in accordance with the practice of most armies of Europe,[2] paid his aide-de-camp himself, receiving from the Treasury 9s. 6d. a day for the purpose. He also kept table for him. When Smith was appointed a.d.c. to Brig.-Gen. Sydney Beckwith, Beckwith said to him, 'Can you be my aide-de-camp?' 'Yes', said Smith, 'I can ride and eat.'[3] With the permission of the Commander a general might keep an extra aide-de-camp above the establishment, whom he might pay if he could afford it but for whom he received no allowance. Aides-de-camp were invariably young men, some not yet out of their teens, sons, as often as not, of the general, or close relations, or sons of friends or men of interest at home to whom he wished to pay or repay a favour. The appointment was a personal one and lasted only for so long as the general held the command. During that time, however, his duty consisted in making himself useful, writing letters, riding messages, issuing invitations, and generally easing his general's burden.

[1] Wellington to Lieut.-Gen. Lord Charles Stewart, Brussels, 8 May 1815 (*Disp.* viii. 66). It is to be noticed that, apart from any other consideration, this letter was written soon after he took command and before he had assembled a staff more to his liking, for, as Brig.-Gen. Sir J. E. Edmonds pointed out in *J.S.A.H.R.* xii. 239–47,Wellington's *Staff Officers* were by 18 June a quite experienced body.

[2] Cf. Feldzeugmeister Baron Anton von Mollinary, *Quarante-six ans dans l'Armée austro-hongroise, 1833–1879*, Fr. trs. (Paris, 1913), i. 48 and n. (cit. hereafter as 'Mollinary').

[3] *The Autobiography of Lieutenant-General Sir Harry Smith*, ed. G. C. Moore Smith (London, 1901), i. 35 (cit. hereafter as 'Smith').

Some were well-known characters in the Army: such, for instance, as Tyler, a Welshman of huge proportions, a 'very popular Amphitryon', who, as manager of Picton's household, carried in his head the best recipes and testified to them by his bulk.[1]

The Brigade-major, the chief staff officer attached to a brigade, tended to come from a different class of soldier. While almost all the a.d.c.'s came of well-connected families and some from the first families of the land, brigade-majors, although they were often well connected and had seen service as a.d.c.'s, were more often drawn from the adjutants of regiments, who, until the latter years of the eighteenth century at any rate, were sometimes looked down upon as a class by the regimental officers. They had certain defined duties, arranging duty-rosters, &c., in the brigade, which an aide-de-camp never had. Their pay was the same as an aide-de-camp's, but their relationship with the brigade commander was not on the same personal footing.[2] Once appointed to a brigade they remained with it no matter who commanded it or whether the brigadier was in fact a colonel or a lieutenant-colonel in temporary command.[3] Nevertheless, they were as much part of the general's 'family' as an a.d.c. Harry Smith, on being appointed Brigade-major to Colonel Drummond's Brigade of the Light Division, came up to him and said: ' "Have you any orders for the picquets, Sir?" ' He was an old Guardsman, and kindest though oddest fellow possible. "Pray, Mr. Smith, are you my Brigade-major?" "I believe

---

[1] *A Memoir of the Services of Lieutenant-General Sir Samuel Ford Whittingham*, ed. Maj.-Gen. Ferdinand Whittingham (London, 1868), p. 497 (cit. hereafter as 'Whittingham'). The name of Tyler is not mentioned, but the man is easily indentifiable.

[2] See, for instance, the entry dated Queluz, 19 Sept. 1808, in Gomm's Diary: 'The pay and rank are the same as those of an aide-de-camp: the officer has the rank of major during the time he holds the appointment, and he is not considered as generally belonging to the general's family so much as the aide-de-camp. The situation is more independent.' (*Letters and Journals of Field Marshal Sir William Maynard Gomm*, ed. Francis Culling Carr-Gomm (London, 1881), p. 105, cit. hereafter as 'Gomm'.)

[3] It is interesting to see that Beresford, when commanding the Portuguese army, introduced this system into the Portuguese service. 'Declara . . . Sua Exca. que os Majores das Brigadas deverão ser considerados como oficiais propriamente destas, nas quais se conservarão ainda quando elas mudem de Comandante.' (Ordem do Dia, 10 Aug. 1811.)

so, Sir." "Then let me tell you it is your duty to post the picquets and mine to have a damned good dinner for you every day." [1]

From a brigade, where the military staff might consist of no more than a temporary commander of the rank of colonel and his brigade-major, to a larger formation such as a division, where there might be two a.d.c.'s and two officers from each of the two branches of the staff, there was a great difference.[2] The headquarters of General Hill, who in 1813 commanded three divisions (one British, one Portuguese, one Spanish), was a fairly considerable establishment. The largest of all the generals' establishments was Graham's, whose baggage was commonly said in the Army to need forty mules to carry it. Hope, who took it all over on Graham's departure, reckoned it cost £800, and a further £2,140 per annum to run. As his pay was £1,861. 10s. he was considerably out of pocket. Apart from himself he had six officers to lodge and board, besides, as he said, the two or three who tumbled in every day from the Army who had to be fed. 'We are going to retrench', he wrote, 'but slowly and with becoming dignity.'[3]

Wellington's, in comparison, was enormous. There were seldom less than six a.d.c.'s there, under the control of the chief a.d.c., Colonel the Hon. Alexander Gordon, apart from a number of other officers and a small army of servants. The whole Headquarters was supervised by the Commandant, Colonel Colin Campbell, who had served under Wellington since his Indian days. Arrangements here, though never ostentatious, were on a more august scale, particularly at the end of the war when Headquarters lay in France and were attended by the Duc d'Angoulême and his entourage. On such occasions before a dinner party Campbell might be heard addressing the dishes in his awkward French: 'Biftek, venez ici. Petits pâtés, allez là.'[4] Young men all of them,

---

[1] *Smith*, i. 45.

[2] See Appx. III, which lists the staff attached to a typical division.

[3] Hope to his wife, Hendaye, 22 Oct. 1813 (Linlithgow MSS., Hopetoun House, Box 20, fos. 21–22).

[4] Philip Henry, 5th Earl Stanhope, *Notes of Conversations with the Duke of Wellington 1831–1851* (London, 1889), p. 299 (cit. hereafter as 'Stanhope's Conversations').

some unborn when the wars started and only just remember-
ing Sir John Moore's death, the a.d.c.'s came of the great
houses for the most part, and carried their high spirits into
Wellington's own quarter, where often the Commander
would join in their games. He liked their company and,
though only in his mid-forties himself, was refreshed by their
youthfulness. Some months after Waterloo Lady Shelley
told him she feared he would never settle into the quiet of
private existence. 'Oh yes, I shall', he replied, 'but I must always have my house full. For sixteen years I have always
been at the head of our army and I must have these gay fellows round me.'[1]

However, the families of the Commander and the generals,
though forming the social background for anyone who lived
at Headquarters, took no part in the daily management of
the Army, and so long as the Army remained stationary and
there were no letters to copy and messages to carry—that is
to say, for three-quarters of the year—the life of these men
was fairly idle. The brunt of the work fell upon the civil
departments and the Adjutant- and Quartermaster-General's
staff.

All these departments lived a separate existence. The
Commander's personal staff and his Military Secretary lived
in one building, the A.G. in another, the Q.M.G. in a third,
the Commissary-General in a fourth, the Inspector-General
of Hospitals in a fifth. When Wellington established his
Headquarters on the Spanish boundary at Freineda, as he did
during the winters of 1811–12 and 1812–13, there was no
room for all the departments even in the same village.[2] The
Officer Commanding the Artillery and the Commanding
Royal Engineer put up in Malhada-Sorda, three miles away
to the south, and the medical departments and the Commissary-General were quartered very roughly in Castelo-Bom,
three miles to the north. During the critical period when the
Army lay behind the River Caia in the summer of 1811,

---

[1] *The Diary of Frances Lady Shelley* (*1787–1817*), ed. Richard Edgcumbe
(London, 1912), p. 106.
[2] 2 Oct. 1811 to 5 Mar. 1812 (with intervals), and 22 Nov. 1812 to 22 May
1813.

Headquarters were even more spread out. The villages in this part of the Alentejo are larger and more prosperous, but they are fewer and farther between than in the north; and while Wellington's quarter was the Quinta de S. João, Stewart the A.G. was a mile or two away in the Quinta dos Banhos, Murray the Q.M.G. a quarter of an hour's ride in the other direction in the Quinta das Longas; and the Commissary-General lived a good half-hour's ride away in the Quinta de S. José.[1] Such a wide dispersion does not appear to have interfered with business. Headquarters were rarely located in towns of a size to allow all the departments to occupy contiguous buildings, and even when they were at Madrid[2] Wellington occupied the Royal Palace, with his Q.M.G. at the other side of the city in Godoy's old palace at the corner of the Calle de Alcalá and the Prado. The only occasion when Wellington and his personal staff, the A.G., and the Q.M.G. lived under the same roof was when Headquarters were placed in the Quinta de Gramicha, in front of Elvas, at the time of the second siege of Badajoz, immediately before they moved to the Quinta de S. João;[3] but even then the heads of the civil departments were several miles in rear, in Elvas.

The separate existence which each branch of the staff led, if accentuated by the exigencies of campaigning, was not, however, peculiar to Peninsular practice but arose from the circumstances alluded to in the previous chapter; that, apart from the personal staff, the staff sent out from England owed a double allegiance. The two branches of the military staff and the heads of the Ordnance and civil departments were not attached solely for Wellington's convenience but for the carrying on abroad of the duties of the various offices at home in the public interest. Colonel George Murray, the Quartermaster-General, was not, strictly speaking, Quartermaster-General to Lord Wellington but Quartermaster-General to the Forces serving in the Peninsula under the command of Lord Wellington. That is to say, it was not a personal appointment but an attachment to an Army. It was considered a

[1] 20 June to 24 July 1811.
[2] 13 Aug. to 1 Sept. 1812.
[3] 30 May to 17 June 1811.

'foreign custom' to speak of a commander's Adjutant- and Quartermaster-General.[1]

The divided loyalty of the civil departments is not difficult to envisage, but it is another matter with the military staff. A staff had (and has) no authority beyond that which it derived from its commander, and its instructions to subordinates could be issued only in that commander's name. It is clear this was recognized at the time of the Peninsular War, for all important orders from both the A.G. and the Q.M.G. are prefaced by some such phrase as 'The Commander of the Forces requests that you will', or 'Lord Wellington desires that you will be so good as to'. Indeed in the British army there has never been any other doctrine.[2] Yet it is clear also that at this time these two officers regarded their own departments and the class of business which they transacted as their own preserve, for which they were responsible not to the Commander in the field but to their superiors at the Horse Guards.

In Wellington's Army, in which the Commander had succeeded in cultivating a very high standard of public spirit, this proprietary attitude is not easily detected. But it stood out very clearly in Sir John Murray's Army operating on the east coast of Spain in 1813, where relations between all generals and staff officers were particularly uneasy. Its Quartermaster-General, General Donkin, evidently was regarded, and regarded himself, as having a responsibility in respect of the duties of his own department that was separate from the general responsibility of his commander.[3]

---

[1] See Craig to Col. Ross (Cornwallis's Assistant), Tournai, 8 June 1794: '. . . We may adopt the foreign custom and say "Adjutant-General to *Lord Cornwallis*", thus making it an office attached to the person of the commander, &c., not to his Army.' (*The Correspondence of Charles, 1st Marquess Cornwallis*, ed. Col. Charles Ross (London, 1859), ii. 247.) See also Col. Murray to his sister, Barbados, 24 Sept. 1802, when he was A.G. in the Windward and Leeward Islands: 'Observe that I am Adjutant-General to the Forces (if you will) but not to an individual.' (*Murray Papers* (T.D. 178), viii. 4.)

[2] Speaking of his situation as Chief of Staff to Wellington during the occupation of France, 1815–18, Murray writes: 'My own opinion of it is that there is no authority in it further than as the channel of the Commander-in-Chief's orders; which I should think is the common and only interpretation of authority in staff officers.' Murray to Col. Hardinge, Cambrai, 20 Nov. 1816 (*Murray Papers*, 138, fo. 129).

[3] See the evidence of Donkin in *The Trial of Lieut.-General Sir John Murray . . .* taken in shorthand by W. B. Gurney (London, 1815), pp. 431 et seqq. (cit. hereafter as 'Sir John Murray's Trial').

The sense that each department had prerogatives of its own was also present in Wellington's Army. Colonel George Murray corresponded in his own right with all officers of his own department, attached them where he thought best, employed them as he thought fit, and gave orders on his own initiative on such larger subjects as intercommunication between formations during an operation, and on others which he took for granted as the prescriptive right of his situation on the staff. It was part of a Q.M.G.'s duty, evidently, to see that the Army could retreat to prepared positions in the rear, and so long as Murray had what he called his 'Quartermaster-General-like prejudices'[1] about him the Army would not be at a loss when it was forced to retire, independently of any arrangements of Wellington's. Murray also had been charged by the Quartermaster-General at home to send back accounts of the operations and to employ officers of the department in sketching the battlefields. These accounts were sent off periodically and placed in the Repository. In the manner in which these tasks were performed Wellington never interfered, or, indeed, showed much interest.

Murray and Wellington in the course of years had developed a mode of working together so closely that it is not easy to detect how much each contributed personally to the Army's operations. It is an interesting question and it will be discussed later. In a general sense, however, it may be said Wellington was not averse from allowing his departments their prerogatives so long as they did not interfere with his own intentions. But he rode his Army with such a tight rein that in practice departmental prerogatives were not countenanced. No one who has read it will forget the rebuke the Inspector-General of Hospitals, McGrigor, received when he made arrangements for evacuating sick and wounded without first receiving Wellington's instructions.[2] Stewart, the Adjutant-General, was more deluded by this doctrine of departmental prerogative than anyone else. It was quite usual for an adjutant-general to make intelligence received from the enemy part of his official business,[3] and to that end

[1] Murray to Graham, Lesaca, 7 Aug. 1813 (*Murray Papers*, 45, fos. 67–70).
[2] *McGrigor*, pp. 302–3.   [3] *v. inf.*, p. 119.

he often made it his duty to question prisoners. In the Peninsula, however, Wellington took almost the whole business of intelligence into his own hands, and consequently, when Stewart set up what Wellington calls the 'foolish pretension' that the questioning of prisoners of war belonged exclusively to him as Adjutant-General, there followed the famous scene in which Stewart, haughtiest of Irish nobles and half-brother to the Secretary of State, Lord Castlereagh, Wellington's protector and patron, was reduced to tears.

It happened one day [Wellington said many years after] that some prisoners were taken and my aide-de-camp, happening to be on the spot, examined them immediately and, to save time, brought me the result. But in consequence of this Stewart refused to execute the rest of his duty as to these prisoners and declined to take any charge or care of them whatsoever; and he left them to escape or starve so far as his Department was concerned. This was too much; so I sent for him into my room. We had a long wrangle, for I like to convince people rather than stand on mere authority. But I found him full of the pretensions of this Department of his, although he and it and all of them were under my orders and at my disposal. . . . At last I was obliged to say that if he did not at once confess his error and promise to obey my orders frankly and cordially I would dismiss him instanter and send him to England in arrest. After a great deal of persuasion he burst out crying and begged my pardon, and hoped I would excuse his intemperance.'[1]

However, if Stewart felt it more keenly, both Murray and Stewart felt the restriction on what they regarded as the rights of their office. In a letter to his half-brother Stewart wrote:

I think both the situations of Adjutant-General and Quartermaster-General are not understood in our Army, nor is the business conducted through them in such a manner as to render the offices as interesting or as important as they are in most other armies in Europe. I think this has grown up with us from the system at the Horse Guards, which, by throwing every matter of interest or moment into the hands of the Military Secretary . . ., places both the Adjutant-General and the Quartermaster-General in a great measure under him and after him in all the confidential and secret communications, and all important business of the army. I know this is felt by Murray here as well as

[1] Note of a conversation with Croker at Sudbourne, in the autumn of 1826 (*The Correspondence and Diaries of . . . John Wilson Croker. . .*, ed. Louis J. Jennings (London, 1884), i. 346, cit. hereafter as 'Croker Papers').

myself. . . . With an irregular mode of getting through business the Adjutant-General and Quartermaster-General may pick up at one moment every information and intelligence; at another, they may know nothing and be ignorant of the most essential changes that have been directed (without reference) through the Military Secretary. In short, it is difficult where there is great quickness and where you cannot always be at hand to be as *au fait* as if there were more system and arrangement. . . . The situation and business of Adjutant-General, deprived of close communication with the head of the Army, is reduced to keeping accurately the returns of all descriptions of regiments, making General Returns from these for the office in England or for the Commander of the Forces, corresponding with all the detached officers of the Army, and officers commanding corps, on all casualties that occur, making arrangements for the sick, convalescents, &c. of the Army. . . . This is all most essential in the existence of the Army, but you will admit it does not carry with it interesting or pleasing occupation. . . .[1]

There is a further instance of Stewart's persistent endeavour to preserve what he conceived to be the competence of his Department in McGrigor's *Autobiography*: how on the second day after McGrigor's arrival at Headquarters he was waiting with his papers in the outer apartment of Wellington's quarter when Stewart came up to him, his book under his arm, and told him 'it was unnecessary for me to come to Lord Wellington, that I might come to his office and he would transact my business for me with his Lordship, whom it was unnecessary for me to trouble'. McGrigor replied he had come by Wellington's desire, and he was rescued by the door of the inner apartment opening at that moment, and Lord Wellington's nodding to him and telling him to come in.[2]

In Murray's attitude there is less ambition, more modesty, and no resentment. Yet it is clear that, whereas under Moore Murray had been fully informed of all the confidential intelligence that came into Headquarters and of all Moore's intentions, under Wellington he knew very little and, certainly throughout 1810, was not admitted into his Commander's innermost secrets. The pessimistic views which he entertained on the prospects in Portugal during this period until Masséna's retreat from the Lines of Lisbon are based

[1] Hon. Charles Stewart to Castlereagh, 24 Aug. 1809, cit. in *Fortescue*, vii. 412 n.–414 n.   [2] *McGrigor*, p. 262.

on information and a knowledge of Wellington's intentions no better than that which any general officer in the Peninsula might have obtained. In the last campaign (1813–14) Murray was admitted into Wellington's confidence. The prerogatives of departments then vanished and were heard of no more after the resignation of Stewart. But in the first three years of the war there can be no doubt of their existence.

That Wellington should have eventually possessed a military staff owing him, in effect, much the same personal allegiance as his personal staff was quite exceptional in the British service at that time. Sir James Murray Pulteney, Adjutant-General in the Duke of York's Army in 1793, while acknowledging that he was a staff officer attached to the Duke, even reported independently to the Secretary of State, and though he defended his chief against his detractors and was prepared to criticize instructions sent from home, he did not act exclusively under the Duke's orders.[1] Craig, Murray Pulteney's successor in 1794, similarly made independent reports to the Secretary of State—in fact he had been enjoined to do so freely and fully—on the Duke's conduct of affairs amongst other things, for which purpose, he owned, somewhat naïvely, as it was impossible for him to take the liberty of questioning the Duke of York himself, he must needs have recourse to 'indirect measures' in compiling his information.[2] This was no staff in any sense of the word, and Wellington would not have gone on under such a system. But even he never envisaged staff situations as personal attachments, wherein a staff officer's sole duty lay towards his commander;[3] and he would not have approved of the relationship between Blücher and Gneisenau, and Radetzky and Hess, in which each member of the partnership, commander and chief-of-staff, was ineffective without the other. To the thinking of a contemporary of Wellington's a staff officer could owe a duty to the public as well as to his

[1] Col. A. H. Burne, *The Noble Duke of York* (London, 1949), pp. 90, 97, and 101 (cit. hereafter as 'Burne').   [2] Op. cit., pp. 115–16.

[3] See the 'October Minute', Oct. 1827 (*Disp.* viii. 341). The view of the staff expressed there does not differ very materially from that enjoined in our modern *Field Service Regulations*. But I think that a modern staff officer, after reading the whole of this chapter, would not recognize himself, say, as an A.Q.M.G. attached to a division in the Peninsula.

commander. In Wellington's youth Craig and Fox, the Duke of York's A.G. and Q.M.G., were blamed—justly or unjustly —by the public for the Army's failure in Flanders: just as after his death Estcourt and Airey, Raglan's A.G. and Q.M.G., were held responsible, independently of Raglan, for the disasters in the Crimea.[1] The exclusive personal loyalty of the military staff to which we are nowadays accustomed, and the personal responsibility of a commander, were developments which came later in the century.

No doubt it was vain to expect personal loyalty from a staff of which the commander himself had not had the choosing. Though it is very difficult to say what part, if any, Wellington took in the nomination of his heads of departments, in most appointments of which we know the inner history Wellington seems to have been singularly regardless of his own preferences. At any rate at the outset, he seems to have been prepared to take on men nominated by the departments at home, trusting, rightly, to his own ascendancy to make them work according to his wishes. Charles Stewart, his A.G., Castlereagh's half-brother, he knew, and must have known well enough to be chary of having him by. Fletcher, the Commanding Royal Engineer, and Howorth, the Commanding Officer Royal Artillery, Wellington had never served with, and they no doubt were nominated by the Master-General. Dr. Fergusson and Dr. Franck, his two first Inspectors-General of Hospitals, he may have known of, but they also were probably chosen independently by the Medical Board. Murray, his Q.M.G., he certainly knew and trusted, as they had served together and were on friendly and mutually respectful terms both in the Baltic in 1807 and after Dalrymple's assumption of command at Vimeiro the previous year; but here again the appointment may equally be a nomination on the part of Brownrigg which Brownrigg knew would be agreeable to Wellington, as Murray was the obvious choice. The only appointment, in fact, that we know Wellington wished for he did not get: that of his Commis-

---

[1] I say the Duke of York's and Raglan's A.G. and Q.M.G. for brevity. The official title of Airey, for instance, was 'Quartermaster-General to the Forces serving in the East'.

sary-General. There survives a hurried note from Torrens to Stewart: 'My dear General, Sir Arthur Wellesley has desired me to request that you would *stop Kennedy*, as he means to take him.'[1] Wellington, however, did not take Kennedy in 1809; the Treasury chose Mr. John Murray.

The rule followed was that appointments were made by the King on the recommendation of the Horse Guards (or of the Master-General or the other departments concerned). In practice, however, so far as the military staff is concerned, an expeditionary force sent abroad possessed a staff selected by the A.G. and Q.M.G. at the Horse Guards; and they, having made their recommendations, to some extent delegated to the A.G. and Q.M.G. of the force the power to nominate in their own departments, subject to the approval of the commander of that force.

The officers of the Q.M.G.'s Department, for instance, who took up their duties from 1 April 1809, the nominal date of Wellington's assumption of command, numbered twenty-one: a Q.M.G. (Colonel George Murray), a Deputy-Q.M.G. (Lieut.-Col. De Lancey), five Assistants, and fourteen Deputy-Assistants. All were appointed in accordance with a list prepared at the Horse Guards,[2] which was made up partly of those who were sent out afresh from England, partly of those who were already serving in Portugal under the various commanders that succeeded Dalrymple and Burrard, and partly of those whom the Horse Guards intended to employ but never actually did. As the war went on and the Army expanded, and officers fell sick or went home on promotion or were removed for incapacity, further appointments were made. In the Q.M.G.'s Department eighty-one different officers served at one time or another. All appointments were made in the same way, that is to say, on the recommendation of Murray (or Gordon, Murray's successor in 1812) by Wellington.

Yet the nominations came from a number of different sources. Seven of these officers were appointed at Cadiz by

---

[1] Private note, Horse Guards, 30 Mar. 1809 (*Kennedy Papers*).

[2] 'When Sir Arthur Wellesley came out to Portugal this spring an entire new list of the staff for the Army was made up at the Horse Guards, in the arrangement of which I for one took no part.' Private letter, Murray to Sir Robert Wilson, Lisbon, 16 Oct. 1809 (*Murray Papers*, 59, pp. 4–6).

Graham, who, ardent Scot, surrounded himself with a Scottish staff, in the nomination of whom Murray had no part whatever. Further, there were six officers who never served with the Peninsular Army in the Department. A further seven officers were appointed during Gordon's tenure of office. A further six were already serving at Lisbon where they had remained during the winter of 1808–9. Twenty-six were selected by the Horse Guards at home and sent out without, apparently, a prior request from Murray or Wellington. Twelve officers were nominated by Murray on the recommendation of generals either in the Peninsula or at home. Only six are definitely known to have been nominated on Murray's initiative.[1] Some of the remaining seventeen may have been, but many of them owed their appointment to circumstances of the moment.

It is not, however, to be inferred that Murray was under an obligation to recommend for appointment those whose names had been brought under his notice by others. At least three such were turned down by him for various reasons. And towards the end of the war, when the prestige of the Army was at its height and Murray could to some extent bask in its and his own reflected glory, he even omitted to employ an officer sent out to him by the Horse Guards. This was Lieut.-Col. Northey, a relation of Sir Herbert Taylor's (the King's Private Secretary, a man of immense interest), who had challenged another officer of the Department to a duel when on leave in Cheltenham. He had served as an Assistant in the Corunna Campaign, but when he was sent to the Peninsula in 1813 Murray ignored all applications for his active employment and kept him at Lisbon without any executive function. Others whom the Horse Guards proposed Murray was quite willing to have appointed, even Captain Elliott, whom the Horse Guards sent out merely to deliver him from his financial difficulties at home.[2]

The recommendations Murray received from his friends and the divisional commanders were used by him to supplement his own acquaintance with promising officers. If a divisional commander recommended a man it meant that they both

---

[1] Jackson, Edward Kelly, Mackenzie, Offeney, Reynett, and de Tamm.
[2] Torrens to Murray, Horse Guards, 3 June 1813 (W.O. 3/604, p. 379).

would probably work well together, and Murray was always prepared to sacrifice formality for ease of intercourse. Opportunities frequently came for an officer to be sent by his general on detached service, and if he performed it well he stood a chance of being recommended for employment on the staff when a vacancy occurred. It was in this manner that Leith took notice of Gomm, who was afterwards appointed to the Department and led a most distinguished career; and that Hill took notice of Thorn, Montgomery, Griffiths, Forrest, and Heathcote. To the recommendations of Hill, who for long held a command almost as remote from the main Army as the garrison of Cadiz, and to Graham's, Murray gave almost instant compliance, provided Wellington approved.

In the appointments to the Adjutant-General's Department no doubt a similar procedure was followed, but it is impossible to be certain as no detailed records survive. It is likely, however, that the A.G. at the Horse Guards prepared the original list and proposed others as the war went on, and that Stewart and Pakenham (his successor) brought forward yet others from those already serving in the Peninsula. Potential Assistants and Deputy-Assistants for this Department were perhaps easier to recognize than for the Q.M.G.'s, from amongst the large number of brigade-majors who were already undertaking very similar duties with their brigades.

In both Departments the Horse Guards relaxed their powers of appointment as the Army grew larger; applicants in London were put off on the ground that the Commander-in-Chief left the nomination to Wellington;[1] and apologies were made to Wellington after 1810 for interfering in his patronage on occasions when they made an exception of this rule[2]—as they did for instance when they dispatched Upton to Cadiz, to oblige Upton, who was suffering from some

[1] 'Ever since the Army in the Peninsula has been of such an extent as to furnish its own meritorious candidates for the vacant staff employments upon its establishment, the Commander-in-Chief has ceased to interfere with Lord Wellington in such nominations.' (Torrens to Graham, Horse Guards, 4 Jan. 1813 (W.O. 3/604, p. 46). See also Torrens to Murray 3 June 1813 (W.O. 3/604, p. 379).)

[2] Torrens to Charles Grant, Jun. (afterwards Lord Glenelg), Horse Guards, 14 Aug. 1810 (W.O. 3/597, p. 212).

private affliction which made it necessary he should be out of England.[1]

But the ultimate power of the Horse Guards to recommend and the Crown to appoint was exemplified in the first months of the campaign in Flanders in 1815, when they pressed upon Wellington a staff which he was most reluctant to employ. Why after relaxing this power in the latter years of the Peninsular War they should have reverted to such a stringent use of it is not at all clear. It may have been owing partly to the jealousy the Duke of York is known to have borne towards Wellington, from Wellington's having been preferred to him in the command of the Portuguese expedition in 1808;[2] and there were probably other reasons. The old Peninsular staff had in any case been widely dispersed during the previous year and it was certainly impossible to assemble it again at short notice. The fact remains that in the Waterloo campaign Wellington had none of his old heads of departments. Through the mediation of Torrens, the Military Secretary, who though at the Horse Guards was a devoted supporter of Wellington's, he succeeded in gathering a fairly experienced staff before the fighting began.[3] It is interesting to see that Wellington acquiesced in this overriding power to appoint;[4] and it must be acknowledged that, theoretically, the greatest soldier of his age had the nomination of none but his personal staff at this, one of the most critical moments in the history of Europe.

However, in the Peninsula, Wellington had, by the end of the war, the control of and the responsibility for the composition of his staff (in the modern sense). But just as he kept to the contemporary practice of allowing the two heads of departments to seek out and appoint under the mantle of his authority those officers whom they thought most suitable, he

---

[1] Torrens to Graham, Horse Guards, 3 Apr. 1811 (W.O. 3/599, p. 135).

[2] *Greville Memoirs*, i. 62–63, which is corroborated by Murray to his brother, Lisbon, 30 Sept. 1808 (*Murray Papers*, 22, fos. 169–80).

[3] The subject, so far as the A.G.'s and Q.M.G.'s Departments are concerned is dealt with convincingly in Sir J. E. Edmonds's article in *J.S.A.H.R.*, cit. *sup.*

[4] Wellington to Torrens, Brussels, 21 Apr. 1815 (*Disp.* viii, 48); same to same, 28 Apr. 1815 (*Disp.* viii. 48); and same to same, 5 May 1815 (*Disp.* viii. 52).

allowed them complete latitude in the manner in which they employed them.

In former days an army abroad had consisted of a number of brigades, each with its brigadier and brigade-major; the daily administration of these troops was in the hands of the Adjutant- and Quartermaster-General; and if a decision was needed it was given by the commander himself or by the general of the day, who took his duty in turn with the other generals. At that time a commander could frequently see with his own eyes the whole of his army drawn up in battle, and he needed but a simple staff to convey his orders to it as it manoeuvred in his presence. Perhaps occasionally the A.G. or Q.M.G. might need to detach an Assistant to conduct a column of a brigade or two to some particular point, but on the whole the management of the army could safely be overseen from Headquarters. This simple state of affairs was already beginning to disappear in the last campaigns of the Seven Years War, and bodies of troops of more than one brigade with more permanent commanders were beginning to be used, over whom the same supervision was impossible.[1] The French, early in the Revolutionary Wars, made use of such bodies, and Napoleon had improved on the system and organized not only 'divisions', consisting of two or more brigades, but *corps d'armée*, consisting of two or more divisions, each having its own commander and a staff permanently assigned to it.

The British service had been slow to adopt such a system. Divisions had been known in 1779 and 1780 in America, but even in Flanders and Holland in 1794 and 1795, when the Army was of a considerable size, there had been no larger organization recognized than a brigade, moving, admittedly, with other brigades in 'columns', but columns of which the composition changed weekly or daily according to circumstances. To each column or brigade it was the practice to attach an officer from the A.G.'s or Q.M.G.'s Departments for a particular movement or enterprise, who would

[1] Scharnhorst said that Prince Ferdinand of Brunswick was the first to make use of *Divisions* at the battle of Vellinghausen in 1761 (Lehmann, i. 237, quoting Scharnhorst's 'Von den Vorzügen der Abteilung einer Armee in Armee-Divisionen'). Marshal Broglie is said to have made use of a similar expedient at the same time. (Sir Charles Oman, *Wellington's Army, 1808–1814* (London, 1913), p. 68, n. 2.)

afterwards be recalled to Headquarters and assigned anew
as occasion demanded. The first operation undertaken by a
British Army in which divisions were formed, each with its
commander and its representative from both the departments,
was Cathcart's campaign in Zealand in August and September 1807. And the last operation undertaken by a British
Army composed of nothing but brigades (though even in
this the 'columns' were employed very much as divisions)
was Wellington's Douro campaign in the spring of 1809.

During the interval between the march southward from
the Douro and the advance upon Talavera Wellington formed
his infantry brigades into four divisions, and in the same
General Order[1] directed his A.G. to attach an officer of his
Department to each. A further four infantry divisions and
two cavalry divisions were formed at different periods later,[2]
and to some divisions each department came to attach an
Assistant and a Deputy-Assistant. Hill, whose command
was always larger than any other, had at one time one A.A.G.,
one D.A.A.G., one A.Q.M.G., and three D.A.Q.M.G.s.
The old *ad hoc* attachments were no longer needed, and although Murray always kept a number of officers sketching
in the rear or in advance of the Army, the greater part acted
with infantry or cavalry formations and stayed with them in
very much the same way that brigade-majors remained with
their brigades.

The lists which appear at Appendix I illustrate and give
further details of these attachments. They are intended to
show as far as possible the effective dates at which these
attachments began and ended. The A.G. frequently attached
his officers by a General Order, a fortunate circumstance
when it occurs, as we are without many details concerning
the appointment and, still more, the relinquishments in his
Department. Murray, however, preferred to attach his officers in a less formal fashion, rarely designating them in
General Orders, more frequently by letter or word of mouth.
It is lucky that the greater part of his correspondence survives, else we should be almost entirely without information

[1] G.O., 18 June 1809.
[2] Light Division, 22 Feb. 1810; 5th Division, 8 Aug. 1810; 6th Division, 6 Oct.
1810; 7th Division, 5 Mar. 1811.

on this subject. As it is, the information is not as complete as could be wished.

Nevertheless it is sufficient to show that attachments from both departments were made as convenient as possible to the divisional commanders, and that staff officers who did not pull well with their generals were replaced by ones that did. Graham and Hope were allowed to keep a Scot, Major Macdonald, to act at the head of the A.G.'s Department with their columns; and Murray purposely avoided a formal attachment of his officers on the ground that his doing so made it 'more easy to make such changes as may suit the wishes of the officers they are employed under or the convenience of the service'.[1] The occasion of this remark furnishes a good example of his method. General Cole, recently given the command of the 4th Division, was provided with an Assistant, an officer newly appointed to the Department, Captain Thomas Oliver Anderdon. He was a graduate of the Military College who had been particularly recommended to Wellington by the Horse Guards and to Murray by General Frederick Maitland. After a few weeks' trial, however, Cole found Anderdon too much of a 'fine gentleman', whereupon Murray withdrew him, placed Major Broke in his place and attached Anderdon to Picton, commanding the 3rd Division, who was a close friend of Maitland's.[2] Many of these associations between general and A.Q.M.G. proved lasting and cordial, and Cole's association with Broke was one of the most successful and lasting of all. It continued until Murray needed Broke's assistance in his own office and called him away from the 4th Division just as the campaign started in May 1813. The same cannot be said of Anderdon and Picton. Anderdon was a pretty draughtsman; he served throughout 1810, in the retreat to Buçaco and the Lines; and there is no record of Picton's complaining of him. But about a year after his attachment, when the Army still lay in front of the Lines, he started for some reason applying for leave, which was refused as often as he applied. He then resigned his situation on the staff, and came home without leave, much to the consternation of the Horse Guards, where Torrens, not

[1] Murray to Cole, Viseu, 4 Mar. 1810 (*Murray Papers*, 27, fos. 179–80).
[2] Private letter Murray to Cole, Viseu, 27 Feb. 1810 (*Murray Papers*, 75, pp. 5–9).

often quick to condemn, declared he had 'no hesitation in saying that Captain A[nderdon] ought to be hanged, being nothing more nor less than a deserter'. He was, however, 'as a mark of respect to a worthy and almost broken-hearted father', allowed to sell his company; after which he studied for the law, was called to the Bar, took Silk and became a Bencher of Lincoln's Inn.[1]

An officer of the Q.M.G.'s Department might be employed in one of three ways; he might be attached to a division in the field; he might be employed on an independent mission sketching in the rear or in advance of the army to supplement the scanty information that was obtainable from the maps; or he might be stationed at one of the important hospital or commissariat stations in the rear (such as Lisbon or, later, Santander or Pasajes) to issue routes for reinforcements coming up or convoys of sick going back. How Murray employed him depended upon his aptitudes, the state of his health, or the number of officers available. But, whatever their assignment, they were all at the disposal of the Q.M.G., and however long and intimate the attachment to a divisional commander might have become, and however much Murray may have deferred to the preferences of a divisional commander, it was recognized that the Q.M.G. could withdraw, reattach, or employ on a temporary mission any officer of his Department.

In this respect the Adjutant-General had precisely similar powers. There was not of course the same variety of employment. The business of the Department did not afford opportunities similar to those of the Q.M.G.'s officers detached on sketching duties; and, apart from the few officers in the office at Lisbon and in the A.G.'s own office at Headquarters, there was none occupied in desk duties at the stations in rear, as these were performed by officers detached by the A.G. but not on the strength of the Department. Most of his officers

---

[1] Murray to Anderdon (at Tagarros), Cartaxo, 17 Jan. and 8 Feb. 1811; Murray to Picton, Cartaxo, 3 Mar. 1811 (*Murray Papers*, 60, pp. 208, 210–11, 214); Torrens to FitzRoy Somerset, Horse Guards, 23 July 1811 (W.O. 3/600, p. 77); *Law List*. Anderdon's father was connected with the West India trade. A relation is mentioned in *Farington's Diary*, and the firm was that to which Cardinal Manning's father belonged (E. S. Purcell, *Life of Cardinal Manning* (London, 1895), i. 6). Monumental inscription in Horsenden Church, Bucks.

therefore were attached to formations serving in the field.
But over all he exercised the same powers of superintendence
as the Q.M.G.

Thus, although an officer of either of these Departments
owed a duty to the commander he was attached to, his principal duty was to the chief of his department. This twofold
allegiance did not often conflict, given goodwill on the
part of the Q.M.G. and the divisional commander. It is
true Craufurd once told Murray his D.A.Q.M.G. was too
busy to attend to Murray's instructions; and that Captain
Mackenzie, D.A.Q.M.G. at Lisbon, was once unfavourably
noticed in the daily orders of Brig.-Gen. Peacocke, the Commandant at Lisbon—an action which prompted Murray to
protest on behalf of his own officer.[1] The rarity of such incidents tends to obscure the existence of the divided loyalty.
But it is important to appreciate that these attachments were
not primarily personal, and that they were merely an extension, for the sake of convenience and continuity, of the old
practice of *ad hoc* attachments.

How much the character of a general's staff changed during the succeeding century may be seen in Sir Frederick
Maurice's observations on Moore's retreat to Corunna.

The Duke of Wellington [he wrote in 1904],[2] in his one criticism
of Moore's campaign, says that Moore ought, in anticipation of his
retreat, 'to have sent officers to the rear to mark and prepare the halting-
places for every brigade.' Any moderately respectable divisional general,
or even brigadier, in our own day would be exceedingly astonished if,
when he had received orders and a route for the march of his unit,
officers from Headquarters were sent to prepare the several halting-
places. We should certainly regard that as the work of the divisional
and brigade staffs. If it really was the practice in Wellington's own
Army towards the end of the Peninsular War for Headquarters to
interfere in such a matter, then all that can be said is that it is an
extraordinary illustration of the extent to which Wellington, in his
utter contempt for his subordinate generals, had reduced the whole
Army to the condition of a mechanical instrument in his own hand.

It is unlikely that, at the end of the Peninsular War, when

[1] Craufurd to Murray, Vale, 23 Nov. 1810 (*Murray Papers*, 31, fos. 60–61).
Murray to Peacocke, Headquarters near Elvas, 10 June 1811 (ibid. 60, pp. 227–8).
[2] Maj.-Gen. Sir J. F. Maurice, *The Diary of Sir John Moore* (London, 1904), ii.
376–7.

the tendency in his administration of movements was towards delegation, Wellington would have made use of the expedients he prescribed for Moore. But it is quite mistaken to look upon them as evidence of his contempt for his generals. In his earlier campaigns, before his divisions had acquired all the paraphernalia and his subordinate generals the habits and experience which later enabled them to act independently, sending officers from Headquarters was not merely a legitimate method but the only one by which the commander retained control of his formations. As a matter of historical fact one officer was sent back along the Army's line of retreat to Corunna. A more legitimate criticism would be that Moore, or his Q.M.G., did not send several others.

The civil officers of the Commissariat and Medical Service were attached to formations in much the same way as officers of the military staff. More will be said of them later; it is only necessary to observe here that most of the 300 or 400 officers of these departments were employed in this manner, and that only a few, perhaps twenty, including clerks, were at any one time serving at Headquarters.

Thus the staff of the Peninsular Army, though 850 officers or more, military and civil, served upon it during those five years, was mainly employed with separate formations and on detached duties. Many of the staff saw their commander but once or twice in the whole of their service. Some never saw him at all. Only a very small proportion of it worked at Headquarters in the offices of the heads of departments. The Adjutant-General, for instance, apart from his a.d.c., had usually no more than five: one senior Assistant (usually the D.A.G.), one or perhaps two juniors, and the mainstays of his office: Major Düring, a Hanoverian officer to whom the states and returns were entrusted, and whose quick eye could detect at a glance an omission or a wrong cast in the totals; and Lieutenant Hurford, who had started as a kind of orderly-room sergeant in the A.G.'s office when a sergeant in the Third Guards, had been given a commission, and had remained attached as a 'sub-deputy A.A.G.'.[1]

---

[1] *The Private Journal of Judge Advocate Larpent*, ed. Sir George Larpent, Bart. (London, 1854), p. 52 (cit. hereafter as 'Larpent'). See Hurford's record in W.O. 25/762, No. 263; G.O., 15 May 1814.

Murray (apart from the a.d.c. to whom he became entitled on his promotion to Brigadier-General in the summer of 1811) also had a senior officer with him in his office and one Deputy-Assistant—rarely more, unless an officer or two stayed at Headquarters during an interval between assignments or attachments. Until 18 May 1813 the senior Assistant was Murray's Deputy, Lieut.-Col. De Lancey, who transacted the routine business of attending to demands for camp equipage, transport, and Bât and Forage Money. His place was taken until the end of the war by Lieut.-Col. Broke, who not only attended to the routine business but drafted operation orders as well. He appears to have been a man of more elastic intelligence than De Lancey, whom Murray, considering him better suited as a senior Assistant to a large body of troops, attached to the Left Column of the Army for the last campaign. The junior Assistant was, until June 1811, Captain Reynett, who acted as Murray's secretary, worked with him in the outer room of Murray's quarter, making out routes, copying movement orders, and entering letters into the letter-books. His place was taken by Lieutenant Heathcote, who had been brought up in the life of the small German courts and possessed a useful facility for languages.[1] Heathcote left the office in February 1812 and was succeeded by Lieutenant Freeth, of the Royal Staff Corps, a draughtsman with the draughtsman's untiring hand, who served during the busy period from the third siege of Badajoz until Christmas 1813, when he was appointed to a situation at the Horse Guards. Lieutenant F. M. Read, of the Staff Corps, took his place until the end of the War. Murray's chief clerk was Sergeant Charles Hockey, of the Buffs, who wrote a neat clerk's hand but was never entrusted with the copying of movement orders. And attached to the office, as also to the A.G.'s, was a varying number of orderlies, mounted and unmounted, who carried the orders and messages.

In Appendix II are listed the names of officers, clerks, and

---

[1] Some of Heathcote's letters are printed in *Ralph Heathcote—Letters of a young Diplomatist* . . . (ed. Countess Günther-Gröben), London, 1907. But they are most disappointing and contain no indication that the writer served in the Q.M.G.'s office.

orderlies serving at Headquarters in the autumn of 1813. They are compiled from the returns of those requiring an issue of shoes, blankets, haversacks, &c., which, being a free or 'donation' issue, ensures a fair degree of completeness in the list. We have no list for the Commissary-General's office or for the two Ordnance Offices, and at the composition of these only a guess may be made. What we have is sufficient to show, nevertheless, that, while there were a good many servants and orderlies,[1] the working part of Headquarters was not very large. It was not as large as the comparable parts of Napoleon's Headquarters, which had a ration-strength of about 800.[2] But it was of sufficient size to make it possible for us to appreciate the embarrassment it must have caused to the chief magistrate of any of the small villages in Portugal where it halted. When packed up and on the move its baggage animals were spread along the road in single file for a distance of eight miles.[3]

Though (as will in course become clear) Wellington succeeded in the later years of the war in delegating much of the work that he took upon himself in the first years, it was impossible for the Commander of a British force, constituted in the manner described in the previous chapter, to rid himself of very much of the administrative detail; and his decisions were required upon an enormous number of subjects, ranging from courts martial, horses to be cast, grants of leave, to the number of shoes in a battalion and the purchase of specie. The weight of business therefore imposed on his heads of departments was correspondingly heavy, and it seems fitting that these men should receive particular attention.

With Stewart, the A.G., we are already partially acquainted. He held the situation from April 1809 until resigning it in May 1813. Absent for long periods, he finally left the Peninsula after the fall of Badajoz in April 1812, and

---

[1] Bâtmen, it should be observed, were not personal servants but men in charge of the mules.

[2] Col. Vachée, *Napoléon en Campagne* (Paris, 1913), p. 53.

[3] *Larpent*, p. 214. Reference is made in this paragraph only to the British Headquarters staff and not to the Portuguese, at the moments when Beresford accompanied the Army, nor to the Spanish, which existed side by side with the British from February 1813 onwards.

the Army did not again see this strange figure, in his hussar's uniform covered with orders, until he rode south from Paris bringing news of Napoleon's surrender to Headquarters at Toulouse on 20 April 1814. He was an able man but a difficult subordinate, a 'sad *brouillon*' as Wellington called him, much of whose work during his absences was done by his Deputy, Wellington's brother-in-law, Edward Pakenham. Pakenham, no desk soldier but a good commander of troops, disliked what he wrote of as 'this insignificant clerking business',[1] and from November 1811 until the day after Vitoria, 22 June 1813, was relieved of it. But he then assumed Charles Stewart's post and held it until the end of the war, much against his will but to the satisfaction of Wellington and to the admiration of the Army. He was, moreover, devoted to Wellington, who had had great trouble with the Horse Guards over his appointment, and he brought a personal quality to his official relationship with his chief which had been lacking in Stewart's time.

During Pakenham's absences the Department was sometimes in the hands of Lord Aylmer, who became Deputy in December 1811,[2] sometimes in the hands of the famous intelligence officer, Waters, and for a month or two in the autumn of 1812 it was in the hands of Captain Goodman. That the Department could be entrusted to the charge of such a junior officer testifies to the routine character of its business. There was a moment in fact when Wellington intended it should be managed by a chief-of-staff.

The Q.M.G.'s Department, with the exception of the period from December 1811 to March 1813, was in the hands of Colonel, later Maj.-Gen., Sir George Murray, a Guardsman with a good presence and pleasant manners, a prodigious memory and an aptitude for geography and history which made him take a pleasure and an interest in his surroundings that, with his imperturbability in action, admirably fitted him for his situation. He was the most experienced of Brownrigg's men when he accompanied

[1] Pakenham to Lord Longford, Vilar-Formoso, 22 May 1811 (*The Pakenham Letters, 1800–1815* (ed. Lord Longford), privately printed (1914), p. 96, cit. hereafter as 'Pakenham Letters').

[2] Aylmer was appointed to command a brigade, 23 July 1813, and the deputyship remained vacant for the remainder of the war.

Wellington to Portugal in April 1809, and by the end of the war was probably the best staff officer in Europe. For private reasons he returned home in December 1811, and his place was taken by Colonel Willoughby Gordon, lately the Duke of York's Military Secretary and now the Quartermaster-General of the Forces, who arrived at Headquarters on 2 August 1812. Gordon was an entirely different person. He was an office-soldier, a capable and indefatigable organizer. But his pretensions were such that his colleagues and subordinates withdrew their goodwill, and his indiscretions and shortcomings as a Q.M.G. in the field were so plain that Wellington took advantage of his ill health to allow him home on leave at the end of 1812.[1] Torrens at the Horse Guards, acting with promptitude, managed to get Murray to return before Gordon recovered. During the intervals between Murray's departure and Gordon's tenure of office the Department was run by De Lancey, a loyalist American by origin, a very likeable officer of considerable experience but of limited powers. Graham, under whom he afterwards served, speaks of his habitual *étourderie*, and certainly it seems that his business arrangements, though punctual and satisfactory, had none of the method either of Murray's or Gordon's.[2] It looks also as if he could not rise to his position and that, though the best-tempered of men, to assert himself he entered into long and bitter correspondence with other departments which could not but tend eventually to the disadvantage of his own. With all his faults, however, Wellington preferred to have him as his Q.M.G. in Flanders in 1815 to Sir Hudson Lowe, and at Waterloo he was killed.

Wellington's first Military Secretary was Lieut.-Col. James Bathurst, a brother of the Benjamin Bathurst who mysteriously disappeared at Perleberg in Prussia while returning from a diplomatic mission in Vienna in 1809. Colonel Bathurst had had much experience as an Assistant-Q.M.G. from the first days of the Department's regeneration ten years before. He was disqualified, however, from being an ideal Military

[1] See Sir Charles Oman's *History of the Peninsular War*, vi. 224–6 (cit. hereafter as 'Oman').

[2] Graham to Gen. don P. A. Girón, Hernani, 2 July 1813 (*Murray Papers*, 43, fos. 14–15). Fortescue, ix. 90, quotes a letter from Wellington in which he describes De Lancey as the idlest fellow he ever saw.

Secretary by his quick temper, which was well known to all his subordinates (who referred to him as 'that Turk Bathurst'),[1] and which, moreover, deteriorated under the strain of the immense mass of business that all those departments transacted until his nerve finally broke altogether. The death of his brother, 'a strange, wild fellow, going after women', weighed so heavily on his mind that he eventually brought himself to believe that he was suspected of similar failings and, for some reason of his own, took to riding a white horse, 'a damned violent, vicious beast', as Wellington later described it. Early in December 1810 he was sent from the Army with dispatches to England, but he refused a passage in the first packet at Lisbon, saying that there was a conspiracy against him on board, and bursting out crying before all the ladies as they were coming out of church, who dispersed in the greatest consternation. Wellington had to take the precaution of sending duplicate dispatches in case any further alarm should induce Bathurst to throw his into the sea. The unhappy man eventually recovered to some extent but he could never be depended upon in a responsible situation.[2]

Some months before Bathurst's departure Wellington had appointed one of his a.d.c.'s, Lord FitzRoy Somerset, as his Assistant Military Secretary, and this young man was now brought forward to take Bathurst's place, where he remained until the end of the war. His perfect manners, his good temper, his ability to dispatch complicated business in the hurry and hubbub of active service won him everyone's admiration. Unlike Murray or Stewart he was not, however, a man of strong military views, and his constant occupation at Headquarters and at the Horse Guards, where he continued as Military Secretary to the Commander-in-Chief until the middle of the century, enfeebled his powers of appreciation and decision, and detracted somewhat from his qualifications

[1] Col. George Landmann, R.E., *Recollections of my Military Life* (London, 1854), ii. 194–5.
[2] Torrens to Col. Colin Campbell, Horse Guards, 18 and 24 Oct. and 16 Nov. 1810 (W.O. 3/598, pp. 69, 90–95, 166–7); Wellington to B[athurst], Cartaxo, 29 Nov. and to Charles Stuart, Cartaxo, 3 Dec. 1810 (*Suppl. Disp.* vi. 644–6); *Stanhope's Conversations*, p. 28. In the latter two printed works he is referred to as Col. B., but the identity is quite plain. See also Torrens to Campbell, Horse Guards, 19 Dec. 1810, and 3 Jan. 1811, and to Capt. Pulteney Malcolm, 18 Dec. 1810 (W.O. 3/598, pp. 270, 273, 311).

as a commander-in-chief, the situation to which, as Lord Raglan, he was appointed in the Crimea.[1] But as a devoted, cheerful, and discreet secretary, as he was in the Peninsula, who discharged his business punctually and accurately, he could not have been bettered.

If there is one characteristic common to all these men that cannot fail to attract attention it is their extraordinary youthfulness. Wellington himself was not 40 at the time of his reappointment in April 1809. Murray was 37, Stewart 31, and Bathurst 27. Pakenham was 35 when he succeeded Stewart as A.G., Gordon 39 when he succeeded Murray, and FitzRoy Somerset was a mere 22 when he took over from Bathurst. Officers joined the army young in those days; they were accustomed to taking large responsibilities at an early age, and it is clear they did not regard themselves as young. When Pakenham was promoted Brigadier-General in 1811 he was amused at the constant 'general' that started or concluded every sentence addressed to him. But 'why', he wrote, 'I should be thus taken by surprise in putting on the wig I cannot say, when, unfortunately, it is to be confessed I am 33 and have served near 17 years; but we are all inclined to feel young and act very often so, by Gad'.[2] Old by their standards, however, or young by ours, they were young in body, a fact which explains their ability to sustain the enormous pressure of business that fell upon them, the fatigues of campaigning and the unhealthiness of the climate and the food.

The ages of the officers of the two departments was correspondingly lower. The average of those Assistants to the A.G. whose ages we know was, on their appointment, 30; that of the D.A.A.G.s, $25\frac{1}{2}$. The Q.M.G.'s officers were a little older, the average age of the Assistants being 31 and that of the Deputy-Assistants $27\frac{1}{2}$.

It is the fashion nowadays to describe the army of Wellington's time as officered and staffed by men who owed their position to money and family influence alone, the implication

[1] *Larpent*, p. 309. See also Palmerston's opinion of him in *Panmure Papers*, i. 286; and the Prince Consort's, in Mary Howard McClintock, *The Queen thanks Sir Howard* (London, 1944), p. 44.
[2] Pakenham to Lord Longford, Pedrógão, 13 Aug. 1811 (*Pakenham Letters*, p. 119).

being that they did not rise by their merits and that they were preferred to better officers who had neither wealth nor interest. That this rash assumption may be examined more carefully in so far as it concerns the two military departments a certain amount of evidence has been assembled in Appendix I. It will be seen how difficult it is to generalize upon the origins and upbringing of these men. The A.G.'s list would appear at first sight to contain a large proportion of noblemen, in whose appointment it is too easy to suspect an undue amount of family interest. It contains the large young FitzClarence, 'le petit-fils du Roi Georges', as Wellington called him; and also that well-known figure of the turf and friend of the Regent's, Captain Mellish, a tall, pale man with black hair and drooping moustaches, who, before he squandered his fortune, used to appear at the St. Leger dressed in white, driving a barouche drawn by four white horses, attended by grooms in crimson livery.[1] On the other hand it contains three officers, Elley, Eckersley, and Hurford, who had risen from the ranks, at a time when the gulf between commissioned and non-commissioned rank was wider than it is now. The list is full of contrasts. Most of these officers seem to have come from landed or propertied families, but there are still many whose origins it has not been possible to trace, who may for that reason be legitimately regarded as coming from humbler circumstances. Some almost certainly owed their staff situation to family connexions. But some were brought on by commanders who noticed their ability regardless of their connexions, such as Rowan, who had neither money nor interest. It would be fair to say that all those who had both these assets pressed their preferment to the utmost; but it would be mistaken to suppose that the staff would have been in better hands if birth and interest had not been favoured. Mellish would not have remained A.A.G. to the Light Division under Craufurd if he had been a bad staff officer.

The Q.M.G.'s list is likewise full of contrasts and apparent contradictions. In view of the schooling which 34 of these 81 officers underwent at the Royal Military College

---

[1] J. S. Fletcher, *The History of the St. Leger Stakes, 1776–1901* (London, 1902), pp. 180–90.

this department might be expected to have appealed to a different class of man. Yet it included 7 who had been at Eton, 4 Westminsters, and 2 Harrovians, and there were 7 peers or sons of peers. On the other hand two of the peers' sons were sons of distinguished soldiers, and of the Etonians one was the son of a Poor Knight of Windsor and one was a scholar who had endured the horrors of the old Long Chamber. Moreover, these schools did not carry the same social distinction that they came to later in the century, and the blood that ran in the veins of these men was not particularly blue. In short, this list, like that of the A.G.'s, contains for the most part sons of men of landed property with a sprinkling of well-to-do merchants and professional men. Murray himself was not influenced by claims of kinship or birth *per se*. 'I cannot', he said, 'afford to have any but useful men about me, be they cousins or not',[1] and he avoided showing that he took any interest in them 'than as individual officers in the station in which they are placed and in which they act with the Army'.[2] He laid an emphasis on his officers' possessing good manners,[3] but this was not a principle of selection that would necessarily favour the rich or the well born.

That all these men were ambitious cannot be denied. The lower branches of the staff, Larpent observed, 'are sharp-set, hungry and anxious to get on, and make the most of things, and have a view even in their civilities'.[4] There was more play for ambition in an age in which, by manipulating the complex machinery of purchase, a man could suit his preferences for station and climate, or contract into or out of the rigours of active war, as he felt disposed. But it is very doubtful if the officers Larpent met at Headquarters were any sharper set than the friends he had left behind at the London Bar.

The army was, as a Military Secretary once said, a lottery. Some went up fast, some went up slow; some got more than

[1] Murray to his brother, Freineda, 16 Oct. 1811 (*Murray Papers* (T.D. 178), viii. 5).

[2] Murray to his sister, Mrs. Campbell of Lochnell, Vera, 17 Oct. 1813 (*Murray Papers*, (T.D. 178), viii. 4).

[3] Murray to Col. Abercromby, Lesaca, 22 July 1813 (*Murray Papers*, 43, fos. 220–1).

[4] *Larpent*, p. 69.

they deserved, some less. We are not, however, concerned with individual injustices. We are concerned only if Napier's 'cold shade of aristocracy'[1] (whatever that may mean) prevented Wellington's Army from possessing an efficient staff. Of this, the later achievements in the Peninsula leave no reasonable doubt whatever. If we seek corroboration by comparison we may find it in the admiring testimonials of the representatives of the European armies who saw Wellington's Army at their manœuvres in France after Waterloo, improvised by the Staff at only a few hours' notice, but carried out with the same precision as the manœuvres of the other contingents after weeks of practice and rehearsal.[2] There can be no test of a staff but that of war. Mistakes were made; the weaker elements were ground out in the grim attrition, together with many of the stronger; but the residue, though perhaps small, was by all standards very good. If it is said that undue weight was given to birth in the selection of these men, the only conclusion can be that it was a method which produced excellent staff officers.

[1] Napier's *History of the Peninsular War*, book xi, cap. 3 (cabinet editions, ii. 401), cit. hereafter as 'Napier'.

[2] *Burgoyne*, ii. 223–4; *Delavoye*, p. 765.

III

THE MAINTENANCE OF THE ARMY
IN THE PENINSULA

SINCE the latter years of the seventeenth and throughout
the eighteenth century standing armies in times of war
were subsisted in the theatre of operations principally
by means of depots of provisions collected at the harvest.
Indeed, the very possibility of maintaining a standing army,
during an epoch when agriculture was carried on at little
above subsistence level, depended upon this manner of sus-
taining it. No country in Europe at the beginning of the
eighteenth century could support what amounted to the
imposition of a population of a fair-sized city in its midst;
and armies were dependent upon accumulations of stores
gathered from an area much larger than that which they
immediately occupied. They relied consequently not only
upon the depots themselves but upon regular convoys of
transport and upon the goodwill of the inhabitants. Deprived
of one of these requisites for more than a few weeks they
lost all power of movement; deprived of them all for more
than two days they ceased to be a military force.

In no army had this system been brought to more elaborate perfection than in the French, where it is said to have
been introduced by Louvois. The march of troops within
the kingdom was regulated from one *étape* to the next, where
they received lodging and provisions, along prearranged
routes which remained unchanged until the Revolution,
although improvements in the roads during the intervening
period had made many others more convenient.[1] In war the
depots on the frontier were stocked, and supplies thrown
into the congeries of fortresses by which the northern frontier was protected. These fortified towns, however, regarded
from the administrative point of view, were no more than
elaborate magazines. Though the Low Countries were, so

---

[1] *Encyclopédie méthodique: art militaire,* ii (1785), 315 ff. The *étapes* originally
designated by Louvois were revised in the Ordinances of 1727 and 1737.

to speak, the Centre Court of European war, where all the talents of the most distinguished military engineers of the day could be displayed to their best advantage, and operations were particularly slow and methodical, all warfare in Europe was based upon the accumulation of stores at intervals along the 'line of operations'[1] of each combatant, and the defence or capture of these magazines was the principal preoccupation of each general. 'The object in war', wrote a French military theorist at the end of the eighteenth century, 'is to establish the *lignes d'opération* further forward against the enemy's country, because it is much more important to destroy the places that contain the elements of military power (the magazines) than men, who are nothing without their stores.'[2]

But even before these words were written circumstances were combining to bring about a change in the methods of subsisting armies in the field. The regimen of magazines must always have been recognized as limiting the speed and scope of military operations, and about the middle of the century devices to elude reliance upon depots were proposed by military writers such as Dupré d'Aulnay,[3] which were taken up by Guibert and strongly recommended in his famous *Essai général de Tactique*. The habits of the French soldier as he found him on the eve of the Revolution, prodigal, impatient, physically weak, 'sybaritic', Guibert ascribed to the exclusive adoption of the magazine system, which, he said, prevented the troops from learning to live off the country.[4] Thus from Guibert's time onward the tide of

[1] The *ligne d'opération* was the line of advance along which the depots were formed. It is to be distinguished from the *ligne de communication*, which, as will be shown, was the line by which one part of an army communicated with another, and not our 'lines of communication'.

[2] *Encyclopédie méthodique: art militaire*, suppl. vol. iv (1797), art. 'Système de Guerre moderne'. This article was probably written by Jean-Gérard Lacuée, afterwards Gen. Comte de Cessac (1752–1841), one of those officers who, in Grimoard's words, 'très avide d'avancement et de distinctions', supported the Revolution and proposed sundry new-fangled reforms into the army. His definition of war's object is, therefore, all the more striking.

[3] Louis Dupré d'Aulnay (c. 1670–1758), *Traité de subsistances militaires* (Paris, 1744).

[4] *Essai général de Tactique* (1770), ii. 307. His allusion to the contemporary soldier is very reminiscent of Gibbon's in the *Decline and Fall*, i (1776), cap. i, where he draws attention to the load carried by a Roman legionary, which, he says, 'would oppress the delicacy of a modern soldier'.

military opinion in France set in in favour of some form of requisitioning upon the countryside, a method which it was intended should emancipate an army in much the same way as man was supposed to be freed from his shackles by Rousseau and the rest. The Revolutionary wars that shortly followed came to make the fashionable expedient something of a necessity. The immense armies raised by the Republic and stationed on the frontier could not be subsisted from the traditional depots. Though improved methods of agriculture had substantially increased the yield of every district since the beginning of the century, the economic uncertainties of the time discouraged the farmers from bringing their produce into the open market, and the old methods of supplying the army, whether by *régie* or *munitionnaires*, broke down completely. Recourse was therefore had to requisition as the only means by which the troops could be fed.

The cynic will observe that requisition had been introduced as the principal method of supplying armies at almost the very moment when the political economists in Paris were introducing as one of the inalienable rights of man the 'droit naturel et impréscriptible de la propriété'. This unfortunate coincidence did not escape the commissioners sent from Paris to carry out the requisition. They could only explain it by saying that, though sacred and inviolable, the right could be withdrawn when public necessity demanded and on the condition of a 'juste et préalable indemnité'. This was in 1792, and as the months went by, requisition became more and more the established custom, and people learned that the indemnity was rarely just and never previous. Very soon requisition and even forced contributions failed to supply the troops, and the armies of the French Republic were constrained to subsist themselves by invading the neighbouring states. It was not only for political or military reasons, or out of a zeal for revolutionary proselytizing, but by sheer economic necessity that the French armies carried their operations into enemy territory.[1] So long as the French kept up an army beyond their means, the existence in France of all

[1] Robert Werner, *L'approvisionnement en pain de la population du Bas-Rhin et de l'armée du Rhin pendant la Révolution (1789–1797)* (Strasbourg, 1951), pp. 179, 186, 188, 190.

'droits naturels et impréscriptibles' was subject to the condition that this army should be maintained on foreign soil.

German military writers draw a sharp distinction between what they call the *Magazinssystem*, favoured by most European armies, and the *Requisitionssystem* used by the Revolutionary and Napoleonic armies.[1] It is a convenient distinction, but it must be remembered that the use of one system did not in practice exclude that of the other. Recourse had been made to requisition and even forced contributions throughout the century to supplement supplies from the depots when these failed, as they often did.[2] No military textbook of the time omits reference to the proper way of carrying out a *forage*,[3] which was no more than a requisition carried out by a military party in a manner designed to procure the greatest amount of provisions with the least inconvenience to the population. And in the Peninsula, where the British army was maintained mainly by the *Magazinssystem*, foraging parties were frequent, requisition not uncommon, and even embargo was resorted to. Similarly the French in Spain, though relying on a *Requisitionssystem*, kept up depots for all kinds of stores throughout the country. Requisition had always been avoided because it inevitably antagonized the population, with whose goodwill even a French army could not dispense with impunity. As the principal means by which an army subsisted itself requisition would not have passed beyond the stage of the military theorists' dreams had not standards of living so improved by the end of the century as to make it practicable.[4] In Spain and Portugal, as there had been no rise in agricultural production comparable to that in other parts of western Europe, the *Requisitionssystem* underwent modification, and, indeed, became scarcely recognizable as a *system* at all.

Of the two systems the Depot system was the more

[1] e.g. Capt. C. von B[inder]-K[rieglstein], *Geist und Stoff im Kriege: erster Teil — das achtzehnte Jahrhundert* (Vienna, 1896), p. 267 (cit. hereafter as 'Binder-Krieglstein').

[2] e.g. Tielcke's *Beiträge zur Kriegskunst und Geschichte des Krieges von 1756 bis 1763* (Freiberg, 1781), ii. 31, 64; numerous references in *Beaurain*, and in the *Relation des campagnes de 1745, 1746, 1747*.

[3] Gen. Humphrey Bland, *Treatise on Military Discipline* (London, 1727), p. 235; *Grimoard*, &c.

[4] *Binder-Krieglstein*, p. 267.

expensive, as it involved payment by cash at no very distant date from the transaction; while requisition involved no such obligation and in fact was often no better than confiscation. British armies abroad made greatest use of the former method. Britain was rich, for one thing. The army usually acted in friendly territory, for another.[1] The British soldier has always expected to receive his rations punctually and deteriorates rapidly if he does not—a characteristic for which the more methodical arrangements of the Depot system compensated. And to these practical reasons must be added the further one that the system, being more equitable, was found to answer best in its more emollient effect on the population.

The task of buying, storing, forwarding, and issuing fell mainly upon the representatives of the Treasury who accompanied the army into the field to whom we have already referred: the commissaries.[2] At the opening of the last century the commissary was a civilian—as handling public treasure he had to be—but subject to military discipline: a Treasury official wearing a red coat, who, long after the army had passed by and even embarked for home, stood by his depot to settle all outstanding claims which the contractors and country people brought to him. Having settled them all after issuing notices in the local newspapers, he submitted his accounts to the Auditor-General, who, in his own good time, reported to the Comptroller of Army Accounts, and he to the Treasury, which favoured the commissary (if he were still alive) with a discharge from his accountantship known as a *quietus*. More often than not the auditors found he still owed the public. He then re-examined his accounts, corresponded with his sub-accountants, by now scattered over the face of the globe, and resubmitted them. By this time the original transactions under dispute might be ten or twenty years old; the commissary might have died; in which circumstance the Treasury laid its claims in the name of the public upon his executors and dependants. In Burke's words,

the grand and sure paymaster, Death, in all its shapes calls these accountants to another reckoning. Death, indeed, domineers over

---

[1] Except perhaps the American Colonies, where, however, the war was a civil one rather than a war of independence. At any rate it was a country whose population we wished to have disposed in our favour. [2] *v. sup.*, p. 6.

everything but the forms of the Exchequer. . . . Terrors and ghosts of unlaid accountants haunt the houses of their children from generation to generation, while the Treasury, content with the eternity of its claims, enjoys its epicurean divinity with epicurean languor.[1]

This is no exaggeration of the hazards to which a man's private fortune was exposed when he became responsible for public funds 'imprested', or advanced, to him. The Quartermaster-General to Lord Moira's column (10,000 men) in Flanders in 1794 had ordered a supply of provisions for 25,000 men from a town which the column was not to pass through in order to deceive the enemy as to his strength and intentions; a device which succeeded and helped to save his command from destruction. But neither the success nor the deception recommended itself to the Treasury, which dunned Lord Moira's widow for the extra 15,000 rations for many years afterwards.[2] Commissariat accountants were similarly visited with personal responsibility for their public acts, not punctually but, owing to the small number of auditors, with the most unbusinesslike tardiness. Commissary Kennedy was not discharged from his accounts of the years 1793–5 until 1807. Sir Brook Watson, Commissary-General in the Low Countries during those years, was not given his *quietus* until 1812, five years after his death.

It is not to be wondered at if the men who came forward as commissariat officers[3] were not overscrupulous, and in fact tended to come from the very worst elements of the commercial world. Many joined entirely with a view to the profits that could be made and the ease and comfort to be enjoyed from a life lived amongst piles of good food and embellished with a rake-off from the supplier or contractor. 'Gentlemen,' said one commissary, neither particularly honest

---

[1] *Collected Works and Correspondence of Edmund Burke* (Rivingtons, 1852): Speech on the Plan for economic reform, 11 Feb. 1780 (iii. 378–80).

[2] Col. Arthur Doyle, *A Hundred Years of Conflict, being some Records of the Services of Six Generals of the Doyle Family, 1756–1856* (London, 1911), p. 57.

[3] The grades of the commissariat at the end of the 18th century were: Commissary-General, Deputy, and Assistant. In 1809 the special post of Commissary-in-Chief was created under the Treasury for Col. James Willoughby Gordon, who instituted ranks that had equivalence with military ranks: Commissary-General (Brig.-Gen.); Deputy (Lieut.-Col. and Maj.); Assistant (Capt.); Deputy-Assistant (Lieut.); and Commissary Clerk, a non-commissioned rank but equivalent to Ensign. These were confirmed in 1815.

nor particularly dishonest and a very capable and active man, 'if a commissary is expected to starve in the midst of all his stores, then the devil take the whole business.'[1] The number of commissaries who were dismissed for irregularities, both before and during the Peninsular War, was prodigious. There can have been few professions, crafts, or mysteries in the country which could point, as the Commissariat could, to two men of the highest rank who were serving a sentence in Newgate Gaol.[2] Lord Cornwallis once delicately intervened with the Prime Minister on behalf of a commissary who had been remanded 'in consequence of some inaccuracies in his accounts and vouchers' on the ground that the poor man bore 'a very amiable private character, that in his official situation he only followed the inviting examples of the times, and that I think him an object for as much lenity as the nature of his case will admit'.[3] It was almost expected of a commissary that he would defraud the public.

In view of the temptations that were open to them, the treatment they received at the hands of the regimental officers or brigadiers they were attached to, ever impatient for stores or mules which the commissary could not provide, and the risks they ran if they acted on their initiative in emergencies, it is astonishing that the commissariat should have contained any respectable men. Yet such were certainly to be found among them. Some were sons of bank managers or merchants, who had spent a few years in a counting house in Edinburgh or London, or men of experience in commerce who had fallen on ill luck and looked to a situation of fair security under the government. Perhaps typical of such men was William Dowler, better known to the non-military world as a rival to the Duke of York for the favours of Mrs. Clarke. Born in the parish of St. Clement Danes in about 1773, he had managed his father's counting house for sixteen years, and had then followed the business of stockbroker until becoming

[1] A. L. F. Schaumann, *On the Road with Wellington*, tr. by A. M. Ludovici (London, 1924), p. 38 (cit. hereafter as 'Schaumann').

[2] 'In the Goal [*sic*] of Newgate': Commissary-Generals Alexander Davidson and Valentine Jones. List of Officers, &c., serving in the Department in 1810 (W.O. 61/1).

[3] Cornwallis to William Pitt, Phœnix Park, 13 June 1799 (*Cornwallis Corresp.* iii. 103).

involved in the failure of a financial house in about 1805, when he joined the Department as an Assistant.[1] Erskine, the Commissary-General in Spain in Moore's time, had been captain of the school at Westminster, a M.A. of Oxford, Filazer in the Court of Common Pleas, and a Doctor of Laws.[2] Sir Brook Watson, Commissary-General in Flanders 1793–5, was Lord Mayor of London. And Kennedy, the remarkable man in whose career as Commissary-General in the Peninsula we are particularly concerned, was the son of George III's physician, and a Westminster scholar.

The chief of the Commissariat Department at the time of the Peninsular War occupied a particularly unenviable position. Responsible to the commander of the force for procuring supplies, for hiring or purchasing transport and for negotiating the purchase of specie, and to the Treasury for accounting for every transaction, made in the hurry of a moment yet scrutinized by a perhaps hostile auditor in the calm and lethargic atmosphere of a government office in London, he was also inundated with the daily correspondence of his department. In former days numerous accountants acting under the orders of the commissary-general had been allowed by the Treasury to obtain credit for imprests and accounted directly to the Treasury themselves. But by the time of the war the Commissary-General had been made the sole accountant, and he alone became responsible for all his sub-accountants. This 'exclusive responsibility', as Kennedy called it, was a heavy burden to be added to his others, particularly in view of the fact that, as he wrote, 'those for whom he has to account . . . are appointed and may be removed or dismissed without reference to him, that he has no previous knowledge of their characters, no assurance of their integrity or ability, nor anny certain idemnification for the consequence of their want of these qualities'.[3] Much of Kennedy's burden was shared by Wellington, who was ultimately responsible for the maintenance of his Army and

[1] *Investigation of the Charges brought against H.R.H. the Duke of York* . . . (Stratford's edition, 1809), i. 178 ff. (cit. hereafter as 'Inquiry Proceedings'); W.O. 61/1.
[2] G. F. R. Barker and A. H. Stenning, *Record of Old Westminsters* . . . (London, 1928), *sb.* Erskine, John.
[3] Kennedy to J. C. Herries, Commissary-in-Chief, Saint-Jean-de-Luz, 5 Dec. 1813 *(Kennedy Papers)*.

whose sanction was essential before any step of magnitude was undertaken; but enough has been said to secure our consideration for the individual who carried on his shoulders the responsibilities of a commissary-general.

Robert Hugh Kennedy, a man of boundless energy and enterprise uncoupled, however, with any desire to usurp for himself or his department any powers beyond his own, yet in whose one eye there occasionally burned an ungovernable temper, took over the duties of Commissary-General John Murray on 11 June 1810 and remained at the head of the Department, with a year's interval, until the end of the war.[1] As commissary-general his concern, in a fiscal sense, was the control of the Extraordinaries, while his subordinate colleague, the Deputy-Paymaster-General, who was the representative of the joint Paymasters-General in London, disbursed the Ordinaries. In practice, however, in the Peninsula, as all Treasury money, on whatever account, whether metal or paper, was kept in one Chest at Headquarters,[2] from which payments could not be made without the authority, or warrant, of the Commander except those of a routine nature; and as all money in the Chest passed through the Commissary-General's account, the control of both Ordinaries and Extraordinaries was in the hands of the Commissary-General. The Deputy-Paymaster-General might have the Military Chest in his safekeeping; but if he was required to withdraw money from it, say, to issue the Army's pay to the regimental paymasters, he drew a cheque upon the Commissary-General.[3] And similarly if, as frequently happened, the Commissary-General and the Paymaster-General were separated from one another, the Paymaster-General was under an obligation to render periodically a state of the Chest.[4] Moreover, since Extraordinaries embraced any form of expenditure that was

[1] He was absent from the Peninsula 24 Dec. 1811 until 25 Sept. 1812, rejoining Headquarters at Villatoro on 10 Oct., his place being taken by Commissary-General John Bisset. He was again absent from the Army in Lisbon from 24 Dec. 1813 until rejoining Headquarters at Aire, 11 Mar. 1814, during which time Commissary-General Charles Dalrymple deputized for him.

[2] Perhaps, physically, more than one chest, but nevertheless physical chests.

[3] Kennedy to C.G. Dalrymple, Lesaca, 23 July 1813 (*Kennedy Papers*).

[4] e.g. C.G. Bisset to Assistant-Paymaster-General Gordon, Fuenteguinaldo, 25 May 1812, asking for a state of the Chest, in respect of both Ordinaries and Extraordinaries (*Kennedy Papers*).

not chargeable to regiments in peacetime, the Commissary-General's competence extended over the expenses of the Medical and Purveyor's Departments, in the supply and transport of hospitals and stores.

Over the only other department which had the power to spend money, the civil department of the Ordnance under the Ordnance Paymaster, the Commissary-General had no control, as the Ordnance Department accounted separately for all money voted on its Estimates. It managed its own hospitals, staffed them with its own physicians and surgeons, maintained separate depots of stores (muskets, rifles, bayonets, carbines, sabres, ammunition, and artillery and engineers' stores), over all of which presided the Commanding Officer Royal Artillery and the Commanding Royal Engineer, and their civilian assistant, the Inspector of the Field Train Department.[1] But the affairs of the Ordnance in the Peninsula were small in comparison with those of the rest of the Army, and the Commissary-General supplied all its transport (apart from the horses that drew the guns) on occasions, clothing, even negotiating its bills in the money market to avoid unfavourable competition. Though it is important to notice that all warlike stores were in the custody of the Ordnance, and that issues could be authorized by no one but an Ordnance officer, this department was in many respects dependent on the Commissariat.

Subordinate or independent, no supplying department, no matter how active its chief, could have maintained the Army without enterprising and resourceful Commissariat. The dominant personality in the maintenance of the Army was the Commissary-General; the feasibility of all operations

[1] From Apr. 1809 until the middle of July 1811, the C.R.A. was Brig.-Gen. Edward Howorth; from July till Dec. 1811, Lieut.-Col. Hoylett Framingham; from Dec. 1811 to Mar. 1812, Maj.-Gen. William Borthwick; from Mar. 1812 to Aug., Lieut.-Col. Framingham; from Aug. till 27 Oct. 1812, Lieut.-Col. William Robe; from then till 10 Dec., Lieut.-Col. Alexander Dickson, acting for Col. Waller; from then until 9 May 1813, Lieut.-Col. George Bulteel Fisher; and from then until the end of the war, Lieut.-Col. Dickson.

The C.R.E. from Apr. 1809 until 31 Aug. 1813 was Col. (Sir) Richard Fletcher (Bart.), who was killed at St. Sebastian. He was on leave from June 1812 to Apr. 1813, his place being taken by Lieut.-Col. H. F. Burgoyne, who also acted after Fletcher's death, until the arrival at Headquarters in Oct. 1813 of the next senior officer, Lieut.-Col. Howard Elphinstone.

depended on his ability to provide stores at the right place and the right time; and Kennedy's contribution to the achievements of the Peninsular Army is to be measured in higher terms than by the unhandsome treatment he received at the hands of the Treasury when all the fighting and difficulties were over.

The Commissariat Department was divided into two branches: the Store Department, which procured transport and stores, accumulated and issued them; and the Accounts Department, which checked the accounts of Store Commissaries at the completion of each tour of duty. Both were equally subordinate to the Commissary-General, and both received equal rates of pay (15s. per diem for a Deputy Assistant). But the number of commissaries of accounts who accompanied the Army bore a minute proportion to the whole,[1] and it was generally recognized in the Department that service in the Store Branch was more meritorious and brought a man more under the eye of the Commander.[2] Since it was the branch which procured most of the stores it is with the Store Department that we are concerned when speaking of the Commissariat.

Not all stores, however, were provided by the Commissariat; and to appreciate the extent of the Commissary-General's responsibility in this respect it is necessary to digress on the subject of how all stores were supplied. They are best classified under the heads of the various ways in which they were paid for. First should be mentioned the so-called warlike stores: muskets, the many 'natures'[3] of ammunition, gunpowder, pontoons, &c., supplied and issued, as has been said, not by the Commissariat, but by the Ordnance. Second, the medical and hospital stores, procured by the Medical and Purveyor's Departments and paid for by the Commis-

[1] There was one Commissary of Accounts in Kennedy's office at Headquarters to examine the monthly copies of the accounts of the sub-accountants (C.G. Dalrymple); one (D.C.G. Booth) in the Military Secretary's office to examine the accounts submitted to Wellington for his warrant; and one at Lisbon (D.C.G. Vaux) to scrutinize all vouchers submitted by sub-accountants on the completion of their duties (Com.-Gen. Sir Randolph Isham Routh, *Observations on Commissariat Field Service* . . . (London, 1852), pp. 60 ff., cit. hereafter as 'Routh').

[2] Dowler's evidence in *Inquiry Proceedings*, i. 192, 195.

[3] This old Ordnance word is still in current use.

sariat. Third, clothing. Fourth, Camp or Field Equipment, often called Quartermaster-General's Stores, because, though stored by the Commissariat, they were issued only on the authority of the Q.M.G. or an officer of his department. Fifth, provisions for the men and forage for the horses and mules. And sixth, miscellaneous stores, such as fuel, lighting, stationery, and the whole variety of items outside the ordinary routine of a military existence.

The warlike stores, paid for and supplied by the Ordnance and issued at the request of the A.G. or Q.M.G. made upon the C.R.A. or the C.R.E., may be dismissed immediately. Almost exclusively manufactured at home and sent out in Ordnance storeships, they were in the custody of, as it were, a separate authority which the Commissariat might be called on to assist but never to intrude into. How jealously the Ordnance guarded its preserves may be judged by the occasion when Craufurd, at the time commanding the only troops in the Army in daily contact with the enemy, made a request to Murray for some tools, normally supplied by the Commissariat, but for which Murray, owing to the depots' being out of stock of them, had to make a demand on the nearest Ordnance depot. This was a demand by Wellington's chief staff officer, in Wellington's name, upon a miserable official at a base depot, for stores urgently needed for the one active part of an Army on which the defence of Portugal depended. And yet, as Murray said to Craufurd at the time, he doubted if it would be sufficient authority to the storekeeper to release them.[1]

The Medical and Hospital Stores and the miscellaneous stores may likewise be dismissed shortly.[2] Some of the items were sent out from England, but most of the food for the sick and many replacements were purchased locally by the Medical Department and the Purveyor from imprests advanced by the Commissariat. So far as the supply of medical stores is concerned, these departments never seriously failed.

[1] Murray to Craufurd, Alverca, 11 July 1810. The order to the Ordnance Storekeeper at Almeida runs: 'The Commander of the Forces directs that all the hand-hatchets and hand-bills remaining in the Ordnance Store at Almeida be issued to Brig.-General Robert Craufurd for the use of the British regiments under his orders. G. Murray, Q.M.G.' (*Murray Papers*, 60, pp. 89–90).

[2] See Appx. IV for a list of hospital stores.

No stories survive from Peninsular reminiscences similar to
that of the Walcheren expedition, when the supplies of bark
ran out and were only relieved by the chance arrival of an
American speculator with cargo of it.[1]

Camp Equipment was the miscellany of stores issued to
regiments as a matter of course on disembarkation in Portugal,[2] which transformed them from the elegant soldiers that
went through neat evolutions on Wimbledon Common into
the rough-and-ready, round-shouldered objects that marched
from one end of the Peninsula to the other and gave us the
victories of Salamanca and Vitoria. It was not until a regiment
was fitted out with Camp Equipment that the A.Q.M.G. at
Lisbon gave it its route whereby it joined the Army. These
stores were mostly of the type supplied and forwarded by the
Storekeeper-General in England[3] and committed to the
charge of the Commissariat until issued. Distributed on a
scale drawn up by the Q.M.G., they were supplied out of
public funds and charged to the regiment only in cases of
loss by negligence.

It has already been mentioned[4] that all articles of clothing
(and what were and still are called 'necessaries') were supplied to the soldier by the colonel of the regiment, who
received an annual allowance for this purpose, derived from
a stoppage of the man's pay known as 'off-reckonings'. The
off-reckonings had to suffice, however, not merely for pack-
ing the clothing but also for shipping it and transporting it
to the regiment wherever in the world it might be stationed.
These arrangements took place once a year just after Christmas. It was the responsibility of the Commissariat, therefore,
neither to supply it nor to transport it. Its transport shall be
dealt with later; but it should be noticed here that the wear
and tear of a campaign was too much for these arrangements
in war, and that a commander, having an interest in the state
of his men's clothing, was compelled to provide those articles
which wore worst—shoes, shirts, and pantaloons. The burden of supplying these fell naturally upon the Commissariat,

---

[1] *McGrigor*, p. 241.

[2] See Appx. V for a list of stores issued under this head, and the scale on which
they were issued.

[3] *v. sup.*, pp. 14–15.   [4] *v. sup.*, p. 12.

which procured them, on demand from the Q.M.G., either
by local contract (which was the method employed usually
until 1812) or by shipment from England. Occasionally,
after a particularly severe march, Wellington might order a
'donation' or free issue. But otherwise the cost of new shoes,
over and above the two pairs allowed yearly, was stopped
from the pay of the soldier, who naturally took a pecuniary
interest in the length of his marches. Some men of the 28th,
for instance, engaged in braking some guns down a sharp
incline, were observed to be much disgusted at losing the
heels of their shoes in this work—one pair 'destroyed in a
day without being allowed any consideration'.[1]

If the Commissariat played but a subsidiary part in the
supply of clothing, it was quite otherwise in the matter of
provisions, towards which it devoted the greater part of its
labours. But the Peninsular soldier subsisted on no delicately
balanced diet, and the commissary was under an obligation
to provide daily only the following quantities of these provisions:

For men: 1 lb. of meat.
           1 lb. of biscuit, or $1\frac{1}{2}$ lb. of good wheaten bread.
           1 pint of wine, or $\frac{1}{3}$ pint (English measure) of spirits.

For horses, and carriage and saddle-mules:
           10 lb. oats, barley, or Indian corn.
           10 lb. hay or cut straw.

For mules: 5 lb. oats, barley, or Indian corn.
           10 lb. cut straw.[2]

For his daily ration a soldier was stopped 3s. 6d. a week, but
if, as occasionally happened, supplies of provisions were
insufficient to ensure an issue of the full daily ration, he
could not claim on the Commissariat for the difference.[3] On
the contrary, although the soldier in theory fed himself from
his pay, the cost of meat alone, especially at the end of the

[1] *A Boy in the Peninsular War* [the services of Captain Robert Blakeney], ed.
Julian Sturgis (London, 1899), p. 23. The incident took place on the sharp descent
to Vila-Velha during Moore's advance on Salamanca, Oct. 1808.
[2] Kennedy to C.C. Darling at Espinhal, Vilar-Formoso, 7 Dec. 1812. The
ration varied: sometimes it was 12 lb. of corn, barley, or oats daily, and the men
might receive rice in lieu of bread.
[3] Murray to Spencer, Santa-Marinha, 24 Mar. 1811 (*Murray Papers*, 85, p. 189).

war, rose to such a height that his daily ration of it was calculated to cost about 2s. 6d., equivalent to double his pay.

From the foregoing some of the complexities of the supply of the Army may be deduced, and the different degrees of responsibility which the Commissariat bore in respect of each kind of stores should have become more clear. It is an important first step in understanding this difficult question, as misconception of it has often led to misdirected criticism, not only of Peninsular affairs but of the Crimean and other wars. For the 3s. 6d. it received weekly the government undertook to supply only certain provisions. If the soldier (or the officer) needed anything besides he bought it, if he could afford it, from the camp-follower known as the sutler, who having probably bought in Lisbon had set up shop with his regiment, which he supplied, under favourable conditions, with what the local market could not provide.

Sentiment has so changed during the last hundred years on this subject that it is difficult for us to envisage a period in which a soldier was expected to support himself from his pay and the government supplied only a proportion of his food. But in such countries as Spain and Portugal, if the commissary's responsibilities had extended no farther than it did, his task would have been arduous enough. Portugal, which was the base of operations for over two-thirds of the war, did not produce more than sufficient quantities of these articles for the needs of her population even in peacetime, and in many years had been forced to import on a considerable scale. The Portuguese were not a meat-eating race and the country was unequal to providing the immense quantities of beef which the British army looked to. Moreover, operations were conducted in the Upper and Lower Beira, the most infertile parts of the kingdom; and when the Army came down in 1810 and 1811 to the more fertile province of Portuguese Estremadura, the agriculture here had been deliberately dislocated as part of the defensive policy of 'driving the country'. Therefore the necessity of keeping the Army concentrated for long periods, which was one of Wellington's principal devices to offset the numerical superiority of the enemy, laid a strain on the country which it could not alone support.

In the Low Countries, in western Germany, in Rügen and Denmark, the Commissariat had relied almost exclusively on local merchants who came forward to tender for supplies. In the Elbe expedition of 1805–6, a single contractor of the name of Crelinger had been prepared to supply the whole force, and, until he was stopped, had been prepared to issue provisions direct to the troops without the interposition of the Commissariat. Commissaries coming straight from home to the Peninsula, accustomed only to the contract system, were surprised to find that things were far otherwise here. For the first year, it is true, when provisions were more plentiful, most of the business appears to have been done with contractors. But after the retreat from Talavera the Army occupied less well-favoured districts, where the type of contractor it needed did not exist. There was one Lisbon contractor, however, Henrique Teixeira de Sampaio,[1] who, with his brother F. T. Sampaio, supplied the base depots with immense quantities of provisions throughout the war. The ramifications of these men's business extended to the Barbary coast, Morocco, the Greek Islands, and the United States. Without the assistance of the vast resources of such a capitalist the Commissariat alone would have found it difficult, if not impossible, to subsist the Army. Its organization was not calculated to operate on this worldwide scale, and a smaller contractor than Sampaio could not have remained solvent when subject, as all government creditors were, to the system of tardy settlement. Though he made a substantial profit from his services, Sampaio should receive recognition for his part in maintaining the Army, not only for his enterprise but for accompanying it in the field, as he did in the summer of 1809, as a kind of contracting commissary and paymaster-general.[2]

Contract might be one method of supply but others were necessary to supplement it. At first *embargo* (confiscation under the law) was commonly resorted to, but Wellington early forbade this practice. Requisition was more common,

---

[1] Afterwards 1st Conde da Póvoa (1774–1843). He had been educated in England. Antônio Teixeira de Sampaio, no doubt a relation, was conducting at this time a merchant's business in London at 15 St. Helen's Place (*Post-Office Guide*).
[2] Sampaio to Kennedy, 7 Feb. 1811 (*Kennedy Papers*); *Schaumann*, p. 177.

but it was a disagreeable task and was only employed as a last resource. More than one officer has described the painful feelings with which he lay in wait for a peasant and 'ambushed' his oxen or his carts while he was at the plough; or strode into some riverside port and took possession of the country people's boats, unloaded their merchandise, and substituted the army stores.[1] For the greater part of the war, embargo was forbidden and requisition might only be carried out by or in the presence of a commissary who could settle or give receipts on the spot.

By far the commonest method of obtaining supplies was by ordinary local purchase. The agreement for purchase might take the form of a contract, by which, for instance, Messrs. Rozas & Bayley of Coimbra would undertake to supply so many head of cattle averaging so many pounds a head, at 115 reis the pound,[2] the contractor to forfeit so many dollars on failure to supply. Or alternatively it might take the form of a direct purchase from a merchant in a town near a depot or near the Army's cantonments. When it is considered that the average daily consumption in 1813 was 100,000 lb. of biscuit, 200,000 lb. of forage corn, and 300 head of cattle, the variety and scale of these transactions will be easily appreciated.[3]

By whatever means these supplies were procured, whether by purchase, by contract, or requisition, they were collected at depots at intervals along the roads from the coast to the Army, together with any other stores for which the Commissariat was responsible. The magazine was usually a warehouse rented for the purpose, but it was quite common to use churches for storehouses if the parish priest consented.[4]

[1] See Sir Richard D. Henegan, *Seven Years Campaigning* (London, 1846), i. 20: Lieut. W. Swabey's Diary in *Proceedings of the Royal Artillery Institution*, xxii. 94 (cit. hereafter as 'Proc. R.A.I.').

[2] The price of meat rose steadily from about 90 reis to the pound in 1809 to about 160 in the winter of 1812 to 1813; i.e., taking the milrea (1,000 reis) at the fictional value of 5s. 7½d., the price rose from about 6d. to 11d. To this price must be added the cost of transport.

[3] This was at 17 July 1813. See also Kennedy to D.C.G. Boyes, Castronuevo, 5 June 1813.

[4] *Schaumann*, pp. 16, 232; Álava to Kennedy, Vitoria, 29 Dec. 1813, on the claim of the parish priest of St. Sebastian for 334,700 reales de vellón (*Kennedy Papers*).

The size of each depot depended upon its position. Those nearer the Army might contain two months' consumption; intermediate stations might provide only for detachments of reinforcements marching up to join; and in the Lisbon depots —at any rate at the beginning of 1813—there was no less than seven months' consumption. Depots, moreover, changed their status with the movements of the Army. Celorico, for instance, an important Commissariat station while the Army lay in Upper Beira, became of little account during operations in the Alentejo, when depots around Elvas and Évora would be stocked partly from stores transferred from the north.

The sketch overleaf shows the thirty-seven depots upon which the Army subsisted at the beginning of 1812, immediately before Wellington launched his attack on Ciudad Rodrigo. It shows the routes by which these depots were replenished, and the positions of the various formations and regiments as they lay in their cantonments. It is a characteristic representation of the manner in which the Army was supplied at any period when it was not concentrated; but a sketch of the supply system at moments when the Army was concentrated would not differ materially. The difference in fact would lie in the extent to which each depot was stocked. It will be seen, moreover, that the line of depots (the *ligne d'opération* to which reference has already been made) could be extended or shortened by establishing further depots or emptying existing ones as occasion demanded. In theory, the line of depots might be extended *ad lib.*, and it is true that the system was fairly elastic and allowed freedom of movement at comparatively short notice; but in practice the prolongation of the line was governed by at least three limitations.

One was lack of staff. Each depot was presided over by at least one commissary; some of the more important might have two or three commissaries attached; and there were, besides, four or five senior officers, usually of the grade of deputy, who were entrusted with groups of depots over which they exercised a loose supervision. Thus the service of the thirty-seven depots alone shown on the sketch required the attention of at least sixty commissariat officers and clerks. In addition, each brigade of Anglo-Portuguese infantry, each regiment of cavalry, and each field brigade of artillery had its own commissary permanently assigned to it in the same manner as officers of the military staff—assignments which at the beginning of 1812 would absorb about seventy more commissaries. The maintenance of the Army, therefore, involved the employment of a staff of 130 officers and clerks. From 1812 there were eighty-seven commissaries and 255 clerks (exclusive of storekeepers, conductors, bakers, &c.) on the pay-lists of the Commissary-General in the Peninsula. More depots required more staff, and candidates for commissions in the Commissariat were already in 1812 not arriving in that number.[1]

The second limitation was the supply of transport at the disposal of the Army, what Wellington described as 'the great lever of the Commissariat'.[2] This is a complicated subject and calls for treatment in some detail.

It seems from a study of the system in the Peninsula that there were, broadly, three types of public transport (which in modern military jargon would probably be called échelons). There was, first, the transport which accompanied each regiment and which was issued to it on disembarkation in the same manner as Camp Equipage, on a scale drawn up by the Q.M.G.[3] Throughout the greater part of the war this transport took the form of mules, which were provided for the carriage of such baggage as the camp-kettles, the surgeon's panniers, and the paymaster's chest. The mules were paid for and maintained by an allowance made twice yearly to the officers responsible for their upkeep known as Bât Money.[4] Their number (thirteen for an infantry battalion,

---

[1] C.G. Bisset to J. C. Herries, Commissary-in-Chief, Malhada-Sorda, 12 Feb. 1812 (*Kennedy Papers*); Hon. Sir John Fortescue, *The Royal Army Service Corps: a history of transport and supply in the British army* (Cambridge, 1930), i. 92 n.

[2] *Disp.* v. 86.

[3] See G.O., Abrantes, 19 June 1809, as amended by that dated Freineda, 1 Mar. 1813, when a light tin camp-kettle to be carried by the men was introduced and the camp-kettle mules were turned over to the carriage of tents.

[4] Bât Money at the rate of £28. 5s. p.a. was payable in advance to captains of companies, the surgeon, paymaster, &c., on 1 Mar. and 17 Sept. each year, on the certificate of the Q.M.G. by the Commissariat. But payments both of it and of Forage Money, the allowance granted to all officers keeping horses (usually made simultaneously and known collectively as Bât and Forage Money), were in the Peninsula at least six months in arrear.

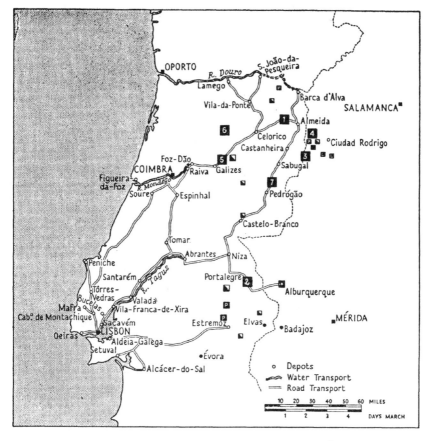

SUPPLY DEPOTS AND CANTONMENTS, JANUARY 1812

fourteen for a cavalry regiment) was fixed by General Order, and they were used exclusively for the purposes for which they were prescribed.

Secondly, there were what were generally referred to as the 'division mules', a number of mules attached to each Anglo-Portuguese infantry brigade, cavalry regiment, and field brigade of artillery, which, under the exclusive supervision of the divisional or brigade or regimental commissary, moved back and forth between the formation or unit and its supplying depot. The number of mules necessary for this employment varied according to the distance between the depot and the troops, and could be calculated on a purely mathematical basis. Given the fact that a mule's load was 200 lb., that it could go 4 leagues in a day, and given the weight of a man's and horse's daily ration, it was not difficult, as Wellington showed, to compute the scale on which mules should be attached to fighting formations. 'A mule', he wrote, in speaking of the transport necessary for a cavalry regiment, will 'carry corn for a horse for 20 days; and, it is calculated, will go upon an average 4 leagues[1] a day. A regiment of cavalry therefore ought to be supplied with mules to carry corn to the horses in such numbers as will bear the same proportion to the number of horses in the regiment as the number of days the mules will be travelling to and from the magazine will bear to 20. Thus, if the regiment is 8 leagues from the magazine the mules will be 4 days going to and from. The number of mules, therefore, which the regiment ought to have to keep up the supply should be one-fifth of the number of horses in the regiment. If the regiment should be 12 leagues from the magazine, the mules will be 6 days going and returning, and the number of mules required to keep up the supply will be nearly one-third of the number of horses in the regiment.'[2] Wellington allowed for an average distance of 12 leagues between troops and depot and the usual number of mules for each infantry

[1] The Portuguese and Spanish leagues were different, and also varied from province to province, but they may be taken as roughly equivalent to four miles.
[2] Holograph memorandum by Wellington headed 'Memorandum for Mr. Kennedy', undated but endorsed 'August, 1811' (*Kennedy Papers*). See also Wellington's Memoranda for the Commissary-General, Freineda, 20 and 21 Nov. 1811 (*Disp.* v. 371–3, 375).

brigade, cavalry regiment, or field brigade of artillery varied between 100 and 150. An infantry division complete with its brigade of artillery (six guns) would therefore possess a train of between 400 and 600 mules.

Thirdly, there was the immense train of bullock-cars that, travelling three leagues a day and plying from one depot to the next in stages, replenished and charged the depots. Stores that were to be carried farther than one stage had to be off-loaded on arrival and reloaded for the next stage. For the carriage of a consignment of stationery, for instance, sent up from Galizes to Headquarters in the autumn of 1812, Mr. Mills had to find transport to Celorico, Mr. Head at Celorico for its transmission to Almeida, Mr. Flanner at Almeida to Ciudad Rodrigo, Mr. Laidley at Ciudad Rodrigo to Rueda.[1] Bullock-cars were the commonest form of transport in this 'third échelon', but over stages nearer the coast great use was made of boats. The Tagus was usually navigable by the smaller river boats known as *fragatas* as far as Abrantes,[2] which became an important commissariat station, and as one officer called it 'the mirror in which the Commissariat Department may be seen.[3] The Mondego was navigable in winter to Foz-Dão, in summer to Raiva. The most important of the three great rivers of Portugal was the Douro, which, flowing between the great vineyards of the port-wine growers, possessed a highly developed system of navigation. In all seasons it was passable for large boats (*matrizes*) to the Vale de Lucaia near Lamego; smaller boats (*trafegueiras*) could reach Quinta dos Carvalhos near S. João-da-Pesqueira, and in winter, and after the Engineers had improved the bed of the river in 1812, it could be navigated safely to the Portuguese frontier at Barca-de-Alva. The dry season (July–October), however, inevitably brought with it a lengthening of the line of land carriage, the need for more bullocks, and the consequent further expense.[4]

The responsibility for procuring all these forms of transport, including mule transport for the Ordnance corps and

[1] Kennedy to the above, Rueda, 5 Nov. 1812 (*Kennedy Papers*).
[2] Scovell's Diary (W.O. 37/6), under entry dated 11 Apr. 1809.
[3] Swabey's Diary, entry dated 13 Sept. 1811 (*Proc. R.A.I.* xxii. 85–86).
[4] e.g. Wellington to Liverpool, Castelo-Branco, 1 Aug. 1811 (*Disp.* v. 194).

the ammunition reserves, was borne by the Commissary-General. In former wars he had shared it with the Q.M.G.,[1] and in other theatres he had been able to depend on the carts of the country people. In Portugal, however, the roads were so bad that by 1810 it had become clear that even the small cart of the Beirão peasant with its solid wheels and moving axles, designed to withstand the rough wear of the country paths,[2] was unsatisfactory for the 'second échelon' transport, and Wellington had ordered for it at least the exclusive employment of mules.[3]

The task of the Commissary-General was by this measure eased to some extent, as in both Spain and Portugal it was customary to carry most merchandise on pack animals rather than by wheeled transport.[4] The whole internal commerce of Spain having been dislocated by the French invasion, the vast system of muleteers, with their mules and asses, in the face of unemployment readily placed itself at the disposal of the British Commissariat in ever increasing numbers as the war proceeded. Mostly Spanish, the muleteers brought varying numbers of mules into the British service, where they were organized into 'mule brigades', which might consist of as few as twenty or as many as fifty mules, each under its own *capataz* or foreman. G. Dias de Lunas, to pick one name out of many, brought in five brigades, two of 28, one of 29, one of 132, and the other of 35 mules. The 'brigade' remained the unit and does not appear to have been split up but assigned in its entirety to the charge of the commissary of a division, who kept account of its service and paid (or at any rate owed) the owner, the *capataz*, and the muleteers at the rate of a dollar a day for each mule and a dollar a day to each muleteer.

While mules formed the transport for what has been called the 'second échelon', the boats and bullock-cars (and

[1] *v. sup.*, p. 27.

[2] Prof. Orlando Ribeiro, *Portugal, o Mediterrâneo e o Atlântico* (Coimbra, 1948), p. 131.

[3] Lieut.-Col. Dickson to Maj.-Gen. Macleod, D.A.G., R.A., Tôrre-de-Mouro, 3 July 1811 (*Dickson Papers*, p. 410).

[4] Alexandre de Laborde, *Itinéraire déscriptif de l'Espagne . . .* (Paris, 1809), pp. cxxi-cxxxv; H. F. Link, *Travels in Portugal and through France and Spain* (Eng. trs. London, 1801), p. 194; Rafael Altamira, *História de España y de la Civilización española* (Barcelona, 1911), iv. 284.

mules also to some extent) composed the 'third échelon', which were equally hired by the Commissary-General to travel by the stage. It is impossible to calculate the quantities but it is clear that those obtainable by the normal means or by requisition, or by demand upon the Inspector of Transport of each province, were insufficient, and at the end of 1811 Wellington ordered the construction at Lisbon, Oporto, and Almeida of some 600 carts upon an improved pattern, which were to be entrusted to drivers and conductors employed directly by the Commissariat. Organized in brigades, sub-divisions, and grand divisions, they became known as the Commissariat Car Train. The first Grand Division was formed in time to assist materially in the transport of stores for the siege of Badajoz in March and April 1812. The second Grand Division was formed on 27 June 1812, after a further 700 'cars of the new construction' had been sent out from England.[1]

Until the autumn of 1812 the Commissary-General also had the assistance of the Royal Waggon Train, a Horse Guards organization, officered and manned by old troopers and n.c.o.'s from the cavalry regiments, which though nominally entrusted to the Q.M.G., had lost its identity amidst the numberless carts and wagons employed by the Commissariat. Possessing the only spring-wagons in the Army, the Waggon Train had whenever possible been detailed for carrying the sick and wounded, but its numbers were so small that it could not be assigned exclusively to any one duty, and it had taken over such miscellaneous tasks as that of carrying the three printing-presses which were sent out to Headquarters in the summer of 1812.[2] When Gordon, the Q.M.G., inspected the corps in October 1812, it consisted of no more than eighty-seven horses and eleven wagons and all in very poor condition.[3] However, it was then transferred

---

[1] [John Edgecombe Daniel], *Journal of an officer in the Commissariat Department*... (London, 1820), pp. 69–70; Memorandum by Wellington, 20 Nov. 1811 (*Disp.* v. 370); correspondence of Capt. Whittle, Royal Waggon Train, engaged in collecting timber at Rochoso for the new wagons, Nov.–Dec. 1811 (*Kennedy Papers*).

[2] One press for the A.G., one for the M.S., and one for the Commissary-General, apparently.

[3] Gordon to Wellington, Villatoro, 9 Oct. 1812 (*Murray Papers*, 63, 87–88).

from the Commissariat to its rightful owner and, reinforced and divided equally between the divisions, it acted thenceforward entirely as an ambulance corps.

Contract, requisition, the Commissariat Car Train, and the Royal Waggon Train: these were the resources upon which Kennedy relied for obtaining the immense quantity of transport needed to carry the multitude of stores from depot to depot. Meat was usually carried up on the hoof under the supervision of the Commissariat (and made pretty tough eating by the time it arrived).[1] But all other provisions whether for the army or the Ordnance were carried on Commissariat transport, together with medical stores and camp equipment and, at the New Year, the clothing of each regiment, the carriage of which, though looked upon as an indulgence to the colonel, became in fact a heavy task shared between Kennedy and Murray.[2]

The system of replenishing the depots was nothing new in an army which was supplied on the *Magazinssystem*, and though perhaps more methodical in the Peninsula, it did not differ materially from the manner in which the army had been subsisted in Flanders twenty years before or, indeed, during any war of the previous century. The novelty of the Peninsular system consisted, firstly, in the extent to which the operation of transport and supply fell upon government servants; and secondly, in the creation of what has been called here the 'second échelon' transport.

In other wars, waged in better-favoured parts of the world, both supply and even transport had been provided mostly by contractors, and the services of the representatives of the Treasury had been called upon merely to order what was required, to check roughly that what was ordered arrived, and in due course to pay. But in the Peninsula, as the Commissary-General wrote, 'it is not with us as was formerly the practice with armies on the continent of Europe. We have

---

[1] *Ross-Lewin*, pp. 150–1.

[2] e.g. Murray to Lieut.-Col. Petrie, commanding the 79th, Fuenteguinaldo, 12 Aug. 1811 (*Murray Papers*, 61, pp. 38–39): '. . . the public departments of the army are under no responsibility in regard to the clothing of regiments, and that it is a matter of indulgence only that such facilities are afforded from time to time in regard to the conveyance and disposal of it as the commanding officers of regiments may request.'

no contractors: everything is within ourselves'.[1] Hence the unprecedented establishment of Commissaries, and hence also the time it took for them to accustom themselves to conditions which were quite outside the ordinary run of Commissariat experience. Sir Brook Watson, Commissary-General to the army in Flanders (1793–5), had been able to conduct his department in ease and comfort from his office in London:[2] Kennedy and Bisset, shivering round a charcoal brazier in a farmhouse on the confines of Portugal, haggled personally with muleteers who were two years in arrear for their pay. The charge of incompetence and inexperience so often brought against these men, not only in this war but in the Crimea, bears a rather different aspect when viewed in this light.

The creation of a permanent body of mule transport attached to each division is difficult to trace. Calling it an 'échelon' is of course modern and has been used here only for the sake of convenience.[3] Something of the kind must have existed both before and after the formation of the divisions in 1809, but the emergence of such a system as has been described does not make itself known until the resumption of active operations in September 1810. A divisional baggage train was certainly in existence in the retreat from the Côa on Buçaco in that month, and it is clearly recognizable as a mule-train during the next operation, in which Masséna was pursued from the Lines of Lisbon in March 1811. The systematic allotment of the train on a scale devised by Wellington becomes apparent during the autumn of that year, and thenceforth the 'division mules' were a permanent feature of Peninsular transport. The gradual transformation of a practice into a system is characteristic of Wellington's method, and in this instance the influence of the Commander is plainly discernible. By allowing the fighting formations to

[1] C. G. Bisset to J. C. Herries, Commissary-in-Chief, Malhada-Sorda, 12 Feb. 1812 (*Kennedy Papers*).

[2] 'Had this service continued or been much more active, much explanation might have been necessary on the situation of a Commissary-Generalissimo residing at home and conducting the extensive operations of Deputies abroad.' Sir David Dundas to Brownrigg, M.S., Delmenhorst, Dec. 1795 (W.O. 1/173, pp. 950–63).

[3] In fact the classification and whole treatment of the transport system used here are only for convenience. It was not recognized at the time and is not, so far as I am aware, to be found elsewhere.

move, as it were, like a horse on a picket-rope, fifty miles from the forward depots, he gave their movements a mobility which the country's lack of resources in their immediate vicinity would otherwise have denied them. It is important, too, to notice that this échelon was organized on a divisional basis. We have already noticed the allotment of staff, both military and civil, more or less permanently to divisions.[1] We now see the division provided with means to subsist itself and to carry its own sick and wounded independently. And we shall later have occasion to observe the division becoming simultaneously a small force with all its own services—a self-sufficient fighting unit.[2]

The third limitation was that imposed by finance. None of these arrangements, whether for supply or transport, would have been possible without money, and not merely credit or paper money but coin. The British Government throughout the whole of the Peninsular War was experiencing great difficulty in procuring specie, and during Kennedy's tenure of office succeeded in dispatching to him a mere £6-million in specie towards the £54-million which he was eventually found to have disbursed. Large contractors' debts could be settled in Treasury bills; even smaller men and muleteers could be satisfied with receipts or vouchers for a time; the officers of the Army could be, as they were, paid half in metal and half in paper currency (which was discounted at rates varying throughout the war between 20 per cent. and 30 per cent.). But the men could only be paid in coin, and the vouchers (or *vals* as they were commonly called) given to the smaller merchants had at some moment to be honoured in the same way, not only in justice, but for the credit of the Army and the solvency of those who supplied it.

The Commissary-General therefore, apart from his other preoccupations, was vitally concerned in devising expedients by which the day of settlement might be deferred without damaging his credit, and for procuring specie. The Treasury

---

[1] *v. sup.*, p. 52.

[2] Wellington, however, did not attach cavalry to divisions in the manner that soon after became customary in, say, the Prussian service, though certain cavalry formations became accustomed to act with certain infantry formations.

was scarcely in a position to assist him except in approving his recommendations. While Colonel Gordon was Commissary-in-Chief (1809–11) his efforts were manfully seconded by his superiors in London; but Gordon, on his appointment as Q.M.G. of the Forces, was succeeded by J. C. Herries,[1] a young gentleman from the City with his own notions of how these things should be done, who gave both Kennedy and Bisset little of the support they needed in their capacities as Treasury officials. As officers serving on a commander's staff, however, they received from Wellington all the backing that a commander dependent on their exertions could be expected to give; but even Wellington at the height of his reputation was unable to intercede decisively with the Treasury.

From the middle of 1809 the usual procedure followed was for a commissary making purchases or hiring transport either to pay the supplier outright from his imprest or to give him a bill drawn upon the Commissary-General, from which it was customary to omit the usance, that is to say, the date at which the bill would be honoured. The merchant, after a lapse of time, would present himself at the Commissary-General's office, or get an acquaintance of his to do so for him, and there he would receive his money. Or, what was more probable in the embarrassed state of the Chest, he would be treated like Snr. Joaquim Pedro Tavares, who was

referred to fifty people without being able to meet the proper authority, and my papers as signed by His Britannic Majesty's commissaries have been hitherto of no utility in the administering of *ad valorem*. My bills have been at Lisbon, where my friends are told they should show them at Headquarters. They accordingly duly appeared there, and there as usual were ordered out of the office to go to the devil or where they pleased.[2]

It was not uncommon for such men as these to go unpaid for two years. Most could not afford to wait so long, and disposed of their bills to large merchants in the towns who could, and who bought them at prices much below their face value.

The credit of the Army suffered accordingly. Not only did

[1] See *D.N.B.*

[2] Joaquim Pedro Tavares to the Adjutant-General, Rossio do Espirito-Santo, Portalegre, 10 May 1812 (*Kennedy Papers*).

muleteers desert, or refuse to come forward, and merchants charge prices reflecting both their profit and the discount on the *vals*,[1] but the exertions of those officers of the Department who were engaged in negotiating commissariat or Treasury bills for specie in the money market were correspondingly embarrassed. The task of negotiating fell, not to the Commissary-General himself, who was at Headquarters, but to his Deputies stationed at the large commercial centres such as Oporto and Lisbon, who treated with the great merchants like Sampaio.[2] For long periods the credit of the Army was so low that it was impossible to procure specie except on unacceptable terms.

Some relief, perhaps, was afforded by importing manufactured articles, and some provisions, from England. This was a practice which became more and more common from 1812 onwards,[3] and assumed considerable proportions after July 1813, when the Biscay ports (Bilbao, Santander, and Pasajes) became available for traffic. The gradual shortening of the communication after this time permitted an increasing dependence on the home market, and Kennedy not only obtained meat from Ireland in the autumn of 1813, but was allowed by Herries to call upon the Senior Commissary at Plymouth to send all disposable vessels to France with forage whenever it became necessary. But experience was to show how hazardous this expedient might be, when bad weather in November and December prevented any of the grain ships from putting in, at a critical moment at which Kennedy had suspended the purchase of all forage in Spain and Portugal and before he had been able to accumulate a reserve from the shipments from home.[4] It was also to some extent offset by the entry of the United States into the war in 1812, which not only deprived the Army of a bountiful source of supply and of the only merchants that would accept Treasury

---

[1] On 29 Mar. 1814 the *val* was worth 74*d*. the milrea at Lisbon, with discount at 23¼ per cent.

[2] D.C.G. Dunmore (1809–12) and D.C.G. Pipon (1812–15) at Lisbon; D.C.G. Mackenzie at Oporto.

[3] e.g. letter Wellington to Stuart, Fuenteguinaldo, 27 Aug. 1811 (*Disp.* v. 237).

[4] Sundry correspondence in *Kennedy Papers* over this period shows how critical the situation was during Dec. 1813 and early Jan. 1814. The whole transport system was in danger of failing through lack of forage.

bills in payment, but exposed the sea communication to the further risk of American privateers.

It is not necessary to examine more closely the manifold expedients to which the Commissary-General and Wellington were reduced. It is necessary only to visualize the effects which the shortage of ready cash had upon operations. It is not often that they are directly visible, since Wellington, and for that matter any general, was constrained to act and plan as his resources permitted. We know, however, that his advance into Spain in the summer of 1809 was delayed for five precious weeks owing to the non-arrival of a treasure ship from England.[1] It may be suspected that there was a further reason why Wellington had to storm Badajoz at the moment he did beyond those military reasons which, indeed, were pressing enough: the besieging force and the formations detached to cover the siege were all subsisted from the magazines of Elvas, Évora, and Estremoz, distant 60 or 70 miles from the most advanced troops—a fact which made this operation the most expensive for its size of any he undertook. And we know, on the evidence of Kennedy, whose activity entitles him to inform us on what was possible and what was impossible, that, but for a device for obtaining specie which brought it in to the Military Chest at the rate of 850,000 dollars a month,[2] the Army in 1813 would not have been able to advance beyond Salamanca by the end of July: at which time it was in fact in the Pyrenees.[3]

It is impossible to speculate upon the course events would have taken if circumstances had been otherwise on any of these occasions. In an army which was as dependent for its maintenance on ready money as Wellington's, the variety of combinations open to a commander who had every resource at his disposal is too infinite for description. All speculations on what Wellington might have done should be indulged in with the knowledge that the Military Chest throughout the Peninsular War was never solvent. The

[1] Wellington to Hon. W. W. Pole, Castelo-Branco, 1 July 1809 (*Camden Miscellany*, xvii (Camden Third Series, lxxix, 1948), ed. Professor Sir Charles Webster, p. 14); *Disp.* iii. 297–329.

[2] Explained in Wellington to Bathurst, Freineda, 21 Apr. 1813 (*Disp.* vi. 439).

[3] Draft letter Kennedy to Col. Sir F. B. Hervey, Wellington's Private Secretary, London, 18 June 1819 (*Kennedy Papers*).

implications of this should have become clearer and should be able to speak for themselves.

Wellington's Army, then, maintained itself with a long, highly organized, and very expensive 'administrative tail'. It was managed from Headquarters; the siting of the depots was decreed by Wellington himself, or Murray, in consultation with Kennedy; and those commissariat stations which were to become also hospital stations or 'passing stations' for sick were equally decided upon by Wellington or Murray in consultation with the Inspector-General of Hospitals. Yet the delegation of duties and responsibilities allowed it to work without excessive interference from the heads of departments. The commandants of hospital stations, hardened old disciplinarians or smart young officers detached from their regiments and appointed by the Adjutant-General to organize the convoys of sick and the detachments of convalescents rejoining from the rear, had considerable powers of their own. The Deputies of the Commissariat Department in charge of a group of magazines, after they had received their instructions as to the stock each magazine was to carry, were left very much to their own devices as to how they could fulfil their duties. We have seen that the Deputy-Commissaries at Lisbon and Oporto could act on their own in negotiating the purchase of specie. The commissaries of divisions, the pick of the commissariat, were likewise at liberty to dispose of their transport as best suited the arrangements of the divisional commander and, unless they infringed Kennedy's standing orders, were almost independent of Kennedy's jurisdiction.

Once, however, the 'commissariat line', as it was called, was established, Wellington allowed no deviation without his orders. His rebuke to McGrigor, the Inspector-General, who on one occasion in 1812 acted on his own and sent a convoy of sick by another route, shows the importance he attached to *system*, which, indeed, was essential in so complex a mechanism.[1]

Experience gained in extended operations revealed that there were other limitations, besides those already described, to the length of the commissariat line. The depot-system

[1] *McGrigor*, p. 302.

required a centralization of information upon the state of the magazines, and, although 'commissary-couriers' recruited from the local population carried these statistics daily to Kennedy, the longer the line the less effective intervention from Headquarters became. When at Burgos in 1812 the Army had scarcely been able to be supported by the tenuous line from Portugal, and Wellington had arranged, while still at Madrid, on 22 August, for a subsidiary supply route to be established from Corunna. The following year, in planning for an advance beyond the Ebro, he anticipated the drawbacks of the Portugal communication; and Kennedy had ordered storeships to lie off Corunna and be prepared for instructions to sail for the Biscay ports, whence a new commissariat line was to be run.[1] The success of the Army's operations proved in the event these measures to be justified. By July, when the troops were in the Pyrenees, it took ten weeks for supplies ordered from Portugal to arrive at their destination. About the middle of that month the Portugal line was abandoned. The Army thenceforward drew its subsistence from Bilbao, Santander, and Pasajes.

Excessive speed in the Army's movement equally dislocated the arrangements of the depot system. Though it might take as little time as two days to establish or suppress a depot, supply in the end was dependent on a bullock-cart which, loaded, could not travel more than 12 miles a day. So long as the Army marched at its usual pace of about 15 miles a day with a halt every so often, the bullocks' pace was quite sufficient and what difference there might be between the two could be taken up by the divisional mules. But sustained marches of 20 miles a day were beyond the limitations of the depot system. This had been clearly shown in the pursuit of Masséna's retreating army in the spring of 1811, when the British troops were brought, after ten days' marching, to a complete standstill for a week during which they waited, half-starved, to catch the sound of the welcome jingle-jangle of the mules bringing their rations from the rear.[2] The circumstances in this instance were peculiar in that the

---

[1] Kennedy to Herries, Lizárraga, 24 June 1813 (*Kennedy Papers*).
[2] Unpublished MS. journal of the Royal Dragoons quoted in C. T. Atkinson, *History of the Royal Dragoons, 1661-1934* (Glasgow, 1935), p. 258.

country they marched through had been twice purposely wasted in six months. More eloquent of the limitations of the depot system was the great advance from Portugal in 1813, which, though prepared for by the Commissariat four months beforehand,[1] nevertheless outran the supplies to such an extent that within three weeks of starting, on 16 June, the transport was unequal to the demands made on it and the Army had to be subsisted on the country.[2] This occurring five days before the battle of Vitoria goes far to answer criticism of the slowness of the pursuit after the battle and to account for the fatigue and frustration which almost destroyed the Army in its moment of victory.

But the effectiveness or ineffectiveness of a system of supply is to be measured not only by the ease with which it maintains its own army. However good a system may be it is not good enough if the enemy's is better.

The Revolutionary and Napoleonic armies were subsisted on a *Requisitionssystem*. They lived on the country they occupied. On entering a new district the Intendant-Général served upon the magistrates of the various towns a formidable bi-lingual document requiring them to provide by a certain time (often 'ce soir avant la nuit') so many rations of bread, so many rations of flour, &c., and finishing with the phrase: 'La présente réquisition est de rigueur. Les justices en sont personellement responsables. Dans le cas de refus ou de retard la Commune de . . . supportera toute la rigueur d'une exécution militaire.'[3] If a magistrate or a farmer refused a sentry was posted before his door and he was charged a dollar an hour while the sentry remained. Requisition for transport was made in a similar fashion, and like all other requisitions made by the French were rarely if ever paid for.

Under no obligation to consult the feelings of a friendly population, the French army could move wherever the country was not exhausted; and as 'exhaustion' to a French

[1] See [P. W. Buckham], *Personal Narrative of Adventures in the Peninsula . . .* (London, 1827), Letters VIII and IX (cit. hereafter as 'Buckham').

[2] Kennedy to Herries, Lizárraga, 24 June 1813 (*Kennedy Papers*).

[3] The originals of three documents of this type served upon the Justicias of Ribera, Fuente del Maestre, and Villafranca by the Intendant-Général of Soult's Army, Los Santos, 13 June 1811, are to be found in *Murray Papers*, 36, fos. 30–34, having been taken up by peasants and forwarded to Wellington on the same day.

intendant meant reduction to the state of a desert, movement could be made without premeditation. Moreover, the French soldier of Napoleon's time, no longer sybaritic, was careful of his food. If issued with fourteen days' rations he could be relied on to save them for so long. He compared favourably in this respect with the British soldier, who was notoriously improvident, and who, though occasionally issued with three days' rations in advance, was rarely entrusted with more than a day's consumption, the rest being retained by the Quarter-master.[1] With such temporary advantages the French armies operated with remarkable swiftness and at little expense over the whole Peninsula.

It would be mistaken, however, to suppose that they could be maintained as armies without accumulations of the many stores which were not to be procured locally. To that extent they were therefore subject to the same handicap as the British. The system of requisition, moreover, carried in itself its own limitations. It inflamed the Spanish countryfolk and fomented guerrilla resistance. While a British force in its encampments or cantonments subsisted on provisions brought from many quarters of the world, the French force opposite them subsisted only on what the country they immediately occupied and, perhaps, 20 miles around, could provide. A prolonged occupation of the same district or a return to an exhausted district were out of the question. Similarly the concentration of a large force could not long endure. Al-though until well into 1813 the French armies, if assembled, could far outnumber the force at Wellington's disposal, concentration, which is the necessary prelude to any effective action, was a game at which Wellington's depot-fed Army was better equipped to play than the French. On at least three separate occasions Wellington forced a superior combination of French armies to retire without fighting merely by remaining concentrated in their front. Though it might bring temporary success, in the long run the French method of supply was no match against a well-managed system of depots.[2]

---

[1] *Routh*, pp. 13–14.

[2] Cf. Clausewitz's chapter (*Vom Kriege*, bk. v, cap. 14) on 'Subsistence', where he writes that the French *Lieferungssystem* was so superior to the *reine Magazinver-*

As Wellington was fond of quoting, 'quand on fait la guerre en Espagne avec peu de monde on est battu, et avec beaucoup de monde on meurt de faim'.[1] After a time even the French, who showed such ingenuity and persistence in exacting the utmost from a district's resources as to astonish their adversaries,[2] were compelled to form depots in Spain. This departure from their usual practice was observed by Wellington in the summer of 1811.[3] But it never supplanted the old system of requisition, and even in 1813 their reliance on the country was so essential that Wellington's close pursuit of their armies, in depriving them of their resources, was an important element in the success of his astonishing advance.[4]

Wellington clearly perceived the weakness in the French system. One of his objects, certainly, was by improving and systematizing the traditional methods of supply of the British army to make it as independent as possible of local resources.[5] He noted with satisfaction the moment when his efforts were so far rewarded as to make the French alter the nature of their military system. He saw that once they were forced back on the resources of France the end was near. The wars had started because France could not support the armies that were raised: they would stop, as they did stop, when they were driven back within their frontiers where the people could not and would not support them.[6]

Viewed in this light Wellington's method of maintaining

pflegung that the armies opposed to them had to go over to it, and, he adds, it is hardly to be expected that anyone will go back to the latter. Clausewitz's whole argument on this subject is vitiated by his ignorance, or neglect, of experience gained in the Peninsula.

[1] Wellington to Dumouriez, Quinta de S. João, 5 July 1811, and Saint-Jean-de-Luz, 22 Nov. 1813 (*Disp.* v. 138; vii. 155).

[2] e.g. before the Lines of Lisbon in the winter of 1810–11.

[3] Wellington to Hon. H. Wellesley, Fuenteguinaldo, 29 Aug. 1811 (*Disp.* v. 248).

[4] See an article by Sir George Murray in the *Edinburgh Review* (1839), lxix. 334.

[5] See the Archduke Charles's verdict, written in the second half of the 1830's as an introduction to the 1811 part of his 'Übersicht des Krieges auf der Pyrenäischen Halbinsel, 1808–1814' (*Ausgewählte Schriften*, iv. 479).

[6] *Disp.* v. 248: 'They are now in a great measure on the defensive and are carrying on a war of magazines. They will soon, if they have not already, come upon the resources of France; and as soon as that is the case you may depend upon it the war will not last long.'

his Army, whatever the difficulties and expense it might in-
volve and despite the occasional failures, was measurably
superior to the French. There is a note of envy to be detected
in this passage from Foy's History of the war: 'La distance
ne fait rien aux maîtres de la mer. On a vu des chevaux anglais
en Portugal nourris avec du foin coupé dans les prairies de
Yorkshire, et les hommes avec des farines apportées d'Améri-
que.'[1] There is of course nothing said of Wellington or
Kennedy. It just happened.

[1] Gen. Foy, *Histoire de la guerre de la Péninsule* . . . (Paris, 1827), i. 310.

IV

THE COLLECTION AND TRANSMISSION
OF INTELLIGENCE

IT is the worst of modern fallacies to suppose, as it might be from the examples given in the foregoing chapter, that all military operations can be explained in purely economic terms. He is an unfortunate man who is *totally* absorbed in the mere struggle for existence; and an army that is preoccupied all the year in its own maintenance cannot properly be described as an army. Equally the army that can strike at will on the right flank, the left, the centre, or the rear as the commander pleases in accordance with the Rules of the Art, as Murray called them, has yet to be seen. This is only to say, of course—what has been said before,[1] yet is often ignored—that a commander's plan is no more than a choice of difficulties. What he would do and what he can do are governed by material considerations. 'Victories in battle win wars', one of the most distinguished and successful practitioners of the craft has said recently.[2]

That being the case, I feel the making of war resolves itself into very simple issues, and the simplest in my view is: what is possible and what is not possible? In trying to discover what is possible and what is not possible I would say that three things matter most. I am assuming, of course, that the weapon is a sharp weapon and not a blunt one. . . . Assuming all that, what is possible will depend first on geography, secondly on transportation, in its widest sense, and thirdly on administration.

The problem and its issues could hardly be put more simply and clearly. But it is permissible for anyone treating of events which took place well outside the memory of living man to refine somewhat on Lord Montgomery's analysis, and to say that a commander has to choose between the

---

[1] War, said Wolfe, 'is in its nature hazardous and an option of difficulties'. Letter to Maj. Rickson, Blackheath, 5 Nov. 1757 (*Beckles Willson*, p. 339).

[2] Field Marshal Lord Montgomery in an address to the Royal Geographical Society, 10 May 1948 (*Geographical Journal*, cxii. 16).

possible and the impossible as he conceives it from his information. Even if a commander has the ability to distinguish between what is relevant and what is not—a gift granted to few men, generals as well—he has ever been at the mercy of the intelligence he has received; and, although he will be criticized afterwards, and occasionally justly criticized, by later generations better informed than he, all criticism, all condemnation, will be misdirected if it takes no consideration of what a commander knew when he made his decision.

At the outbreak of the Peninsular War maps of both Spain and Portugal comparable in accuracy to those of other parts of Western Europe were not to be obtained. What maps there were were infinitely inferior to the geodesic survey of France carried out and published by the Cassini family, and those of the Low Countries based upon Ferraris's survey,[1] the two best-mapped countries of the continent. Mathematics had been neglected for more than a century in the Spanish and Portuguese universities. At Salamanca mathematical study had been deliberately restricted by the Jesuit influence in the governing body *como cosa del diablo*.[2] Until the expulsion of the Jesuits in the 1770's little progress could therefore be made in such a science as triangulation which depended both for its practice and its reputation upon a live school of mathematicians. In default of accurate maps topographical information was drawn from less authentic sources. A young French officer, who later reached distinction (or perhaps notoriety) in his service,[3] has described how the Spanish general, in planning his invasion of Portugal in 1762, compiled his topographical intelligence; how, surrounded by his staff, he questioned them all on the Portuguese roads—one knew from a merchant that the roads from such and such were so and so, and another had heard from a lady at Valladolid that the roads in such a province were

[1] F. M. Josef, Graf Ferraris (1726–1814), who, in various military capacities, supervised the construction of the map of all the lands now comprised in Belgium for the Austrian Government. Only three copies were made, none of which remained in the Netherlands after 1794, but a reduction was engraved by Dupuis and published in 1777 (Sir H. G. Fordham, *Some Notable Surveyors and Map-makers of the 16th, 17th and 18th Centuries and their Work* (Cambridge, 1929), pp. 62–64).

[2] *Altamira*, iv. 357.

[3] Gen. C. F. Dumouriez, *État présent du Royaume de Portugal* [1766] (rev. ed., Hamburg, 1797), pp. xxiii–xxiv.

impassable. 'Tout se passait en conjectures, en ouï-dire, et il
n'y avait pas de projet de campagne faute de connaître
le pays.'

However, information from ladies at Valladolid and the
like, though not eliminated by the time of the war, played
less and less part as the last decades of the century went by.
A sensible improvement came in the immense compilation
of information, derived from many different sources, printed
in the series of maps known collectively as 'López'. These
were published province by province from 1765 onwards by
D. Tomás López (1730–1802), who had learned his art in
France under Lacaille, d'Anville, and Dheulland, and by
his son, D. Tomás Maurício López (1776–1835), who continued the publication and the revision of the original plates
after his father's death. 'López' was the basis of all maps of
Spain in currency at the time of the war.[1] Corrected and improved by map-publishers throughout Europe (Artaria in
Vienna, Collin and Mentelle in Paris, Stockdale and Faden
in London), his maps gave a tolerable representation of the
ground and a moderately accurate notion of distances which
would satisfy a traveller. But they were not based upon a
trigonometrical survey, and the methods used for indicating
the quality of the roads were almost useless to a general or a
military topographer.

In Portugal, though there had been a revival of interest in
maps and charts, fostered by Pombal, the effects of the revival were confined to the learned academies and did not
reach the public. Francisco Antonio Ciera, a Piedmontese by
origin, had measured two long bases in Portuguese Estremadura between 1793 and 1802, and a number of officers of
the Portuguese Royal Engineers were permanently assigned
to the preparation of the 'Carta Geográfica do Reino' from
1799 onwards.[2] In this respect the Portuguese were probably ahead of the Spaniards. But for some reason, no doubt
the bankruptcy of the State, these researches had yielded
nothing that was of use to the traveller and very little that

[1] See *De Laborde* (1809), pp. cx–cxi: '. . . dans un pays dont on connaît à peine
la configuration et sur lequel on n'a que des cartes moins parfaites encore que celles
de López (qu'il est d'ailleurs impossible de se procurer). . . .'
[2] Cristóvão Aires, *História . . . do Exército Português. Provas* (Lisbon, 1910), v.
156, 239, 243–4.

was of advantage to the army or to the commander of an allied force. The survey of the neighbourhood of Lisbon, carried out by Major Neves Costa as the basis for his proposal of fortified lines to cover the capital, proved to be inaccurate and misleading.[1] The only tangible result of this interest in topography was the so-called 'Mapa Militar', compiled by one of the officers concerned in the 'Carta Geográfica', Major Lourenço Homem da Cunha d'Eça, and published in the year of Vimeiro by Eloij de Almeida.[2] It was a large map in two sheets, more reliable than López's *Portugal* (1778), but, as experience in the war was to show, containing several inaccuracies and distortions.[3]

To supplement the information to be obtained from maps the guides and road-books available were not of a very high order. The best description of Portugal was P. João de Castro's *Roteiro Terrestre de Portugal*, published sixty years previously. There were also the same priest's *Mapa de Portugal*, published over the years 1745 to 1758, and António de Oliveira Freire's *Descrição Corográfica do Reino de Portugal*, published in 1755. Careful officers, such as Dickson of the Artillery, took pains to possess themselves of these works,[4] but none of them is listed among the Q.M.G.'s documents, and their value must have been doubtful. For Spain great use was made of what is always referred to as 'the Spanish Road-Book'.[5] This may have been one of several in existence: Campomanes's *Itinerário* of 1761, Bernardo Espinalt's *Guía General* of 1804, or Juan Muñóz Escribano's *Guía General*

---

[1] Wellington to dom M. P. Forjaz, Alfaiates, 24 Apr. 1812 (*Disp.* v, 609). Neves Costa is considered by Portuguese writers to be the 'inventor' of the Lines of Tôrres-Vedras. But the advantage of such a line must have been apparent to any competent general, particularly to one who, like Wellington, had been faced with the prospect of forcing the naturally strong country in front of Lisbon. The decision to construct the Lines and the method of constructing them are admitted to be Wellington's.

[2] 'Carta militar das principaes estradas de Portugal. Por L. H.' (whom the *British Museum Catalogue* identifies as Lourenço Homem), Lisbon, 1808. It is the basis of the map contained in Capt. G. W. Eliot, *Treatise on the Defence of Portugal* (London, 1811).

[3] e.g. *Dickson Papers*, p. 49, entry dated 31 July 1809.

[4] Ibid., p. 81.

[5] e.g. Hope to Murray, Elvas, 19 Oct. 1808, and pencil Memorandum Wellington to Gordon, Madrid, 22 Aug. 1812 (*Murray Papers*, 22, fos. 264–5, and 38, fos. 143–4). In the latter instance reference is almost certainly being made to Espinalt's work.

of 1796; or it may have been an early edition of Santiago López's *Nueva Guía de Caminos*.[1] Whichever it was, it was found to be untrustworthy at an early stage in the war, and it does not appear to have been used except for determining halts on well-established routes. In fact none of these books could be of very great value to a commander in the field.

We are fairly well informed of the maps and guides used by regimental officers and staff officers in general and the Q.M.G. in particular. The atlas of López's maps (printed by Faden) which Moore carried with him is still in existence. We know with what justice he complained when at Salamanca of the bad maps of Spain, and can appreciate his anxiety to borrow a copy of Brion's post-roads—an offer of Charmilly's which Moore three days later declined when a copy of Mentelle's map came into his possession.[2] Stockdale's version of López did not find its way to the Peninsula until December 1808 after Moore had left Lisbon.[3] Nantiat's map of Spain, published by Faden on 1 January 1810, must have been in the hands of the Army early that spring, as one of Beresford's a.d.c.'s, Warre, was asking his family for a copy in that March.[4] Faden's Map of Spain and Portugal in four sheets which, when pasted together, 'would fill the whole side of a moderate-sized room', was a prized possession for which officers, when buying the effects of their dead comrades, were prepared to bid 21 dollars, or £4. 10s.[5] Murray had a complete set of López, a Mentelle, a Carta Militar, and a Faden.[6] He also possessed a fairly complete set of Cassini, which, as a matter of fact, he ordered up too

[1] The earliest edition of this I know of is that of 1812.
[2] Col. Venault de Charmilly, *Narrative of the Transactions* . . . (London, 1810), pp. 12–13. Hope had the benefit of Mentelle from the beginning of his march.
[3] Donkin to Murray, 5/6 Dec. 1808 (*Murray Papers*, 24, fos. 137–40).
[4] Warre to his father, Coimbra, 21 Mar. 1810 (*Letters from the Peninsula 1808–1812* (ed. Rev. Edmond Warre, London, 1909), p. 116).
[5] *Royal Military Chronicle* for Dec. 1810 (i. 111); *Eliot*, p. 118; Swabey's Diary (*Proc. R.A.I.* xxii. 247). Letter of an officer of the 34th, 9 June 1811 (*Hist. MSS. Comm.* (*Hastings*), iii. 293). He does not say it was a Faden but it sounds very similar.
[6] List of the Papers, Books, and Maps in the Quartermaster-General's Office, Lisbon, 15 Aug. and Dec. 1810 (*Murray Papers*, 28, fos. 249–56; 31, fos. 134–41); Reynett to Mackenzie, Alverca, 24 July 1810 (ibid. 103, p. 94).

late from Lisbon for it to be of use to him in the advance from
the Nive in the spring of 1814.[1]

Anyone who has the curiosity to compare these maps with
a modern Portuguese or Spanish map will not be astonished
to learn that neither these nor the guide-books mentioned
above were the sole sources of topographical information.
Every provident soldier kept memoranda of the roads he
had marched by, and lent them to his friends for them to
copy when duty took them on a strange route. They varied
in quality. The following memoranda made by a soldier
marching from Lisbon to rejoin his regiment was of little
value, say, to a Quartermaster-General:

Two leagues from Lisbon on the right, at the Casa de Pasto	good vino
Half a league beyond on the left	strong akadent[2]
At Rio-Maior, at the end of the town, on the left, a small house	right strong vino
At Leiria, a shop going up to the Bishop's palace, on the right	good akadent
Two leagues beyond Pombal on the left	horrid rot-gut stuff
Half a league further, white house (without a bush)	right good stuff
On entering Coimbra, on the right	good cheap vino[3]

However, though this might differ in content it did not
differ in design from those other memoranda made by

[1] Murray to Geddes (at Lisbon), Saint-Sever, 4 Mar., and Murray to Hope, Saint-Sever, 5 Mar. 1814 (*Murray Papers*, 48, fos. 37, 48–49).

[2] i.e. *aguardente*, spirits.

[3] *Colburn*, 1829 (Part I), p. 572. It is enclosed in a letter from a Hussar officer, dated Barcelonne, 16 Mar. 1814, who says it was shown to Wellington for his amusement.

careful officers such as D'Urban, Dickson, and Scovell which may yet be read among their papers.[1]

Portugal and Spain remained at the time of the Peninsular War unexplored territory. Some information could be obtained from officers of the Portuguese and Spanish armies, and more still from muleteers and shepherds and the like in the immediate neighbourhood. But Portuguese officers in particular were unfamiliar to an astonishing degree with their own country, and since one of the essential requirements of this kind of intelligence is that it should be centralized and ready to hand at short notice, such sources could at best be described as haphazard. The only dependable manner of collecting information was by constant reconnaissance, sketching, and map-making carried out by officers acting under the orders of a staff officer at Headquarters.

This officer was the Q.M.G., who, as carrying the responsibility for everything appertaining to marches, had had this task throughout the eighteenth century even at periods when the Adjutant-General had acted as the commander's chief assistant for operations.[2] It had always been the Q.M.G. who hired the guides and the pioneers, or, if these had been organized as military units, superintended their recruitment and kept them at his disposal. For this purpose Murray had in the Peninsula the assistants and deputy-assistants of his own department and the officers of the Royal Staff Corps.[3] Some A.Q.M.G.s and D.A.Q.M.G.s were[4] attached to divisions and had other duties. But these attachments in no way absolved them from the task of reconnaissance, whether for the benefit of the divisional commander or Murray; and those not attached to divisions were indistinguishable in this respect both as to duty and pay from the officers of the Royal Staff Corps. Even Whittingham, who never served with the British Forces in the Peninsula, could not escape Murray's net and, when sent to act with the Spanish armies, was

[1] *The Peninsular Journal of Lieut.-General Sir Benjamin D'Urban, 1808–1817* (ed. I. J. Rousseau, London, 1930), *pass.* (cit. hereafter as 'D'Urban'); *Dickson Papers, pass.*; and W.O. 37/6–7B. The routes in *Eliot* were no doubt obtained from memoranda of this kind.

[2] *v. sup.*, p. 11.

[3] The Corps of Guides formed by Murray in 1808 and 1809 are mentioned below, pp. 125–6.   [4] *v. sup.*, p. 54.

instructed to send all the maps and information of Spanish Estremadura and Andalusia he might lay hands on.[1]

Each of these officers received his instructions from Murray, whose interest in his surroundings and people and strong historical sense fitted him for holding as he did the sole responsibility for the collection of such information for his commander. Towards the end of 1810 Murray compiled and issued for the use of his officers a number of standing instructions about the form in which reports were to be presented and the types of information that were most valuable.[2] He had already compiled instructions of this kind when he was D.Q.M.G. in Ireland in 1806 and 1807. In both these and the Peninsula instructions there may be detected the influence of those issued thirty years previously by General Rôy, who, though perhaps better remembered for his work towards the foundation of the Ordnance Survey and the measurement of the bases on Hounslow Heath and Romney Marsh, deserves recognition as probably the most experienced scientific officer in the British army before the Revolutionary wars. There may also be detected in them the influence of Jarry's lectures on reconnaissance duties and the teaching imparted by other instructors at the Royal Military College at Wycombe. There is a similarity between Murray's instructions and a document which fell into his hands in 1811, the orders issued to a reconnoitring officer by the senior French Engineer officer with Soult's Army,[3] and it is interesting to reflect that these and Murray's were both, as it were, related by marriage.

To the reports and sketches brought in by these officers were added memoranda by Portuguese and other officers on particular areas and features and also of past campaigns. The accumulated information was either kept in the Q.M.G.'s

[1] For Whittingham see Appx. I; letter Murray to him, Abrantes, 12 June 1809 (*Murray Papers*, 74, fos. 4–9).

[2] Murray to all A.Q.M.G.s and D.A.Q.M.G.s at various dates between 22 Nov. and 19 Dec. 1810 (*Murray Papers*, 97, pp. 43 et seqq.). Murray's Peninsula Instructions were printed by Col. Gordon, Q.M.G., in his 'Instructions for the Officers of the Quartermaster-General's Department', London, 1814, pp. 67–87.

[3] Circular No. 84 to Capt. Vauvilliers, commanding the Engineers, 4th French Division, Los Santos, 8 June 1811, signed by Beaufort d'Hautpoul on behalf of Col. Valazé, 'commandant en chef le génie de l'Armée' (*Murray Papers*, 36, fos. 10–11).

office at Headquarters or sent back to be stored in the
A.Q.M.G.'s office at Lisbon, where it was usually copied by
the draughtsman and the copies sent to London for inclusion
in the Military Depot. It is difficult, without entering into
detail, to give an idea of the intensity of these activities.
There were rarely less than six officers engaged at any one
time in reconnaissance and sketching.[1] By the end of 1810
almost the whole of central Portugal had been mapped on a
scale of four miles to the inch. The labours of these men
freed Wellington and Murray from dependence on the
printed maps and road-books to an extent which it is impossible to assess but which must have been very material.

The subsequent history of these topographical surveys is
an interesting one. When the war was over Murray obtained
permission from the Treasury for an officer to reside in Spain
and Portugal for four years to complete the sketches of the
battlefields which had been begun during the war for the
Military Depot. The task was entrusted to a draughtsman of
outstanding ability, Captain Mitchell (afterwards Sir Thomas
Livingston Mitchell), whose finished drawings were published, after many vicissitudes, by the London geographer
James Wyld, in 1841, at the very best period, as it chanced
to be, of English lithography. Wyld's *Atlas containing the
principal battles, sieges and affairs of the Peninsular War*, together with a *Memoir* annexed to it (consisting of a text of the
movement orders prepared at the same time by Murray)
is an elaborate and monumental work of almost unimpeach-
able accuracy which has by some means or other escaped recognition as a prime source for the topography of the war. If
it is evidence of the intense activity of the topographers of
Wellington's Army, it can also be looked upon as the last
manifestation of the old Q.M.G. Department's preoccupation with military topography, military science, and military
history.

How little Murray depended on the printed maps and
guide-books and how much he relied upon the information
brought to him by his officers was shown in his planning of

---

[1] Bainbrigge, de Tamm, Pierrepont, and Balck of the Department, and Tod,
Freeth, Staveley, Colleton, Willermin, Sturgeon, and Read of the Staff Corps were
those most frequently mentioned.

the advance in 1813. The greater part of the Army was routed through the Portuguese provinces north of the Douro which had hitherto received little attention from reconnoitring parties, and was therefore almost unknown. Murray sent two officers from each of three British cavalry brigades,[1] and one from two of the divisions to examine the roads as far as the frontier; one D.A.Q.M.G. (Bainbrigge) to examine the Trás-os-Montes between the Sabor and the Douro, a second (Broke) in the country between the Sabor and the Tua, and a third officer (Mitchell)[2] to examine the region north of the Douro from its junction with the Esla to Benavente.[3] Four officers were also sent to examine the passages of the Douro. Within five weeks the information collected by these men had been collated; the routes were issued; and before another fortnight had passed the troops had moved from their cantonments to the assembly area and had crossed two large rivers with the loss of only half a dozen men, a few horses, and two wagons, without losing a day of the time allowed.[4] This achievement (a complete surprise to the French, as it proved), by which over 50,000 men with artillery, countless horses, baggage animals, and bullocks were moved punctually over 150 miles of roads, upon none of which Wellington nor any of his principal staff officers had ever set eyes, is sufficient testimony of the experience these men had acquired and of the reliance that could be placed upon them in default of other information.

It is not easy, however, to draw general conclusions from a direct comparison between the effectiveness of Wellington's topographical intelligence and that of the French. The only instance of its marked superiority was the operations which preceded the battle of Buçaco (27 September 1810). By that time the British Army had occupied and extensively reconnoitred the whole theatre of these operations for eight months.

---

[1] Confidential letter Murray to Cathcart (A.Q.M.G., Cavalry), Freineda, 20 Apr. 1813 (*Murray Papers*, 64, pp. 148–50).

[2] Afterwards Sir Thomas Livingstone Mitchell (1792–1855), the famous explorer of Australia. See *D.N.B.*

[3] Murray to Bainbrigge, Freineda, 31 Mar. and 8 Apr.; to Broke, 6 Apr., and to Mitchell, 8 Apr. 1813 (*Murray Papers*, 97, pp. 169–74, 174–81).

[4] 1st Division lost one day in the first crossing but it assembled at the second crossing point (over the Esla) punctually.

The French on the other hand were entering territory on which they might have informed themselves in 1807 and 1808 but had omitted to. Masséna therefore relied on precisely that information which Wellington was so careful to avoid using without further confirmation: printed maps— in this case López—and Portuguese officers, the Marquês de Alorna (who had been governor of the province), General Pamplona, and others.[1] These led him to march his whole army by the worst road in the country,[2] only to be confronted by Wellington, occupying one of the strong positions which had been examined thoroughly by British topographical officers since the beginning of the year. It is sometimes said and often implied that Masséna's discovery of the pass of Boialvo through the Serra de Caramulo after his repulse at Buçaco took Wellington by surprise. It is clear, however, from the maps and sketches in Murray's hands at the time of the battle that the pass of Boialvo was well known at British Headquarters, and that if Wellington was surprised it was not by its existence but by its not being occupied by a force he had ordered there to defend it.[3]

So long as operations were carried on in and near Portugal Wellington's topographical information, after January 1810, was probably superior to his adversary's, although, admittedly, Buçaco was the one instance where the French were seriously embarrassed by the lack of it. When the British Army came into difficult country which it had not been possible to reconnoitre, as Graham's Column did during the three or four days immediately following the battle of Vitoria, it correspondingly suffered. But it recovered quickly. And, it can be said with justice that there were no occasions on which the movements of the British Army were either materially embarrassed for want of a knowledge of the country, or seriously misdirected by wrong topographical information.

---

[1] The sources of Masséna's information and the errors consequent upon them are studied in detail by T. J. Andrews in *Eng. Hist. Rev.* (1901), xvi. 472 ff. See also Gen. Paul Thiébault's *Mémoires* (Paris, 1893–5), iv. 456, 488.

[2] *Disp.* iv. 89.

[3] The left flank of the Buçaco position was made the subject of a particular reconnaissance by Murray's instructions to Maj. Hon. R. L. Dundas (O.C. Royal Staff Corps), Viseu, 14 Jan. 1810 (*Murray Papers*, 96, pp. 30–35); Murray to Cotton, Convent of Buçaco, 24 Sept. 1810 (ibid. 82, pp. 105–6).

Arthur Wellesley, 1st Duke of Wellington by Thomas Heaphy. Heaphy visited the headquarters in late 1813 and made a number of studies of the leading officers which he later used in a grand painting of Wellington and his staff. (© *National Portrait Gallery, London*)

Sir George Murray by Thomas Heaphy. Murray's pleasant manner and admirable efficiency made him invaluable as Wellington's Quartermaster-General. (© *National Portrait Gallery, London*)

Rowland Hill 1st Viscount Hill by Thomas Heaphy. Kind and good humoured, Hill was the most dependable of Wellington's subordinates, often employed in detached operations. (© *National Portrait Gallery, London*)

Sir George Scovell by Thomas Heaphy. Scovell's work deciphering French codes allowed Wellington to read confidential enemy dispatches captured by the Spanish guerrillas. (© *National Portrait Gallery, London*)

Sir Edward Pakenham by Thomas Heaphy. Pakenham was Wellington's brother-in-law and a fine fighting soldier, who was killed leading the British attack on New Orleans in 1815. (© *National Portrait Gallery, London*)

General Charles William Stewart, 3rd Marquess of Londonderry. A dashing cavalryman by nature, Stewart was often bored by the routine nature of his work as Adjutant-General. (Engraving by W.J. Colls after Sir Thomas Lawrence). (*Philip Haythornthwaite*)

Sir William Howe De Lancey. De Lancey was Murray's deputy as Quartermaster-General and filled his place for much of 1812 when Murray was at home. He was Wellington's Quartermaster-General in 1815 and was mortally wounded at Waterloo. (Artist unknown) (*Philip Haythornthwaite*)

Field Marshal the Duke of Wellington giving orders to his generals and staff previous to a general action in 1813 by Thomas Heaphy. (© *National Portrait Gallery, London*)

Regimental baggage on the march, a pre-Peninsular scene but typical of the sort of hired transport used throughout the period. (Engraving after W. Pyne, 1801). (*Philip Haythornthwaite*)

'Official' army wagon: Royal Wagon Train, 1812 (engraving by I.C. Stadler after Charles Hamilton Smith). (*Philip Haythornthwaite*)

A battalion halts on the march (engraving by J. Hill after J.A. Atkinson). (*Philip Haythornthwaite*)

Outpost encampment overlooking Ciudad Rodrigo (print after Thomas S. St Clair). (*Philip Haythornthwaite*)

Crossing the Mondego in pursuit of Massena, 1811 (print after Thomas S. St Clair). (*Philip Haythornthwaite*)

Crossing the Tagus at Villa Velha (print after Thomas S. St Clair). (*Philip Haythornthwaite*)

Wellington's headquarters before the Battle of Vimeiro, typical of the sort of substantial building in which the headquarters could be established (after a sketch by Colonel G. Landmann). (*Philip Haythornthwaite*)

The Battle of Busaco, a revealing artist's impression showing the 'reverse slope' tactic of British volley and counter-charge. (Engraving by C. Turner after Thomas S. St Clair). (*Philip Haythornthwaite*)

Siege battery at Badajoz. (Artist unknown) (*Philip Haythornthwaite*)

The great Battle of Salamanca, 1812 (woodcut, published by J. Pitts, September 1812). (*Courtesy of the Council of the National Army Museum, London*)

Battle of Vittoria, 1813 (watercolour, possibly by Lieutenant-Colonel Thomas McNiven, 1814) (*Courtesy of the Council of the National Army Museum, London*)

Such reconnaissances as have been described not infrequently took detached officers close to or even behind the enemy's cantonments, and it was natural that much of the information that came into the hands of the Q.M.G. was not of a purely topographical nature. It could include the so-called 'secret' intelligence of the enemy's dispositions and movements on the one hand. On the other, the Q.M.G.'s correspondence contained more or less routine reports of the dispositions and intentions of the British subordinate commanders. This great mass of information really defies all classification; and it would be unprofitable to attempt it were it not necessary to inquire which branch of the staff, if any, it was that had the responsibility of the collection or collation of intelligence other than topographical.

Routine intelligence of this kind was obtained partly by the cavalry patrols that moved out every morning 10 or 15 miles towards the enemy's lines and returned in the afternoon or evening with a report to the commanding officer or the divisional commander of the enemy's movements; and partly by the cavalry (and occasionally infantry) outposts that, remaining stationary for days, weeks, or even months, at more or less fixed spots in front of the British cantonments, kept a close watch on the French. These were regular duties carried out in all seasons as a matter of course. Old officers such as Sir Edward Cust, looking back to their young days in the Peninsula, recalled with nostalgia the pleasing hours they had spent on outpost duty during the summer months.[1] This network of 'posts of observation', as they were called, formed a sensitive fringe of capillaments at the edge of the main army as it lay peacefully in its quarters, absorbing and transmitting information as nerve-fibres transmit sensation to a body.

The posts and patrols relied not so much upon their powers of observation as upon their ability to tap the rumours that passed from village to village or information picked up from the roving guerrilla bands. News did not travel far in Spain and Portugal, but within narrow limits it travelled

[1] C. F. Adams, Jr., to Henry Adams, Sulphur Springs, Va., 8 Aug. 1863 (*A Cycle of Adams Letters, 1861–1865* (ed. Worthington Chauncey Ford, London, 1921), ii. 68).

with astonishing speed and accuracy; and the main purpose of the posts of observation was that they should be advanced near enough to the enemy to catch these fleeting rumours before they evaporated beyond the range of local interest. Moreover, every commander of a detached division or brigade made it a duty to 'establish a correspondence', that is, to seek out what they called 'confidential persons' who would be prepared, usually for a consideration, to furnish information either through the outposts or by a direct correspondence with the divisional or brigade headquarters. It was for such an object that Cole sent his Swiss a.d.c. Roverea from Guarda into the country around Aldeia-da-Ponte, S. Martín de Trebejo and Penamacor, where Roverea succeeded in selecting two reliable 'confidential persons', a schoolmaster at Penamacor who knew the French-occupied district of Plasencia, and a merchant at Vilar-Maior, whose business frequently took him to Salamanca.[1] From Cole's headquarters, or Hill's, or wherever the 'correspondence' had been established, the information was transmitted to Wellington.

It is clear at any rate that the collection of intelligence was not centralized in the sense that scouts were sent out exclusively from Army Headquarters and that they reported back exclusively to Wellington or the staff. Indeed it could not be so, and it was best that it should not be. The local commander, whose interest it was to have timely intelligence, usually heard first; and he in his turn informed Headquarters and his neighbours. The exploits of the famous scouting officers of Wellington's, Grant, Waters, and others, to which Napier has devoted so much attention, have tended to obscure the humdrum activities of the many humble persons who daily supplied the Army with ordinary but no less essential information.

It is clear also that, apart from patrols and posts, the Army's secret intelligence system depended very largely upon the people of the country. Occasionally useful information was obtained from deserters and prisoners. But intelligence of this kind came principally from Spanish and Portuguese sources, and though directed through military channels it was itself mainly collected by civilians such as Dr. Curtis,

---

[1] Cole to Murray, Guarda, 30 Jan. 1810 (*Murray Papers*, 27, fos. 53–56).

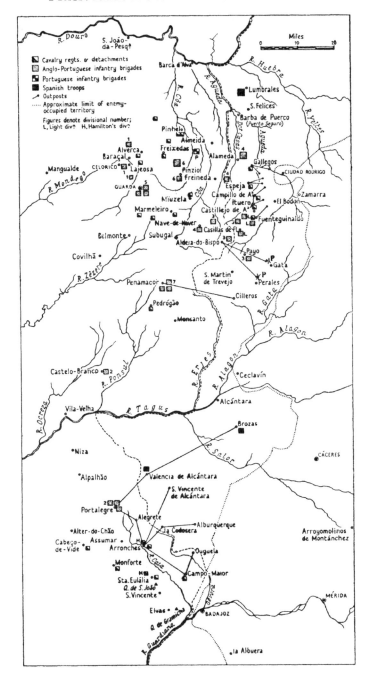

SITUATIONS OF OUTPOSTS, ETC., 1–8 OCTOBER 1811

Rector of the Irish College at Salamanca, or guerrilleros and others. It in no way detracts from the achievements of such men as Grant and Waters and the lonely officers stationed at the posts of observation to say that they moved in a friendly country where their presence was unlikely to be betrayed and where information, not always accurate, admittedly, would be readily proffered. Nor does it detract from the loyalty of the inhabitants to observe that the information had usually to be paid for. When it is considered how it was obtained, that each intercepted dispatch had probably cost the life of a French orderly, and that a guerrillero on a 'cutting out' expedition took his life, and perhaps his family's, into his hands, payment will not seem out of place. The torn and crumpled scraps, some stained with blood, which may be seen among Scovell's papers,[1] remain as evidence of the implacable hostility which worked for Wellington during these years over the whole no-man's-land between the armies. And not only worked for Wellington but for the destruction of the French. The *afrancesado* party could provide nothing similar for French generals on the same scale.

The information was there to be had, and the secret intelligence 'system', if it may be called such, lay in placing the men where it could be tapped and transmitted. The famous scouting officers may consequently be distinguished from the reconnoitring officers and patrols only in the degree to which their posts of observation were advanced into enemy-occupied territory. Some indeed were no more than officers on reconnaissance. Captain Somers Cocks and Lieutenant Lovell Badcock,[2] left behind on the slopes of the Serra da Estrêla to see which road Masséna would take in his advance on Coimbra (whether that through Fornos on the north bank of the Mondego or that by Cortiçô and Pinhanços on the south bank), were merely acting as observing officers on a rather particularly dangerous and interesting service. At the other end of the scale there is the example of Lieutenant George Hillier, posted far into Spanish Estremadura during

---

[1] W.O. 37; see also *Oman*, v. appx. xv.

[2] Murray to Cotton, Gouveia, 3 and 7 Sept. 1810 and 'Memorandum for Captain Brotherton and Lieutenant Badcock, employed to watch the motions and observe the force of the Enemy', Gouveia, 5 Sept. 1810 (*Murray Papers*, 60, pp. 145–6, 149–53, 155–6). Cotton selected Somers Cocks in place of Brotherton.

the anxious days of the second siege of Badajoz in June 1811, when Wellington was expecting at any moment to be confronted with a superior combination of French armies and his dispositions depended entirely on the speedy conveyance of intelligence.[1] Hillier's range of vision virtually extended far beyond the range of his glass, since he corresponded with a confidential person in Cordova and also seems to have maintained communication with Madrid. Officers in Hillier's position gave Wellington a decided advantage over the French. It was at about this period that Wellington wrote: 'The French armies have no communication and one army no knowledge of the position or circumstances in which the other is placed; whereas I have a knowledge of all that passes on all sides.'[2]

The best known of these detached officers are: the two Grants (Lieut.-Col. John Grant, Loyal Lusitanian Legion, and Captain Colquhoun Grant, 11th),[3] Lieutenants John Ayling, 40th, George Hillier, 29th, Samuel C. Grey, 71st; Captains H. S. Blanckley, 23rd, Waters, Somers Cocks, 16th Light Dragoons, James Jones, 87th, John Burrows, 57th, Andrew Leith Hay, 29th, Lewis Rumann, 97th; Captains José O'Ryan and Tomás Connolly, Major Pierre Baradiu and Lieutenant Ange Auberge of the Spanish service, and Captains José Clemente Pereira and Beirimhof Daubrawa of the Portuguese. There must have been many others, as Leith Hay, who has described his adventures when engaged on this duty, gives the impression that the whole country was studded with confidential persons; and a young commissary, sent into León early in 1813 to make preparations for the forthcoming campaign, mentioned in his letters the presence

[1] Murray to Cotton, Near Elvas, 7 June 1811 (ibid. 85, pp. 182–3).
[2] Hillier to Murray, Hornachos, 4 p.m., 9 June 1811, and Hill to Murray, Almendralejo, 1 p.m., 9 June, enclosing one from Fernando de la Rocha, Hornachos, 8 June 1811 (ibid. 36, fos. 12–15, 17–18; Wellington to Liverpool, Elvas, 23 May 1811 (*Disp.* v. 43).
[3] It is sometimes not easy to distinguish between these two in references to them. In *Disp.* John Grant is usually referred to as Lieut.-Col. Grant. He was captured near Plasencia in Sept. 1811, but was released by Temprano's guerrilleros a few weeks later, and probably returned to England then. Colquhoun Grant, promoted Bvt.-major, 30 May 1811, may safely be identified if his rank is mentioned. He was captured in Apr. 1812, but after many vicissitudes succeeded in reaching the Peninsula again before Feb. 1814, when he was appointed to the Q.M.G.'s Department, *vice* Sturgeon, killed.

of men employed 'on observation' in almost every town he entered.[1] It is difficult to speak adequately of the achievements of these men as, to avoid detection, they never stayed long in any one place; they committed as few names to paper as they could, and most of such documents as there were have been purposely destroyed. But their usefulness in helping Wellington to find out 'what they are doing on the other side of the hill',[2] as he expressed it, must have been very considerable.

One of the ways in which these officers employed on detached service were kept in touch with Headquarters has been described by a young officer of the 29th, Lieutenant Leslie.[3] During the advance into Spain in the summer of 1809 Colonel Murray, he says, suddenly summoned him from his regiment to Headquarters at Plasencia. There, Murray told him what was expected of him and sent him round to the A.G., Charles Stewart, who gave him a sealed packet of confidential dispatches to carry to Captain Rumann at Alba de Tormes or wherever he might be. Leslie was then given 200 dollars by the Commissary-General[4] for Rumann; and from the Military Secretary he received an order on the Junta of Plasencia to provide a guide and a horse. Leaving Bathurst's office, Leslie returned to Colonel Murray, who gave him a further packet of dispatches,[5] a written memorandum of the route he was to take and of the distance (said to be five leagues), and a verbal injunction to find Rumann and return to Headquarters with all speed. Business over, Murray gave him a cordial invitation to dinner, which he very readily accepted. He set out at 5 p.m. that day (15 July) and, having found Rumann, not at Alba de Tormes but Barco de Ávila, he returned to Headquarters in the afternoon of the 17th.

[1] A. Leith Hay, *A Narrative of the Peninsular War* (Edinburgh, 1831), ii. 116–38; *Buckham*, pp. 139–44.

[2] Sir James Graham to Charles Arbuthnot, Grosvenor Place, 5 June 1839 (*Correspondence of Charles Arbuthnot*, ed. A. Aspinall. Camden Third Series (vol. lxv, London, 1941), p. 204).

[3] Col. Charles Leslie of Balquhain, *Military Journal* (Aberdeen, 1887), pp. 127–33; *Murray Papers*, 95, pp. 36–37; 99, p. 90; and 58, p. 50.

[4] The text in *Leslie* says 'commanding' general. It is clear from the relevant letters in *Murray Papers* that this is a mistranscription for 'commissary-general'. The warrant was issued by Col. Bathurst.

[5] Only one letter, as a matter of fact.

Leslie's experiences, though of no great moment in the history of the war, nevertheless afford an insight not only into the defective state of topographical knowledge at Headquarters at that time,[1] but into an incident that must have been repeated on hundreds of occasions. Although this was not the only way in which information was passed back—the task seems as frequently to have been entrusted to couriers—it was evidently quite usual. The most interesting part of Leslie's story is its revelation of the interlocking responsibility of the various departments at Headquarters in regard to intelligence. No less than four departments had a concern in the arrangements, and it is clear that not one (at any rate at this stage) had an exclusive responsibility. If it was the Military Secretary's, as Stewart complained,[2] then it is evident that the A.G. succeeded in interfering. If it was the A.G.'s, as his competence over prisoners of war might lead one to expect and as some commanders allowed it to be,[3] then it is evident that the Q.M.G. with his monopoly of the topographical business had an important contribution to make.

The answer to the problem appears to be that a commander himself retained the principal care of his intelligence service, though it was open to him to delegate the whole or part of it to a branch of the military staff. General Donkin, Q.M.G. to the force at Alicante, stated that before Sir John Murray's arrival he had charge of the secret intelligence department, and that Murray, on assuming command, took that branch of the service into his own hands, relieving Donkin of it entirely.[4] Wellington, for his part, appears also to have taken the secret intelligence department to himself. As he saw a very large proportion of the incoming letters which the heads of his departments brought to him for his decision, it is not surprising that all reports of enemy movements, no matter what source they came from, whether from the outposts, the divisional or allied commanders or officers on detached service and the rest, were brought to him as well. Nor do these

[1] The distance between Alba and Plasencia is nearer 18 leagues than 5.
[2] v. sup., pp. 43–44.
[3] e.g. Smith, as D.A.G. to the expeditionary force sent to North America under Ross, was in charge of the secret service (Smith, i. 198); v. sup., p. 42.
[4] Sir John Murray's Trial: Murray's evidence, pp. 330 et seqq.; Donkin's evidence, pp. 249–446, 460, 461.

reports appear to have been summarized, abstracted, or collated before they reached him, but were taken before him as they stood.[1] What collating was done was almost certainly done by himself, or at any rate in his office. And when he mislaid the keys of his boxes, as he did for about a week at the beginning of May 1811, the intelligence department of the Army may be said to have put up its shutters for the time being.[2] When intercepted enemy dispatches in cipher were brought in no one member of the staff attempted their decipherment. Had he anyone with him for the purpose? he was asked after the war. 'No', he replied, 'I tried: everyone at Headquarters tried: and between us we made it out.'[3]

What evidence there is, taken in conjunction with Charles Stewart's grievance that the A.G. in the Peninsular Army had no interesting business and with Murray's ignorance of his commander's intentions during his first period with the Army,[4] tends to show that during the first three years of his command all intelligence came to Wellington and that the appraisal of it was his and his alone. Nevertheless, in the latter half of the war, certain habits become discernible which may be said to have hardened into a practice, bringing the Q.M.G.'s Department more than any other to concern itself with intelligence. For instance, it became usual to send all ciphered correspondence to Scovell, an A.Q.M.G. and Commandant of the Corps of Guides, who showed an aptitude for decoding. But it is to be noticed that Scovell does not speak of his first successful attempt until November 1811,[5] and the series of decoded dispatches remaining among his papers does not start until March 1812.[6] Indeed, it is during 1812, after Stewart's departure, that a marked inclination on Wellington's part to redistribute the duties of the staff becomes noticeable. He favoured the introduction of

[1] This is borne out by his occasional complaints of illegible handwriting, amongst them that of Erskine (*Disp.* iv. 559), with which any modern transcriber will sympathize.

[2] Wellington to Charles Stuart and Beresford, Vilar-Formoso, 30 Apr. and 8 May 1811 (*Disp.* iv. 780, 793).

[3] Conversation on 10 Aug. 1836 (*Stanhope's Conversations*, pp. 77–78).

[4] *v. sup.*, p. 44.

[5] It is included under date of 24 Nov. (W.O. 37/7A), but it may have been a few days earlier or later.

[6] See *Oman*, v. appx. xv, pp. 612 et seqq.

a chief of staff, an appointment which he was disposed to confer on Colonel Willoughby Gordon until this busy gentleman showed himself unfitted for it.[1] And after George Murray's return in the spring of 1813 the Q.M.G. took a larger share of the intelligence business. He was allowed a slightly wider interest and, in contradistinction to the earlier years, enjoyed a complete participation in the intelligence his commander received.

This is not to say, however, that Murray controlled the intelligence department. Murray had concerned himself in the counter-espionage measures proposed early in 1811 when the French were before Lisbon; and he had always carried on a correspondence with certain of the observation officers and not with others—what grounds there were either of principle or expediency for this distinction it is impossible to say—but this practice was never extended into becoming an exclusive responsibility. It is clear that the Q.M.G.'s Department under Wellington never was primarily equipped to handle secret intelligence in the same manner that it handled the topographical;[2] nor is there any definite indication that Wellington intended to relieve himself of the main burden of the business. All that can be said is that he found it convenient to take Murray into his confidence and allow the Q.M.G.'s Department rather than any other to assume some of the tedious tasks. It should be noticed that in the Waterloo campaign he appointed Colquhoun Grant, an A.Q.M.G., to the head of an 'Intelligence Department';[3] and it is probably fair to assume that, in the latter months of the Peninsular War, his practice under the press of business was turning towards the organization of such an office within the framework of the Q.M.G.'s Department. As it was, however, both in the

[1] Wellington to Bathurst and the Duke of York, Villatoro, 29 Sept., and Rueda, 31 Oct. 1812 (Suppl. Disp. vii. 433–44, 465). Wellington appears to have read Grimoard, who was in favour of reverting to the staff organization of the Ancien Régime.

[2] There are some notes of Murray's among his papers, probably dating from 1805 (5, fos. 1–30, 56), regarding the duties of the Q.M.G. which indicate that the Department, as reorganized by Brownrigg and others in 1803, was intended to take over the secret intelligence. But as it is not certain whether these notes are proposals or instructions, and as they cannot relate to Peninsular practice, they cannot be admitted as evidence.

[3] Wellington to Torrens, Brussels, 29 Apr. 1815 (Disp. viii. 50).

Peninsula and at Waterloo, Wellington was his own Director of Military Intelligence.

Intelligence is of little value unless it is timely, and Wellington, from a fairly early period in the war, insisted on precision and punctuality in the dating of reports and their transmission, both to him and to different parts of the Army.[1] We have already observed how those in the peculiar situation of observing officers were kept in touch with Headquarters, and we may turn now to the more routine methods used in daily intercourse. The Army made use partly of the civil postal service of Portugal and partly of its own resources within itself: letter-parties from the cavalry and infantry and the newly formed Corps of Mounted Guides.

The Portuguese post-office was not a go-ahead institution. An attempt had been made to bring it up to the standards of that of other European countries in 1798. But the lack of postal traffic, owing to the absence of a flourishing inland trade, and the bankruptcy of the treasury had brought these improvements to naught, and in 1804 the service had reverted to a jog-trot carriage of mails by post-mules and messengers on foot along two main routes. The first was from Lisbon to Oporto, with branches at Castanheira for Castelo-Branco, and at Coimbra for Almeida. The second was from Lisbon to Elvas, with a branch at Montemor-o-Velho for Vilar-Real-de-Santo-António. The post left Lisbon every Monday, Wednesday, and Saturday at 6 in the evening.[2] These arrangements formed the structure upon which the system of military communications was built up while the Army was in Portugal, that is to say, during the years 1809 to 1813. The Portuguese post-mule was a reliable beast and the mails travelled with as much expedition as the country permitted in all seasons.[3]

But it will be seen from the sketch opposite that there was room for improvement both in the frequency and in the routes if the post was to serve an army disposed along the eastern frontier. Wellington from 1809 onwards had

[1] G.O., Santo-Quintino, 11 Oct. 1810.

[2] Godofredo Ferreira, *A Mala-Posta em Portugal* (Lisbon, 1946), pp. 33–60.

[3] William Thomas, *Memoirs of Portugal, Historical and Medical* (London, 1819), p. 35.

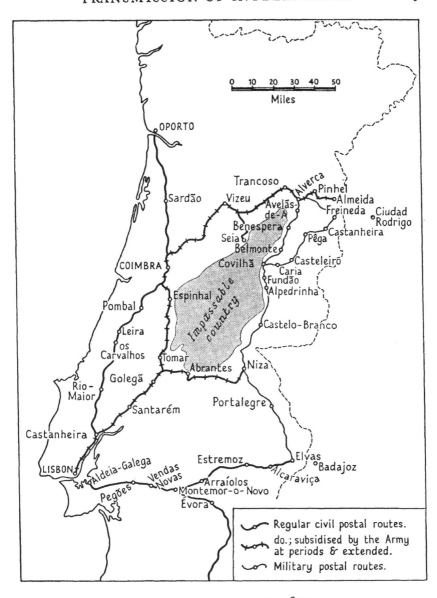

POSTAL ROUTES, DECEMBER 1811

arranged with the postal authorities for at least a daily service from Headquarters to Lisbon. It would appear also that the routes were extended to serve some of the advanced formations and to keep up the communication (when the Army was divided) between the force in the Beira and Hill's force in the Alentejo, by the new road running close under the western extremity of the Serra da Estrêla through Espinhal, Tomar, and Abrantes. The expense of all these additional posts were paid for by the Commissariat, and the extended service appears to have been in full working order by April 1810.[1] In July 1810 it took about three days for a letter dispatched at Headquarters at Celorico to reach Lisbon. When, after April 1811, the Army took up its advanced positions beyond the Portuguese frontier and the lateral communication between the Beira and the Alentejo could no longer be kept up through Espinhal and Tomar, a new line was run through Fundão and Castelo-Branco, to the east of the Serra da Estrêla. This was a military line of communication[2] maintained entirely by letter-parties furnished from the cavalry regiments, and carrying the military mail on a time-table agreed between the regiments and Scovell, who was in charge of the Military Post-Office. It took about two days for a letter posted at Portalegre to reach Headquarters at Freineda.

Letter-parties, both cavalry and infantry, were detachments of a n.c.o. and six or so men placed half-way between certain points or formations. It was the responsibility of the Q.M.G., both when the Army lay in cantonments and during active operations, to place these parties at convenient intervals, and there is hardly one operation order issued by Murray in which the duties of intercommunication are not specifically allotted.[3] It was a task which fell heaviest on the cavalry, and depleted their strength as fighting units to a very material extent. Cotton in 1814 complained that one of his brigades (Lord Edward Somerset's) had no less than thirteen letter-parties out, exclusive of what the 7th Hussars furnished

[1] Wellington to Charles Stuart, Viseu, 11 Apr. 1810 (*Disp.* iv. 14); G.O.s, Seia, 14 Apr. and Viseu, 21 Apr. 1810.   [2] *v. sup.*, p. 67, n. 1.
[3] Good examples are to be found in the Movement Orders printed in *Memoir annexed to an Atlas containing the principal battles, sieges and affairs* . . . (London, James Wyld, 1841), pp. 162 ff., cit. hereafter as 'Wyld'.

to keep up the communication between Headquarters and Beresford's force detached to Bordeaux from Saint-Sever.[1]

By this time operations were being carried on on a very extended scale. From the date the Army left Portugal until the end of the war it relied exclusively, so it seems, upon its own resources. The Spanish postal system does not appear to have been made use of very much—indeed, there was little call for it when the Army lay in the Pyrenees—and the French system does not appear to have been used at all. In the final year of the war therefore the postal service was principally furnished from the Army's own resources.

Apart from letter-parties these consisted in: mounted and foot orderlies[2] attached temporarily to Headquarters or for-mation headquarters; the Corps of Mounted Guides; and, very occasionally, in a system of semaphore signalling.

The orderlies need no further description. Their numbers fluctuated; they were frequently changed and their duties may be easily guessed at. The Corps of Mounted Guides, however, deserves special mention. They were a body of men raised locally by the Q.M.G., as all Q.M.G.s had done in the past, from the peasantry or deserters. Murray had entrusted the raising of such a body (consisting of a sergeant, a corporal, and sixteen men) to Scovell in September 1808 for Moore's campaign.[3] Most of these, to judge by their names, were Italian deserters from Junot's Army, the majority of whom, after being evacuated at Corunna, returned to the Peninsula and formed the nucleus of the Corps when Mur-ray persuaded Scovell to re-form it in May 1809.[4] The establishment was raised during the war from 8 officers and 34 n.c.o.'s and men until it reached a strength of 12 officers and 193 n.c.o.'s and men in the spring of 1813.[5] It was at this

---

[1] Cotton to Murray, Saint-Germé, 8 Mar. 1814 (*Murray Papers*, 48, fo. 81).

[2] These are the soldiers listed among the officers and clerks of the various depart-ments in Appx. II.

[3] Letter of Instruction written in Scovell's hand and signed by Murray, 26 Sept. 1808 (*Scovell Papers*, W.O. 37/10, p. 5).

[4] 14 (out of 30) listed in a muster of July 1810 (*Kennedy Papers*) were men who had received pay at Corunna in Jan. 1809, when the Corps consisted of 25 men, the establishment having been augmented on 16 Dec. 1808 (W.O. 37/10, 37/4; *Murray Papers*, 54, p. 68).

[5] G.O.s, Oporto, 23 May 1809, and Freineda, 23 Apr. 1813; Scovell's Diary (W.O. 37/6) under entry of 24 May 1809.

time organized into two troops, but this was evidently only an administrative arrangement, since the larger part of the Corps was split up and attached to the different divisions in the same manner as the Waggon Train and the various branches of the staff. The original purpose of the Corps had been to furnish a reserve of guides who should lead columns on the march through unreconnoitred districts. But at an early stage in the war it appears to have been given over almost if not entirely to the carriage of dispatches in difficult and unknown country under the supervision of its Commandant, who also supervised the whole system of military communications.[1] Guides for formations there certainly were, but these were volunteers or pressed men from the local peasantry whom provident staff officers took care to have at their disposal.[2] The Corps of Guides was a useful and highly experienced body of men. Their officers varied in quality, but there were some, particularly those who had volunteered from the Academic Battalion of Coimbra, who afterwards rose to eminence in the service of their country.[3]

Lastly, there were at least four periods during the war when the ordinary service of orderlies and guides was supplemented by the use of semaphore signalling. The first was in the summer of 1810, when the Army remained stationary awaiting the onset of Masséna's Armies after they should have reduced the fortresses of Ciudad Rodrigo and Almeida. Wellington, consciously or unconsciously taking advantage of the old medieval *atalaias*,[4] or watchtowers, on the Portuguese frontier on which to establish telegraphs, had been able to maintain a correspondence with the outlying parts of his Army and even with Colonel Cox, the governor of Almeida, while the town was besieged. This communication was satisfactory until the very last vital moment when bad weather

[1] Until Apr. 1813 Lieut.-Col. Scovell; until his death, 19 Mar. 1814, Lieut.-Col. Sturgeon; and thereafter Maj. Colquhoun Grant.

[2] e.g. *Smith*, i. 87, who says he always had three or four *paysanos* at hand in charge of a guard.

[3] e.g. Agostinho Albano da Silveira Pinto (known to Hill as 'Cornet Albino'), a distinguished polymath (1785–1852); and Rodrigo da Fonseca Magalhães (1787–1858), known as 'Cornet Rodrigo', who later became involved in the revolutionary movement of the post-war years.

[4] Gen. João de Almeida, *Roteiro dos Monumentos Militares Portugueses* (Lisbon, 1945), i, caps. 1, 3, 10, 11; *Disp.* iv. 196, 199, 203, 209, 224, 236, 248.

intervened and obscured the telegraphs. All the apparatus was dismantled when the Army retired from its forward positions in September.

The second period was that during which the Lines of Tôrres-Vedras were occupied. Wellington had made arrangements with Admiral Berkeley in the summer of 1810 for officers and men from the Fleet to man telegraph stations situated at prominent points within the Lines, and he had asked for copies of Home Popham's 'Telegraph Vocabularies' to be supplied to him. Home Popham's *Marine Vocabulary* (1800, 1803) was the standard signal-book in use by the navy at the time. From it, indeed, had been derived Nelson's famous signal to the Fleet on joining battle at Trafalgar, and it was now to become the medium of communication on another no less momentous occasion. Two copies of the vocabulary used in the Lines have survived.[1] They proclaim their naval origin by such phrases as No. 2103: 'I have sprung my bowsprit but cannot fish it at sea' (not a frequent topic of conversation in the Lines); but their containing under additional numbers the place-names of Sobral, Alenquer, Alhandra, Santarém, and others shows that they were adapted for use during this period of the war.

At about that time Wellington had been in telegraph communication with the Spanish garrison of Badajoz, 130 miles away and under siege, until its unworthy governor surrendered. A few months later, while the Army occupied the Caia position in the summer of 1811, a system of signals, less articulate than semaphore and consisting of a combination of regimental colours hoisted on the citadel of Campo-Maior and rounds of gunfire,[2] had been devised to give notice of certain anticipated emergencies during that anxious period of tension.

In 1810 the signals had been entrusted to army officers, but it was clearly not intended that the arrangements should subsist beyond the moment when the need for them should cease. The fourth period, the period of the investment of Bayonne (December 1813 to February 1814), is consequently

---

[1] These vocabularies, together with the dictionary mentioned below, were presented to the War Office Library by the present Duke of Wellington.

[2] Memoranda by Murray, 24 and 25 June 1811 (*Murray Papers*, 68, pp. 36–42).

of particular interest, since it was then that a system of signals was established on a divisional basis which is clearly the ancestor of the modern divisional signals. A divisional telegraph-officer was appointed, and an intelligent n.c.o. and three privates attached, all receiving additional pay, who were to take charge of the apparatus (poles, flags, balls, and dictionary) and carry it wherever the division moved. The dictionary, a less elaborate affair than Home Popham's *Vocabulary*, was designed for use by the 'unlearned' (as Wellington called those who were to use it) without the assistance of the navy; but the principle was the same. It is evident that the telegraph sections of the divisions that were instituted on 12 January 1814 were intended to become an integral part of the divisional organization as much as Artillery, Engineers, Staff Corps, Medical Department, Commissariat, and Staff; and although circumstances did not call them into operation after the greater part of the Army left the neighbourhood of Bayonne in February 1814, their brief existence deserves recognition as yet another example of the means for independent life with which Wellington equipped his divisions.[1]

Occasions on which dispatches and orders were delayed and went astray were not, unfortunately, unknown. There was the orderly dragoon who during the retreat on Corunna got drunk and lost the order for Fraser's and Hope's Divisions to carry on to Corunna instead of turning off to Vigo. More serious consequences followed the misdirection of the letter written immediately after the battle of Vitoria in 1813, ordering Graham's column to take a road by which the retreat of a large part of the French Army might have been cut off.[2] And it is clear that the imperfect state of the communication between the various parts of the Army, in the operations in the Pyrenees of July that year, contributed a great deal to the embarrassing and potentially dangerous situation which arose when Soult made his first attacks. This originated mainly from the state of mind in which the Army,

---

[1] Instructions by Murray, Saint-Jean-de-Luz, 18 Dec. 1813 and 12 Jan. 1814 (*Murray Papers*, 91, pp. 53–56, 77–79). The director of the Light Division's telegraph was Lieut. George Simmons, 95th (*A British Rifleman* (ed. Col. Willoughby Verner, London, 1899), p. 335). See also Col. R. Batty, *Campaign . . . in the Western Pyrenees . . .* (London, 1823), pp. 102–3.

[2] *Wyld*, p. 104 n.

not excluding Headquarters, indulged during the first three weeks of July, and which it never allowed itself again. Otherwise, such failures as there were only served to show how the stupidity of comparatively humble persons may invalidate the best of systems. When it is considered that Wellington's information service depended on the receipt and transmission of tens of thousands of orders, reports, and messages, the odd dozen or so failures are not, perhaps, surprising.

V

THE QUARTERING AND
MOVEMENT OF THE ARMY

THE concern of the Q.M.G. in regard to camp equipage, regimental transport, and the transport of clothing, his exclusive responsibility for topographical intelligence, and the ill-defined part he played in the collection of secret intelligence have already been described. Though these tasks took up a large proportion of his time they were, however, subsidiary and accessory to his principal function as a staff officer: that from which he took the title of his appointment, the encampment and quartering of the army. Quartering had been his main preoccupation since the institution of his office late in the seventeenth century, and he had retained it unimpaired in all active service during the whole intervening period.

The movement of troops on the other hand was a duty that became his prescriptive right only after the reorganization of the Q.M.G.'s Department in 1803. During the eighteenth century the commander had issued his movement orders as often as not through the A.G.; and although the Q.M.G. was naturally interested in what these orders were, since he would have to quarter the troops at the end of the march, a movement order seems to have been treated like any other order, as one whose execution the A.G. enforced. The A.G. had acted in this manner in the Minden campaign. Murray Pulteney and Craig, A.G.s to the Duke of York in 1793–5, and Hope, A.G. to Abercromby in 1799 and 1801, were clearly in a similar position.[1] It is interesting to see that in the army of the United States, which apportioned the staff-duties substantially as they existed in the British service in the 1770's, the Quartermaster-General had little or no responsibility for movements. The American Q.M.G. in the course of years progressively lost what military attributes he

---

[1] v. sup., p. 11; Burne, pp. 83, 170–1, et al.; Linlithgow MSS. (Hopetoun House), Boxes 2 and 3.

had started with until, by the time of the Civil War, he was not very different from a British commissary-general; and it was the A.G. (or a chief-of-staff) through whom Lee and McClellan issued their movements orders.[1] In the British service the Q.M.G. went through precisely the opposite process, and although he subsequently lost his responsibility for operational movement, in Wellington's time all his training was directed towards his being able to advise his commander in the theory and practice of the art of war. 'War is first and foremost a matter of movement', it has been said,[2] and Wellington, in following the new usage of issuing movement orders through his Q.M.G., established him as the principal staff officer of the Army.

In the eighteenth century the military year was divided into two parts: the campaigning season, which ran from about May to October, and the season of winter quarters, which occupied the remainder of the year. The campaigning season was spent under canvas, and winter quarters in cantonments, that is to say, with the troops billeted in houses. This division of the year was a response to the dictates of nature. An army could not move until green forage was on the ground; winter was spent in immobility, while the animals were fed on hay and the recruiting parties were sent back to beat the drum for recruits to fill the gaps made in the ranks and replace horses lost during the summer. Military finance was ordered in such a manner as to correspond with this universal practice and the 200 days' Bât and Forage period represented in fiscal terms the length of a campaign.[3] At no time, however, had the practice been strictly adhered to. Throughout the century there had been occasions when operations were carried on—to the cost of those who did so— into the depths of winter, and the Revolutionary armies at the end of the century had broken all the rules by making war across the ice and marching and fighting in deep snow. The French armies now made extensive use of bivouacs and huts

---

[1] *The Legislative History of the General Staff of the Army of the United States* (*its organization, duties, pay and allowances*), ed. Maj.-Gen. Henry C. Corbin, A.G. (Washington, D.C., 1901).

[2] Lieut.-Col. G. F. R. Henderson, *The Science of War* (ed. Capt. Neill Malcolm, London, 1905), p. 1.

[3] *v. sup.*, p. 84, n. 4.

improvised from branches of trees.[1] It was a form of quartering that would have recommended itself to Guibert in its allowing a greater freedom of movement and a more rapid concentration. But it played havoc with armies. The new rude method of warfare reflected not so much an improvement in the means of subsisting armies as a decline in the value of a soldier's life (reckoned as a matter of pounds, shillings, and pence), which came with the immense surge of volunteers that, joining the French armies one week and lying dead of exposure or wounds the next, were replaced at comparatively little expense by more volunteers and more conscripts the week after.

The British soldier on the other hand, despite the various recruiting acts of the war period, was always an expensive man to replace; and if there had been no humanitarian reasons and reasons of ordinary prudence and economy for keeping him in good health, there were others equally cogent against exposing him in bad quarters and hazardous enterprises. The 'states' of February 1812 show the price in sick his onslaught upon Rodrigo in January had cost Wellington. But it is impossible to visualize him committing his troops to a prolonged bivouac before the Lines of Lisbon, and it is difficult to imagine him exposing them to a situation in which it was necessary to winter in front of Sebastopol. While not cosseting his men, Wellington was careful, so far as the standards of the age allowed, of their lives. By French standards he was niggardly and unenterprising.

He kept, as much as possible, to the traditional practice of cantoning his army in winter, and while campaigning he was constrained to hut his men in bivouacs as the French did theirs. But, as he confessed afterwards, bivouacking was bad for troops. It prevented them from getting regular rest. They got into the habit of sleeping for an hour at a time or when they felt drowsy. 'Nothing', he said, 'wears out the troops so effectually.'[2] It was not, however, until the last campaign in Spain that he succeeded in ridding the Army of the bivouac.

---

[1] Cf. Corporal Todd's (12th Regiment) Journal in the Seven Years' War, ed. C. T. Atkinson (*J.S.A.H.R.* xxix. 118–27, 158–69).

[2] *The Diary of Frances Lady Shelley*, ed. Richard Edgcumbe (London, 1912), pp. 155–6, a note of a conversation which took place in Sept. 1815.

The transport system was already sufficiently over-burdened, and the change was effected by adopting a light tin camp-kettle which could be carried by the men, and turning over the camp-kettle mules to the conveyance of tents.[1]

Equipped with tents, the Army changed its habits. Many units spent most of the remaining year of the war under canvas, even during the unpleasant winter in the neighbourhood of Saint-Jean-de-Luz. The encampments of this last year were not, however, the regular lines of tents and streets, ruled out by the Quartermaster-General and his assistants in the manner prescribed by the rules of castrametation, that the armies of Marlborough or Cumberland had known. Murray and his assistants from Wycombe were familiar enough with castrametation, but circumstances favoured the adoption of what the rules recognized as 'camps of convenience'.[2] Wellington's only rule was that the Army should encamp, wherever possible, out of sight of the enemy, so that they should not calculate its numbers. 'Could Marlborough have risen to see one of our straggling and irregular mountain camps', a regimental quartermaster said afterwards, 'I know not what his feelings would have been. He would, I fear, have thought we had sadly degenerated.'[3] In a sense Wellington's reversion to the use of encampments after they had been discarded in continental armies might be regarded as retrogressive. But in the improvement it effected in the efficiency of his Army he was demonstrating, not for the first time,[4] that old methods could be brought up to date and made superior to the newfangled notions that came in with the Revolution. 'Any officer who served through the Peninsular War', one of his soldiers wrote later,[5] 'will bear testimony to the immense saving of health and life resulting from the adoption of tents and encampments by the Duke of Wellington in the latter years of that war, as distinguished from its

[1] v. sup., p. 84, n. 3 and Appx. V. The Portuguese units, however, were not issued with tents and had still to be cantoned and hutted.

[2] The hutted camp of Tôrre-de-Mouro, occupied by part of the Army from 19 June to 19 July 1811, was a camp of convenience.

[3] William Surtees, Twenty-five years in the Rifle Brigade (Edinburgh, 1833), p. 189.

[4] His retention of linear tactics is another instance, and his adherence to a system of depots another.

[5] Colburn, 1837 (pt. ii), p. 22.

commencement, and the sickness and loss sustained by the French from never putting their men under canvas in the field.'

For almost five years, however, the Army's quarters alternated between huts (and bivouacs) and cantonments. Huts and bivouacs were only resorted to on marches and on occasions when there were no buildings nearby; and it is probably true to say that, until March 1813, when tents were introduced, three-quarters of the soldier's year was spent in cantonments, or, as the army of 1914–18 would have called them, billets.

All arrangements for quartering were the exclusive responsibility of the Q.M.G. and the officers of his Department. Laying out the encampments for his division, designating suitable bivouac sites, marking off streets in towns, were the daily routine of an Assistant.

When the troops were placed in cantonments the usual mode of taking up quarters was for the quartermasters of the several corps to proceed in advance to the town, where an officer of the Q.M.G.'s Department, having divided the place into districts according to the different brigades, gave over to each quartermaster certain streets for his corps. The quartermaster then selected the best houses for the commanding and other field-officers, marking the same with chalk; then the next best for the captains, and so on. Those for the men had the number they were destined to contain also written in chalk on the door.'[1]

Chalking names on a door was an unpopular drudgery left to the junior Assistant. 'Thorn has swelled out amazingly,' wrote the A.Q.M.G. of Hill's Corps, 'he has now become above marking doors, &c.'[2] When a British expeditionary force was sent to Portugal in 1827 they found the names of well-known officers written in chalk on the doors which had remained untouched since 1813.[3]

After these preliminaries the men were marched to their quarters, the officers went back to their houses in the com-

---

[1] *Leslie*, pp. 187–8. See also Capt. Sir J. Kincaid, *Adventures in the Rifle Brigade* . . . (London, 1847), pp. 23–24; Introduction to the *Selected General Orders* (ed. Lieut.-Col. J. Gurwood, London, 1837), p. xxxv.

[2] Tweeddale to Murray, Berlanga, 30 Aug. 1812 (*Murray Papers*, 38, fos. 155–6).

[3] *Colburn*, 1829 (pt. i), p. 566 n.

pany of their servants, and on the appearance of the *patron* the officer's servant took charge of proceedings. A conversation similar to the following then took place: 'Shove off, Señor, ondigesta el salo? ondigesta el cama? cama bono for official inglesy, es bon Christiano; quero pong, vino, montecy, akydenta for soldados, quero leche, oily for de lampy, you intende; me parly bon spanole. Shove off, Señor, shove off.'[1]

Assistants soon learned to estimate the quartering capacity of a town or village. They could ask the local magistrate for the number of *fogos* it contained, the public buildings, convents, and churches, and from that calculate the living accommodation and stabling the place would offer. Scovell, whose notes and routes are to be found amongst his papers, appears to have reckoned eight men to each house of a typical Portuguese village.[2] Waller, A.Q.M.G. of the 3rd Division, reckoned an average of no more than six.[3] The subjoined table shows the proportions of men to houses as they appeared in practice when the 3rd Division was cantoned in some villages near Ciudad Rodrigo in January 1812. It will be seen that they are in excess of Scovell's or Waller's estimates, a fact which is to be attributed to omitting the capacity of the public buildings from the calculation.

Cantonment	Houses[4]	Church	School	Ayuntamiento	Troops cantoned	Proportion of troops to each house
Martiago	180	1	1	1	1,046	6
Zamarra	95	1	1	..	957	10
La Atalaya	42	1	1	1	947	22
Villarejo	16	1	1	..	315	20
Las Agallas	70	1	..	1	584	8
Herguijuela	60	1	1	1	646	11

Taking up cantonments for the Headquarters of the Army,

[1] Maj. John Patterson (50th), *Camp and Quarters* (London, 1840), i. 244.

[2] W.O. 37/11.

[3] Waller to Murray, Moimenta-da-Beira, 26 Apr. 1813 (*Murray Papers*, 39, fos. 94–100).

[4] Cantonments of the 3rd Division, 26 Jan. 1812 (*Murray Papers*, 38, fo. 32), imposed on the statistics of the villages from Pascual Madoz, *Diccionario geográfico-estadístico-histórico de España y de sus posesiones de ultramar* (Madrid, 1848). As there was no census between 1797 and 1857, Madoz's statistics can be taken as roughly correct for 1812.

or the staff of a large division such as Hill's, was a more
complicated business. It had always been a responsibility of
the Q.M.G.'s, but in the past it had usually been entrusted
to a functionary known as the Fourrier de la Cour, a superior
type of the running footmen who, at least in the French and
Austrian services, were sent on ahead to bespeak quarters
for noble officers.[1] Fourriers, together with draughtsmen,
pioneers, guides, and artificers, had originally been intended
to form part of the Royal Staff Corps when it was first
organized by the Q.M.G. for his assistance in 1800. But
they never made an appearance in the field, and in the
Peninsula quarters for the 'General Staff' of the Army were
taken up by a Deputy-Assistant of Murray's Department
attached to Headquarters for the purpose, Captain Dawson
Kelly, who also acted in this capacity in the Waterloo campaign and during the occupation of France, 1815–18. Kelly
left the Peninsula in 1812, and his place was taken by
Lieutenant William Butler Hook, not an officer of the
Department but doing duty under Scovell's superintendence.[2]
Headquarters took up a considerable number of buildings
and, as Wellington preferred living near his Army to occupying a quarter in a sizeable town, many of the small villages of
Portugal and Spain could not hold more than two or three of
the Departments.[3] Even in a town of the size of Portalegre all
quarters had to be considered as vacant when Headquarters
moved there, 'no individual having any right to occupy any
quarter in the place allotted for the Headquarters of the
Army' without Kelly's (or Hook's) sanction.[4]

An interesting and unusual light is shed on the manner in
which Headquarters moved into a new place by the narrative of Brother José de S. Silvestre, a monk of the Discalced
Carmelite monastery of Buçaco, which was occupied by
Wellington from 21 to 29 September 1810.[5] It reads like

1 J. E. Weelen, *Rochambeau, Father and son*, trs. Lawrence Lee, New York,
[1936], p. 110.
2 Murray to Pakenham, Saint-Jean-de-Luz, 24 Nov. 1813 (*Murray Papers*, 46,
fos. 147–8; *Suppl. Disp.* viii. 399). Hook had a commission in the Mounted Staff
Corps on its formation in 1813, and died at Plymouth, 29 July 1829 (*Colburn*, 1829
(pt. ii)).   3 *v. sup.*, pp. 39–40.
4 Murray to Kelly, 20 July 1811 (*Murray Papers*, 61, p. 4).
5 It is translated and printed in Lieut.-Col. G. L. Chambers, *Bussaco* (London,
1910), pp. 142–76.

the irruption of a modern army into the chronicle of Jocelyn of Brakelond. These monks had taken a vow of silence and had withdrawn from the world into the solitude of the convent, which is buried deep in the midst of an immense dark forest, as all their predecessors had withdrawn, with the expectation of never once setting eyes on a layman again. At one o'clock in the morning of 20 September they were woken by the arrival of an a.d.c. of Wellington's who asked to see the Abbot. The Abbot showed him the convent and the chapel and ordered the monks to whitewash and clean the best room for the General. 'Our day ended in fear', writes the unhappy brother, 'for we now saw ourselves obliged to tolerate things never before known in this house.' At 8 on the 21st the Quartermaster-General[1] arrived, who gave out a roll of officers to whom and whom only quarters had to be given. There were 50. At 9 o'clock Wellington entered the convent. 'We showed him his room. It did not please him, in spite of its being the best, because it had only one door. He chose another more secure, for it had two. He ordered us to wash the place, and to dry it by lighting a fire.' The other staff officers were meanwhile taking up quarters in other rooms of the convent and in the other small hermitages that were scattered singly in different parts of the great forest. (Murray, we know, occupied a little hermitage about five minutes' walk from the convent.) Except for the cell of the Prior, Brother Antonio of the Angels, 'which nobody wanted, because it was found full of lumber, rags, and old iron', and the Abbot's, all were taken by the Staff, and the monks slept in the church and the sacristy and elsewhere. If that disturbance were not enough, Wellington asked that the bells should not be rung at night. Matins had therefore to be held at 8 in the evening. Worse still, 'he broke up the confinement for all kinds of persons, which had never been done since the foundation of the convent'. On the 27th the battle was fought out at the very gates of the monastery enclosure.

The authority by which the Army was quartered in particular places, and, indeed, the authority by which any battalion, detachment, or even a single soldier, moved from one

[1] I am inclined to think this was Dawson Kelly rather than Murray.

place to another, was the Route, which was issued by the
Q.M.G. or an officer of his Department and by them alone.
If there was but one activity of the Q.M.G.'s known to the
highest and lowest in the Army it was his issue of routes.
When Wellington in a fit of impatience told an officer he
might go to hell, the latter's friend was heard to mutter that
he would go to the Q.M.G. for a route for him.[1] The route
was often a confidential document, usually sent in duplicate
by two separate messengers, always requiring acknowledge-
ment and always made out by an officer. Though occasionally
'discretionary' routes were issued, in which the dates of the
marches were not specified, the route more frequently listed
the dates and halting places; and routes for detachments (of
sick or convalescents or reinforcements) usually bore the size
of the party as well, and the depots at which rations could be
drawn from the Commissariat. Without the authority of the
route, no unit or detachment could be fed at the public expense or quartered by the magistrates. All these routes[2] were
entered into the 'Distribution Books' at Headquarters, and
as a statement of the stations of the units and formations,
known as a 'General Distribution', was periodically drawn up
in the Distribution Book from information sent in by the
divisional Assistants, all information as to the disposition of
the Army was conveniently centralized in the Q.M.G.'s
hand and readily available to his commander.

The Q.M.G. being responsible for all types of movement,
whether movements of troops in the back areas or movements
in front of the enemy, there was no distinction of responsibility drawn between orders issued, say, to the skeleton of a
regiment marching for embarkation at Lisbon and an operational order issued in the heat of battle. Indeed, except for a
few days in 1809, the ordinary route, or a combination of
routes, served to move the whole Army in the comparatively
simple marches it undertook until the pursuit of Masséna in
the spring of 1811. The advance across the Douro, the advance on and the retreat from Talavera in 1809, the retreat

---

[1] *Larpent*, p. 96. The friend was probably Lieut.-Col. Framingham, the C.R.A.

[2] All issued at Headquarters at any rate, and copies of some issued by the
A.Q.M.G.s at Lisbon, Coimbra, Pasajes, &c. Some routes of detachments are
entered in the 'Day Books'.

on Buçaco, and the retreat to the Lines in 1810, were all controlled by simple orders issued daily for this division and that division, this brigade and that troop of artillery, to march from such a village to such a town. Except in so far as they rarely provided for more than one or two days ahead, these orders can hardly be distinguished from any of the Q.M.G.'s routes.

After 8 March 1811, however, the movement orders issued by the Q.M.G. became more complex. They began to embrace tactical dispositions on the field of battle; and, whereas previously, if further explanation beyond the bare statement of a formation's destination appeared necessary, Murray had supplied it in a short note to the divisional or brigade commander concerned, Murray henceforward tended to include it in the body of the movement order itself. From this time onwards the distinction between a route and a movement order appeared more clearly. The so-called 'arrangements'[1] of the Q.M.G. became more and more comprehensive as the war proceeded until they reached their peak of comprehensiveness and complexity in the 'arrangement' for the crossing of the Bidassoa in October 1813, which—we are not measuring terms too precisely—must be one of the most, if not the most, comprehensive movement orders for a successful 'set-piece' operation ever issued by a staff officer.

Too much emphasis should not, however, be laid upon this transformation nor upon the date at which it became easily discernible. A few orders of the Q.M.G.'s in the days immediately preceding the battle of Talavera, some orders immediately preceding the occupation of the Serra de Buçaco, and the order for the evacuation of the Serra, the order for the unfought battle for Santarém on 18 November 1810, are not unlike those issued after March 1811. Similarly Murray continued throughout the war to add explanations in letters to the formation commanders, particularly to Hill,

---

[1] This was the word which Murray habitually used. The 'dislocation' of the Q.M.G.'s vocabulary of the previous century had gone out, and 'disposition' was ambiguous, as being applicable to the situation of troops either as they were or as they were to be. 'Distribution' was the normal word used in Peninsular times of the situation of troops at a given moment. Murray's 'arrangement' avoided all ambiguity.

Graham, Cotton, and Cole, whose commands were usually more independent. The transformation was probably unconscious, and certainly gradual; and what change there was is not necessarily to be ascribed to an alteration in the nature of the Q.M.G.'s responsibility, nor to a change in the manner by which Wellington issued his orders, nor solely to a growth of confidence on Wellington's part in Murray's abilities, to a waxing of these abilities themselves, nor to any administrative change in the distribution of orders. It arose from the changed circumstances: the more frequent assumption of the offensive; the augmentation of the Army; and partly through that subtle change in the habits of thought and outlook of subordinate commanders and men which during 1811 made the Army a 'manoeuvring army'.[1] If an operation order similar to that for the crossing of the Bidassoa had been issued in 1809 or 1810 it is difficult to imagine its being carried out with precision and, above all, success.

Operation orders of this kind were more suited to an offensive movement when the initiative lay with Wellington, and Wellington's gradual assumption of the initiative after July 1811 no doubt goes far to account for their adoption. But the growth of the Army undoubtedly contributed to the use of a method that would reduce the paper work in the Q.M.G.'s office, where there were rarely more than four officers available to copy orders.[2]

The usual practice observed during the whole of the Peninsular War was for marching orders to be issued in the evening previous to the march, at about 5 p.m., and the troops to start before dawn in order to avoid the full heat of the noonday sun. Most marches could be accomplished by midday, and the troops, on arriving at their destination and having received their camp-kettles or pitched their camp, would set about their dinner. To preserve this routine, the whole business of writing and copying the orders and carry-

[1] Scovell's Diary (W.O. 37/7A), entry of 24 Nov. 1811: '[   ] thinks the position of Buçaco . . . the strongest he ever saw and is of opinion that, had the Army at the time of the battle been as it is now, a manœuvring army, Masséna would have suffered severely for his temerity in presenting a flank when he turned us after the action.' There is reason for identifying [   ] with Murray.

[2] v. sup., p. 57. At the time of the Bidassoa crossing these officers were: Murray himself, Broke, Freeth, and Murray's a.d.c., Charles Moray.

ing them to the different formations had to be done between the afternoon of one day and three o'clock the next morning. Speed was essential. Either the orders could be copied at the Q.M.G.'s office and portions of them extracted for each subordinate commander before they were sent out; or a 'pass order' could be taken round each formation by one or perhaps two messengers, and each formation staff could copy from it the parts that related to itself. Which of these two courses was adopted depended upon the circumstances rather than any rule. The 'pass order' required fewer orderlies or officers; on the other hand, the time spent by the Q.M.G.'s office staff in copying would equally be spent by the divisional staffs in making their extracts, and, unless the divisions were in close proximity to each other and Headquarters, the pass order was probably not a great time-saver. In practice it seems to have fallen into disuse, and after April 1811 pass orders are not often met with.

The speed with which the whole mechanical process was gone through was intimately related to the number of subordinate formations and their distance from Headquarters. In the early days this had not been such an important consideration. Though the Army at the time of the Douro campaign had been organized in formations no larger than brigades, it had acted in but three (not widely separated) columns, and the Q.M.G.'s addressee-list was short. But by the time of the pursuit of Masséna in March 1811 the Army was composed of eight divisions; and although one (the 2nd) was beyond Murray's immediate concern, the remaining seven were split into more than seven groups, each requiring separate attention. The dockets on a pass order of this period which was transmitted to seven out of the (at least) eleven[1] formations provide a useful indication of the time it took for orders to reach their destination. It is a movement order issued at Vila-Sêca after the fight at Casal-Novo, and though unfortunately bearing no hour, it must have been issued very late but before midnight on 14 March 1811. Murray ordered it 'to be passed from the 3rd Division to the Light Division, and thence to the 6th Division, thence to the 1st Division

---

[1] The 3rd Division, the six recipients listed below, and additional orders to Hawker, Nightingall, Cole, and Pack (*Murray Papers*, 33, fos. 160, 161, 163–4).

and to the rear of the column—to be passed to the 5th Division by the nearest division to it'. It received the following dockets:

> Received by the Light Division from the 3rd, and passed as ordered, 3 o'clock a.m.—H. Mellish, Captain, D.A.A.G.
>
> Received by 6th Division and passed to the 1st at [*illegible*] 6 a.m.— S. B. Auchmuty, D.A.A.G.
>
> Received by the 1st Division and passed to the 5th Division at 7 o'clock a.m.—F. von Drechsel, Brigade-major.
>
> Received by the 5th Division and passed to Colonel Ashworth's Brigade at ½ past 7 o'clock a.m., 15 March.—H. Craig, Captain, D.A.A.G.
>
> Received by Colonel Ashworth's Brigade at ¾ past 7 o'clock a.m., 15 March 1811.—A. P. Quindeland, Brigade-major.
>
> Received by part of the 7th Division, from Colonel Ashworth's Brigade, 3½ o'clock [p.m.]—H. Belson, Brigade-major, 7th Portuguese Brigade.[1]

In this instance the formations were fairly concentrated. Yet about eight hours elapsed before all immediately concerned had received their orders; and when the Army was dispersed, as it habitually was in the latter years of the War, the time taken in drawing up, extracting, and carrying orders was very considerable. The copying alone of each complete order for the Bidassoa crossing cannot have taken less than six hours.[2]

Who made out these orders? and how much of Wellington is there in them and how much of his Q.M.G.? Since all operation orders without exception were issued over the Q.M.G.'s signature and bear no outward indication of their authorship, it is not an easy question to answer. Yet, if there is one activity of a commander's that lives after him it is the movement of his troops, and it is vital that of all questions this at least should be answered.

---

[1] *Murray Papers*, 33, fos. 156–7. The order as printed in *Wyld*, pp. 50–51, and from there copied in *Disp.* (1852), iv. 666 n. is the pass order (altered) combined with instructions added by Murray to those copies sent separately to Hawker, Nightingall, and Pack. The 7th Division was only partially formed at this date, consisting only of the Chasseurs Britanniques, the 12th, 7th, and 19th Portuguese Infantry and the 2nd Caçadores. The 85th was at Leiria, the 2/88th at Pombal, and other regiments farther in rear. None was involved in tactical movements until a fortnight later.

[2] This is not to say that each of the nine recipients received the order in its entirety.

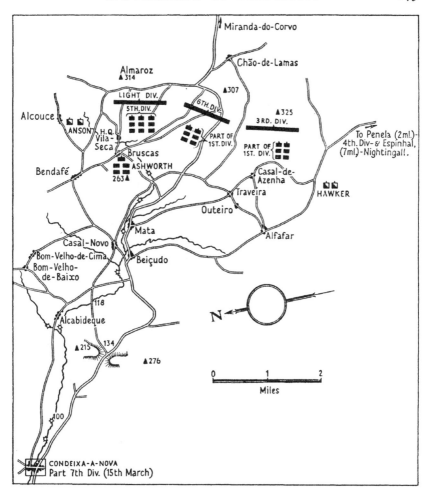

POSITION TAKEN UP BY THE ARMY, AFTER THE FIGHT AT CASAL-NOVO, FOR THE
NIGHT OF THE 14–15 MARCH 1811

During Murray's absence in 1812, while De Lancey and Gordon took his place, it is quite clear what happened. Wellington wrote in his own hand a memorandum setting out exactly what movements were to take place, and handed it to the Q.M.G., who did very little more than issue it as it stood. The orders for the attack on the hornwork of Burgos Castle[1] were written on scraps of paper in pencil by Wellington as he sat in one of the forward trenches: the order as issued by Gordon was a word for word copy. Others might need slight alteration. A typical example of a memorandum of this period is that reproduced as No. 1 in Appendix VI, one of the daily movement orders made during the advance on Madrid after the battle of Salamanca. No. 2 (a), the Q.M.G.'s order derived from it, was, as a matter of fact, the first order Gordon issued, as he had only arrived at Headquarters three days previously. He had only to rearrange the orders contained in Wellington's memorandum in a way that would ease the clerical work of making abstracts for the divisional commanders (no one divisional commander receiving the document in full), to add times and various details, to specify the routes of the columns about which Wellington was not certain, and to address an additional memorandum to Bisset on the subsistence of the troops in Cuéllar (No. 2 (b)).

This is an example that may be taken as characteristic of the relationship between Wellington and the chief of his Q.M.G.'s Department throughout 1812. It is certain beyond all reasonable doubt that no operational unit or formation was moved unless Wellington had given a previous order, and that usually in writing. The organization of the communications in rear was also prescribed by Wellington. He drew up in great detail a scheme by which Gordon was to arrange the routes by which the clothing was to be carried up from Portugal.[2] He instructed Gordon to devise the stages in the route along which the new communication from Corunna was to run.[3] Both Gordon and De Lancey had little

[1] The originals are in *Murray Papers*, 38, fos. 170–4; the Instructions of Gordon's in ibid. 88, pp. 130–2, Villatoro, 19 Sept. 1812 (*Suppl. Disp.* xiv. 119–20).

[2] Memorandum for the Q.M.G., 12 Sept. 1812 (*Murray Papers*, 38, fos. 159–62; *Disp.* vi. 68–70).

[3] *v. sup.*, p. 97. Memoranda Gordon to Wellington and Wellington to Gordon, 22 Aug. 1812 (*Murray Papers*, 38, fos. 143–4).

more to do, so far as troop movements were concerned, than copy out what Wellington had given them in a memorandum.

It is fair to assume that his employment of De Lancey in 1815 was very similar. If it was, as seems almost certain, it throws a very different light upon the so-called 'De Lancey Memorandum', a document said to have been drawn up by De Lancey, presumably for Wellington's assistance, on 16 June 1815, in using which Wellington is supposed to have deceived Blücher into fighting at Ligny.[1] Foreign writers of a later day, accustomed to staffs that did much of their generals' thinking for them and made decisions which no staff officer of Wellington's Army would ever, except in exceptional circumstances, have presumed to take upon himself, have described this document in such phrases as 'the most misleading statement ever drawn up for the information of a commanding general'.[2] It is inconceivable to anyone who has studied Wellington's methods to suppose that he could be 'misled' to such an extent on a matter on which he himself had given the orders. He would have detected a mistake of such magnitude without a moment's reflection.

During Murray's tenure of office (1809–11 and 1813–14) it is clear that the manner in which the Commander and his Q.M.G. worked together was different. Few memoranda of these years in Wellington's hand similar to that reproduced at Appendix VI (1) have survived. There is one for the projected attack on Santarém on 19 November 1810 which was never carried out.[3] There is the famous order Wellington wrote on the coping of the bridge at Sorauren during the fighting of 27 July 1813.[4] There is an order for the occupation of Pau by a force under Fane in March 1814.[5] All these

---

[1] *Disp.* viii. 142–3. See Maj.-Gen. C. W. Robinson, in *Journal of the Royal United Service Institution* (1910), liv. 582–97, with whose conclusions I agree entirely.

[2] John C. Ropes, *The Campaign of Waterloo* (1892), pp. 86, 113.

[3] Memorandum, Cartaxo, 18 Nov. 1810 (*Murray Papers*, 31, fos. 41–44).

[4] Instructions dated 'at the bridge near Larrasoaña', 11 a.m. 27 July 1813 (ibid. 44, fos. 114–18; *Suppl. Disp.* viii. 122, printing from the copy Murray had made for Pack). Only copies survive. The mistake of *Larrasoaña* for *Sorauren* may therefore be not Wellington's but the copyist's. See *Oman*, vi. 660–1.

[5] Printed in *Disp.* vii. 350 n.: Instructions for Maj.-Gen. Fane, contained in Murray to Hill, Saint-Sever, 6 Mar. 1814 (*Murray Papers*, 48, fos. 65–66; 91, pp. 120–2).

were issued by Murray almost exactly as they stood. There are besides a few brief notes instructing Murray to issue orders for certain movements. These again were issued precisely as Wellington had required. If a correspondence arose between Murray and a subordinate commander as to how the latter should act in certain eventualities, it is apparent that Murray consulted Wellington before answering. Murray's draft orders for the evacuation of the Serra of Buçaco have survived, and contain Wellington's corrections and amendments.[1] In fact all the documents in Murray's papers indicate that Murray did not, any more than De Lancey or Gordon, issue movement instructions unless it was at the instance and with the full and previous concurrence of his commander.

Yet the almost total absence of memoranda by Wellington requires explanation. It might be that they all were destroyed. On the other hand, they may never have existed. That they were, or have since been, destroyed is unlikely. Many papers certainly have been lost, but almost everything relating to movements Murray carefully preserved against the moment when, as he intended, he would write a history of the Peninsular operations. Common prudence would have led him to keep the orders his commander had given him, and the survival of such Wellington memoranda as remain suggests—it does no more—that he would have kept them if they existed. The editors of Wellington's dispatches give no help. The copies printed in the later editions of the *Dispatches* were derived from the Memoir published by Wyld, the geographer, who used a text specially prepared by Murray. The 2nd Duke of Wellington's edition of the *Supplementary Dispatches* includes many movement orders, especially those from 1813 onwards, but though he printed them direct from the originals among Murray's papers, he followed an unscholarly practice by which he placed the more important over Wellington's signature and the less important over Murray's or no signature at all, regardless of the fact that they were all issued over Murray's. To establish the manner in which Wellington conveyed his wishes to Murray it is

---

[1] Instructions dated Buçaco, 28 Sept. 1810 (ibid. 29, fos. 170–4; *Disp.* iv. 300–1 n.).

consequently necessary to have recourse to the ocular testimony of some witness and an examination of the manuscript
drafts.

We are fortunate enough to possess the acount of a reliable
eyewitness, Captain Harry Smith, who saw Wellington and
Murray together one day late in October 1813, when the
forward movement known as the battle of the Nivelle was
being planned.[1] Wellington used often, he says, to visit one
of the Light Division outposts on the Rhune, and once he
stayed unusually long, talking to Colborne.

The Duke was lying down and began a very earnest conversation.
General Alten, Kempt, Colborne, I and other staff-officers were pre-
paring to leave the Duke, when he says 'Oh, lie still.' After he had
conversed for some time with Sir G. Murray, Murray took out of his
sabretache his writing materials, and began to write the plan of attack
for the whole Army.[2] When it was finished, so clearly had he understood the Duke I do not think he erased one word. He says 'My Lord,
is this your desire?' It was one of the most interesting scenes I have ever
witnessed. As Murray read the Duke's eye was directed with his tele-
scope to the spot in question. He never asked Sir G. Murray one question, but the muscles of his face evinced lines of the deepest thought.
When Sir G. Murray had finished the Duke smiled and said 'Ah,
Murray, this will put us in possession of the fellows' lines. Shall we be
ready tomorrow?' 'I fear not, my Lord, but next day.'[3]

The draft that Murray was writing has not, unfortunately,
survived. However, some similar notes, evidently written by
Murray in an uncomfortable position or with cold hands for
the Bidassoa operations a month earlier, are still extant, and
accord perfectly with such a scene as Smith has described.[4]
On the latter occasion the notes made on the ground served

[1] *Smith*, i. 142–3. Smith was the brigade-major of the brigade of the Light
Division commanded, in Skerrett's absence, by Colborne.

[2] More probably only for that part of the Army which attacked the Petite
Rhune.

[3] This last interchange cannot be quite accurate, as the orders drawn up after
this reconnaissance (which must have taken place about 22 or 23 Oct.) were issued
on the 25th and were made contingent upon the fall of Pamplona. Pamplona did not
fall until the 30th, and owing to bad weather the attack had to be postponed suc-
cessively until 10 Nov. Smith's report is correct to the extent that the movement
required two days' notice (*Suppl. Disp.* viii. 335; *Murray Papers*, 46, fos. 46–98).

[4] Unheaded, undated notes, one set for the movements of the Left Column
(*Murray Papers*, 46, fos. 45–46), and one for the movements of Longa's troops and
the Light Division (ibid. fos. 53–55).

as the basis for a draft movement order which was submitted to Wellington and corrected by him; a further draft was drawn up by Broke, which, after being corrected by Murray and perhaps also taken before Wellington, was copied for issue to the troops in the form in which the order now stands.[1] The only indication visible in the manuscripts of Wellington's intervention in these proceedings is his observations on the 'memorandum of the Q.M.G.'[2] which, inasmuch as Broke's draft incorporates them, is presumably the first draft in Murray's hand.

That Smith was describing the manner in which Wellington and Murray habitually worked together in this last year of the war there can be little doubt. Wellington sketched out his intentions verbally and left Murray to reduce them into his somewhat inelegant yet businesslike and unambiguous prose; and the order, after Wellington had approved it, was issued to the troops. By this time the two men had collaborated cordially for several years, and Murray was reputed to be the only officer who was received into Wellington's unlimited confidence.[3] Is it possible to accept this relationship as characteristic of the earlier years of the war? The documents suggest that it is.

The draft order which appears at Appendix VII comes from the earlier period. The part printed in roman type is written by Murray either in a hurry or in some uncomfortable posture: that in italics is in better ink, and is consistent with its having been written at a desk. It is impossible to be certain, of course, but it is tempting to guess that the former was taken down by Murray in conference with Wellington in the manner described by Smith over two years later; and that the latter was added when Murray returned to his quarter, by way of extenuating and explaining the bare instructions of the first part. The whole forms the order more or less as it was issued to the formations concerned.[4]

---

[1] Ibid., 46, fos. 9–15, 39–42, 23–28; 90, pp. 217–35; *Suppl. Disp.* viii. 285–92. Broke's having written the final draft may have been owing to an illness which kept Murray in his bed from about 1 Oct. to the 4th. The orders were issued on the 5th.

[2] *Murray Papers*, 46, fo. 56; *Suppl. Disp.* viii. 299.

[3] *Henegan*, i. 316 (spring 1813).

[4] The text of the order as printed in *Wyld*, pp. 51–52, and *Disp.* iv. 670 n. has been much altered.

Some pencil notes of Murray's (Appendix VIII (1)), on the back of a copy of a movement order belonging to the later period, appear to be of the same nature. They certainly form the basis of the orders issued on 11 June 1813 to the Right Column of the Army (2); and once again it is tempting to suppose that Murray took down a note of Wellington's directions on a spare copy of an order that happened to be in his pocket, and extended and elaborated them later.

All this is pure conjecture, but it rests on numerous indications of a similar character. It is consistent with other small pieces of evidence revealed by a study of the many other manuscript drafts both of the earlier and of the later period; it explains the almost total absence of memoranda from Wellington; it accords with the only positive evidence that has come down to us; and, moreover, it is supported by what is known of the intercourse between Wellington and Murray. Murray, unlike De Lancey and Gordon, had had a wide experience of active operations as a staff officer, and, with the exception of the Mediterranean theatre, had served in responsible situations in all the expeditions based on this country for ten years before he landed in Portugal in 1809. He was a man of independent ideas and the quality of his military views had already been proved in the impartial test of practical warfare. That Wellington did not always agree with these views we know, and that Murray did not always agree with Wellington's views, especially during 1810, we know also. But there is sufficient evidence of a general kind to make it possible to say that Wellington found it profitable to discuss business with Murray and that he missed Murray's help and advice when, in 1812, they were not there to be had. In a letter to Murray he betrayed the keen disappointment he felt at Murray's absence. 'I acknowledge', he wrote, 'that when I first heard of your intention to quit us my sentiments were not confined to concern and regret.'[1] It is a confession in which we are able to recognize a deeply mortified and very angry commander. Napier, who at the time of writing his history was carrying on a private feud with Murray, sought to discount the assistance Wellington received

[1] Wellington to Murray, Fuenteguinaldo, 28 May 1812 (*Disp.* v. 677). See also letter same to same, Paris, 23 July 1815 (ibid. viii. 214–15).

from him by implying that Wellington managed as well without him in 1812 as he had in the years before and after.[1] But Napier was in no position to know. It is a matter on which Wellington alone can speak, and he has not spoken. We know that even when he had Murray by him his personal supervision of the Army's movements was very strict. But there can hardly be a doubt that, in comparison with writing the orders himself, the kind of intercourse that Smith observed between the two on the Rhune relieved Wellington of an immense proportion of the drudgery of command.

While it is possible to hazard a guess at the part Murray played in the composition of the movement orders, his contribution towards his commander's decisions has become inextricably fused in the decisions themselves. This is as Murray would have wished, and it is unlikely that many instances of his intervention in Wellington's plans will ever be isolated. Wellington is reported later to have said that he never offered battle without Beresford and Murray and other generals begging him on their knees not to.[2] And long after the war, he told Croker that in 1813 Murray, among other generals, advised him to go no farther than the Ebro in his advance towards Vitoria.[3] These are both vague and unsupported statements, of which the latter at least appears to be a garbled account of something which is contradicted by contemporary evidence.[4] Murray for his part is reported by his family to have said there was only one occasion on which he had offered advice to Wellington and it had not been taken—again an incident during the advance of 1813, but earlier than the crossing of the Ebro, on about 9 June, when he urged Wellington not to push his right forward so much as to alarm the French into securing their routes to the French frontier.[5] This seems more likely, but the evidence is as open to question as that for Wellington's statements.

[1] *Napier*, bk. xix, cap. vii (Cabinet Editions, iv. 408).

[2] *The Journal of Mrs. Arbuthnot, 1820–1832* (ed. Francis Bamford and the Duke of Wellington, London, 1950), i. 212 (7 Feb. 1823).

[3] *Croker Papers*, i. 335–6 and n. (17 Jan. 1837).

[4] See *Oman*, vi. 360–1. What evidence there is in Murray's papers supports Sir Charles Oman's view.

[5] Manuscript biographical notes made by Mr. John Murray Gartshore, Murray's nephew, in the 1870's or 1880's (*Murray Papers*, T.D. 178, xi). He supports it by a report from Hill, Villalaco, 8 p.m. 9 June 1813 (*Wyld*, p. 93, n. 2).

Only three instances of Murray's intervention in Wellington's arrangements can be established with any certainty. The first is his proposal, made the day after the battle of Vitoria, to send Graham's Column by a mountain road in pursuit of the part of the French army that had escaped by the direct route towards Bayonne.[1] The second is his taking upon himself, while Wellington was absent from Headquarters, to warn two divisions to be ready to move from the centre of the Army towards the rear on the afternoon of 25 July 1813.[2] The third is an episode which occurred on the evening previous to the battle of Buçaco.[3] Having, he said, closely watched Masséna and his staff all day of 26 September, he was certain that the roads to Coimbra by the chapel and by Santo-António-do-Cântaro would be the principal points of attack. As Wellington's dispositions had been made on the assumption that the main ridge of Buçaco was too strong to attack and that the most dangerous blow would be struck on the left flank of the position, Murray went to Wellington, who had gone to bed, and he, though scarcely believing that the French would attack the ridge, gave orders for reinforcing the line at the points Murray named. On Murray and Wellington arriving on the ground the next morning, not only had the enemy made the attack on the ridge but had actually gained possession of the summit and the 88th were firing on them in column.[4]

There is no reason to doubt the truth of this story, Murray and Scovell being both reliable sources; and of the other two there is ample confirmation. But whether they are to be regarded as characteristic of Murray's relationship with Wellington or exceptional incidents warranting no general

---

[1] *Wyld*, p. 104 n.; *Oman*, vi. 455.

[2] *Wyld*, pp. 110–11; *Oman*, vi. 643. Unfortunately the Letter-Book for the period 21 July 1813 to 13 Jan. 1814 is missing which evidently contained several important letters that were not copied into the Distribution Book (Vol. 90). It should be noted Murray did not actually move these troops until Wellington returned to Headquarters.

[3] Scovell's Diary (W.O. 37/7A), entry of 4 Nov. 1810.

[4] This incident has been described more fully than its importance warrants because it has not appeared in print before. It raises some difficult questions, as neither of Picton's letters on the battle (his *Memoirs and Correspondence*, ed. H. B. Robinson (1836), i. 316–20, 330–6) nor Wellington's dispatch mention these last-minute alterations. Fortescue's account (vii. 514) contains them, but it does not otherwise quite square with Picton's letters. Murray's papers offer nothing.

inference it is hard to say. They might have taken place on every day of the common existence of these two men and we should be none the wiser. The disappointing conclusion must be reached that what was discussed between them behind the closed doors of Wellington's inner apartment will never be known.

The impression, however, remains that on all the business arising from the movements of the Army Murray had opinions already formed; that though he allowed himself, or was allowed, very limited powers of decision, and, like other heads of departments, took most questions before Wellington for his approval, Murray's recommendations were taken up by him; and that Wellington found discussion with Murray profitable. Murray's constant attendance upon him, the sentiment that prevailed generally at Headquarters that Murray was only second to Wellington,[1] and other indications all point to Wellington's high estimation of his abilities. It would be wrong to regard him as a kind of *éminence grise*, prompting in the background, a staff officer of the Prussian model, like Scharnhorst, a *stiller Gelehrte*, or Massenbach, reciting pedantic appreciations in a loud voice after a heavy dinner and sending his general to sleep. It would be equally mistaken to look upon him as merely a 'zealous and competent chief clerk'.[2] Even De Lancey and Gordon would scarcely fill that description. He was something between the two extremes: something that allowed Wellington, who directed his Army himself yet had to delegate much, to describe him as 'a very able man and an admirable Quartermaster-General'.[3]

[1] *McGrigor*, p. 343; *Henegan*, i. 316; *Larpent*, pp. 86, 188, 199; *Letters of Sir Augustus Simon Frazer* (London, 1859), p. 225.
[2] Oman, *Wellington's Army*, p. 157.
[3] *Croker Papers*, i. 337.

VI

WELLINGTON AND HIS STAFF

THE description of the business carried out by the staff at Headquarters is now finished. It is in no sense complete. If it had been the intention to allot space in proportion to the volume of the work each department undertook, the Medical Department has been unfairly neglected; the Adjutant-General, with the auxiliary services performed for him by the Deputy-Judge-Advocate-General, the Provost and his guard and the Cavalry Staff Corps, has received but scant attention; and the Quartermaster-General has absorbed a disproportionate amount of the limelight. But the Q.M.G., though second in dignity, was the first in importance, and while a modern adjutant-general, if translated into Wellington's Headquarters, would be able to assume his duties with little sense of unfamiliarity, a modern quartermaster-general would be lost in the multiplicity of strange responsibilities that he would be expected to bear. The emphasis has been laid upon those peculiarities of procedure that seem strange to us and upon those tasks that appear to us in retrospect to have been the most important.

Unless active operations interrupted the routine it was Wellington's practice to see each of his heads of departments daily. He rose at six every morning, wrote until breakfasting at nine, and immediately after was waited on by the A.G., the Q.M.G., the Commissary-General, the Inspector-General of Hospitals, the Commanding Officer of Artillery, the Commanding Royal Engineer and occasionally the Deputy-Paymaster-General, and by any other officer he wished to see on business such as Colquhoun Grant, or the Judge-Advocate, Larpent. This occupied him until two, three, or four in the afternoon.[1] He would then order his horse and ride until about six, or, when at Freineda, he might be seen walking up and down the little square in front of his quarter in his

---

[1] *Tomkinson*, p. 108 (written in the summer of 1811 when Headquarters were at the Quinta de S. João); *McGrigor*, pp. 262–3; *Larpent*, p. 52.

grey greatcoat, talking with anyone he wished to. Everyone who came to him found he dispatched business with remarkable facility, especially on the days he went hunting. 'He is very ready', Larpent wrote after his first week at Headquarters, 'and decisive, and civil, though some complain a little of him at times, and are much afraid of him. Going up with my charges and papers for instructions I feel something like a boy going to school.'[1] McGrigor, who arrived at Headquarters to replace Dr. Franck as Inspector-General soon after the siege of Ciudad Rodrigo in January 1812, at first used to wait on Wellington with a paper in his hand bearing the heads of the matters on which he wished to take the Commander's orders. 'But', he says, 'I shortly discovered that he disliked my coming with a written paper; he was fidgety, and evidently displeased when I referred to my notes', so McGrigor put aside his paper and arrived every morning with his business arranged in his head.[2] Wellington retained his astonishing capacity for getting through work until late in life, and a French ambassador who knew him when Prime Minister told an acquaintance that in thirty minutes he could transact as much with him as he could with a French minister in as many hours.[3] Masséna in his heyday[4] and Napoleon both appear to have possessed the same extraordinary facility.

The close collaboration between Wellington and his staff has, like his relationship with Murray, tended to obscure the extent to which each of his heads of departments contributed personally towards the administration of the Army. If he was offered advice by the responsible staff officer concerned (whether civil or military), he probably acted on it; and it is consequently not easy to detect in his dispatches how much they reflect the views of his staff, and how much his own peculiar opinions. It is an interesting question, but it is not of such importance as if we were discussing some piece of literary plagiarism. Wellington held the view that he took the responsibility for everything that he required of his Army and everything that he demanded of the Secretary of State,

[1] *Larpent*, p. 35.   [2] *McGrigor*, p. 263.
[3] *A Portion of the Journal kept by Thomas Raikes, Esq., 1831–1847* (London, 1856), ii. 69, Sébastiani's statement (1835).   [4] *Thiébault*, iii. 81–83.

irrespective of whether the suggestion was initiated by himself or one of his staff. In estimating Wellington's contribution towards the successful administration of his Army it should, in fairness both to himself and his heads of departments, be said that there is, for instance, a good deal of Kennedy in his opinions and directions on the subject of commissariat affairs, and a good deal of McGrigor in the medical; and it is not difficult to quote occasions on which he was guided by Dickson and Fletcher just as he consulted Murray on operational matters. But once the advice was accepted the decision was his responsibility and his alone.

In making use of his staff in this manner, Wellington showed himself to be of the new school, but it cannot be said that he was an innovator, as, for instance, it might be said of him in respect of his use of ground, or of Gustavus Adolphus in his cavalry tactics and his use of light artillery. In the previous century much of a general's burden of responsibility had been lifted from his shoulders at critical moments by councils of war, which were committees composed of the general officers and the A.G. and Q.M.G. Councils of war had punctuated and underlined, as it were, every step of importance taken in the wars and expeditions of the period: at Rochefort, at Saratoga, in the Low Countries in 1793–5. For the Helder expedition of 1799 a council of war had not only been enjoined upon the commander of the British contingent by the Secretary of State, but its composition had been precisely laid down beforehand.[1] As late as 1809 Lord Chatham summoned a council of war before evacuating Walcheren. But by the time of the Peninsular War councils of war were passing out of fashion. Dalrymple had summoned an assembly of officers to discuss the terms that should be agreed with the French after the battle of Vimeiro in 1808, but this was not a proper council of war. Moore never resorted to it. He was inclined to consult others outside his staff, such as Anstruther, and there are indications that he was influenced by the opinions of senior officers in his immediate entourage to an extent that

---

[1] Lieut.-Gen. Sir H. E. Bunbury, *Narratives of some passages in the Great War with France, 1799–1810* (London, 1854), p. 43 (cit. as 'Bunbury').

accounts in some degree for the outspoken criticisms of his decisions when he ultimately made up his mind. This attitude went right through the Army and may be said to have contributed to the destruction of discipline on the retreat to Corunna.[1] But in no sense can these consultations be described as councils of war. They were a legitimate use of professional counsel—very much in the manner which, according to General De Guingand,[2] was favoured by General Auchinleck when commanding the Middle East forces in the second World War. On the whole Moore, and, so far as we know, Cathcart, made use of their staffs in much the same way that Wellington treated his.

As to composition Wellington was given the same staff as that which any of his contemporaries would have received. Its duties have already been described. It unfortunately cannot be compared with Marlborough's, as in the interval the competence of the departments had changed;[3] and Marlborough's employment of his Q.M.G., William Cadogan, cannot be equated with Wellington's of Murray, who was kept perpetually at his commander's side.[4] The allocation of work was so altered during the Revolutionary period that comparison is possible only between the staffs of expeditionary forces that left this country after 1803. The use Wellington made of his departments is more to be distinguished by his views on the responsibility of the staff officers than by any innovation of the work that they undertook. He lived in the lonely isolation which must hedge a commander of no matter how large or small a force. He confided in few and he admitted none to his counsel but such as were responsible for their advice. His reasons may be seen in his attitude to seconds-in-command, which the military authorities at home, not having altogether abandoned the council of war tradition, persisted in appointing. He would not admit their existence.

[1] In contrast notice the rebuke administered by Haig during the retreat from Mons to his chief-of-staff, who gave vent to his exasperation in the presence of other staff officers. (*The Private Papers of Douglas Haig, 1914–1919*, ed. Robert Blake (London, 1952), p. 87.)

[2] Maj.-Gen. Sir F. W. De Guingand, *Operation Victory* (London, 1947), p. 90.

[3] An observation by Murray himself, in his introduction to his edition of *Marlborough's Letters and Dispatches* (London, 1845), p. x.

[4] This comes out clearest in references to Cadogan in the *Correspondence ... of ... Marlborough and Antonie Heinsius* (ed. B. van 't Hoff, The Hague, 1951).

To Sir Brent Spencer, who had received this appointment in Portugal, he said he 'did not know what the words "second-in-command" meant, any more than third-, fourth- or fifth-in-command'. He told him 'I would have no "second-in-command" in the sense of his having anything like a joint command or superintending control, and that, finally and above all, I would not only take but insist upon the whole and undivided responsibility of all that should happen while the Army was under my command'.[1] Moore and other generals of the new school would have agreed. Wellington was not innovating, any more than Lord Montgomery may be said to have innovated when he took command of the Eighth Army and employed his staff in the manner General De Guingand has described.[2] But Wellington and the success that attended his method of command gave the mortal blow to the council of war. When Wellington was a subaltern the anonymous author of the *Advice to Officers* had written for the benefit of generals: 'as no other person in your Army is allowed to be possessed of a single idea it would be ridiculous, on any occasion, to assemble a council of war, or at least to be guided by their opinion'.[3] That had been sarcasm in 1787: in 1815 it would have raised a smile only as a quaint antiquity.

The only innovation that Wellington attempted to introduce into his staff was the institution of a chief-of-staff. It would, he hoped, enable him to delegate much of the routine business. But Willoughby Gordon proved himself unsuitable, and after a trial of only a week or two the project was dropped. That Murray afterwards, in 1813 and 1814, became almost a chief-of-staff (without, however, assuming any of the prescriptive functions of the A.G. or the Military Secretary) indicates that Wellington, impelled by the size of his Army,[4] was aiming towards a greater degree of delegation.

[1] *Croker Papers*, i. 343-4 (conversation of about Dec. 1826). See also Wellington to Beresford, Freineda, 2 Dec. 1812: 'Every officer in an army should have some duty to perform for which he is responsible. . . . The second-in-command has none that anybody can define, excepting to give opinions for which he is in no manner responsible . . .' (*Disp*. vi. 188).

[2] *De Guingand*, pp. 187-93.

[3] *Advice to the officers of the British Army* (London, 1787), p. 2. It is commonly attributed to Capt. Francis Grose, but there is some doubt about the authorship.

[4] Cf. *Clausewitz*, bk. v, cap. 5.

It is an indication that is borne out by his appointing Murray as his chief-of-staff when he commanded the Allied contingents in France after Waterloo,[1] when he was at liberty to construct a staff after his own liking for that purpose. But Murray was never such a chief-of-staff as Lord Montgomery used, and Wellington throughout the Peninsular War adhered to the traditional staff whose composition has already been described.

Just as Wellington inherited the same staff as his contemporaries so he took over the men composing that staff who had been chosen to assist him. In this respect he was at no advantage over any other general of the time. It might indeed be argued that he was rather at a disadvantage. He was far from being *persona grata* at the Horse Guards, and if he had not received support from his former a.d.c., Torrens, who was now Military Secretary, it is impossible to say what men might have been thrust upon him. As it was, enough has been said to show that his patronage was limited, and acquiescence on the part of the Horse Guards in his preferences was not always to be expected even at the height of his reputation. To say that 'when he had found his man he stuck to him'[2] is misleading, as it implies that he was at liberty to search for staff officers. Although perhaps in theory he had the appointment of junior officers, and even civil officers, to the departments in the Peninsula, in practice they were nominated by the heads of those departments, and the nomination of those heads was securely retained by *their* heads in London. The only two staff officers he fought with the Horse Guards to hold were Colonel Edward Pakenham, his brother-in-law,[3] and Colonel Colin Campbell; on the latter's appointment Wellington was so insistent that the innocent victim was nicknamed by Torrens 'God's Curse'.[4] The Peninsular staff appointments came mostly from London,

---

[1] Murray was Chief-of-Staff to Wellington as Commander-in-Chief of the Allied Army of Occupation as well as Q.M.G. to the British contingent.

[2] Oman, *Wellington's Army*, p. 157.

[3] Torrens to Wellington, 18 Dec. 1809 and to Charles Stewart, 18 Jan. 1810 (W.O. 3/595, pp. 230–40, 357–8).

[4] Torrens to Calvert, 6 May 1810 and to Wellington, 10 Feb. 1811 (W.O. 3/596, p. 323; W.O. 3/598, p. 407). Campbell had been appointed D.A.G. in Malta.

though in the later years he was allowed a larger share of the patronage.

It is fairly certain that if Wellington's preferences had been consistently consulted a different type of officer would have been favoured. The immense augmentation of the army in the years of the Revolution and again after 1803, the temper of the time, and perhaps also the natural disposition of the Duke of York and his staff, had led the Horse Guards to accept officers from a class of persons which in ordinary circumstances would have been denied advancement in the service. Whatever the causes, the Horse Guards at the period of the Peninsular War was prepared to promote officers without money or interest on a greater scale than in the days of the King's administration before the wars. Officially the emphasis was upon merit, and the foundation of the Royal Military College had been an attempt, praiseworthy in its intentions, to give effect to this policy. The great revolution of sentiment had passed Wellington by—indeed, he had been out of the country while the revolution was at its height. The good officers who had been thrown up he acknowledged; but sufficient inducement and backing were not, he thought, given to those who combined merit with money and interest, or, as he called it, 'family, fortune and influence'; the products of the Military College he (like other eminent commanders fifty or sixty years after) stigmatized as 'coxcombs and pedants'. If the Horse Guards had allowed Wellington full discretion his staff would have been composed of young men, certainly of no less ability but of more distinguished lineage, men such as Cadogan, Somers Cocks, and the others who already composed his personal staff.[1] But, as we have seen, the Horse Guards did not materially relax its powers of appointment, and the staff of the Peninsular Army cannot be said to have been Wellington's in the sense that it was of his choosing. Far more remarkable than his sticking to his man when he found him was his sticking to men who had been found for him; that having been presented with these men, even thirty-four coxcombs and pedants, and while

---

[1] Wellington to Torrens, Celorico, 4 Aug. 1810 (*Disp.* iv. 205); Torrens to Beresford and Wellington, Horse Guards, 28 Aug. 1810 (W.O. 3/597, pp. 259-60, 263-5).

entertaining his own prejudices, he should have made them work so successfully to his wishes.

His power to dominate was extraordinary. Generals fresh from an inspiring campaign in Hyde Park, who received the customary invitation to dinner with the Commander on their arrival in the Peninsula, discovered immediately that informal consultations were not in order here. One such was heard to offer his opinion on the critical situation in which he felt the Army to be. If, he asked, explaining his movements on the tablecloth, the French moved here, and then did this and then did that, which they would inevitably try, what would your Lordship do? 'Give them the most infernal thrashing they've had for some time', replied Wellington.[1] To reduce a man such as Charles Stewart to tears; to tame Craufurd; to bend Willoughby Gordon, the most inveterate busybody, and make of him the most subservient of tools, willing to undertake anything for 'the Marquess' (always 'the Marquess'); to cleanse Headquarters of all spirit of party—such achievements testify to no common ascendancy. A general's staff, the officers of the military and civil departments, owed, as we have seen, what has been described as a double allegiance, and in this respect Wellington's differed at the outset in no way from any other. This double allegiance was noticeable in the subordinate formations and particularly in the civil departments, which had financial responsibilities that derived from the parent departments in London and affected the private fortune of the men concerned. But, however easily discernible it may have been in the first years in the Peninsula, by the end of the war, though necessarily present, Wellington, by sheer personality, had purged it of any of its harmful influence. In the Crimea forty years later the divided loyalty of the civil staff was one of the principal causes of the notorious maladministration. Heads of departments declared on oath that they did not know where their responsibilities ended and another department's began. There were unimportant instances of this in the Peninsula, but if the Commander of the Forces got to hear of them the culprit was immediately visited with his wrath.

[1] Mark Boyd, *Reminiscences of Fifty Years* (London, 1871), p. 5. The incident was related by Sir John Waters.

If there were any abstract qualities that Wellington insisted upon, they were permanence and system: permanence to give experience, system to avoid equivocation. They may be seen in all his arrangements for the administration of his Army. His repeated complaints of general officers and staff officers going home on leave; his wish to keep all soldiers who had served a campaign or two, even to the inconvenience of the administration of the individual regiments; his emphasis on obedience to orders; the detailed written instructions to his subordinate commanders—more numerous than those issued by any commander before him, even including Napoleon; all these are the outward indications of the value he placed upon an inexorable adherence to method.

No better illustration of his love of system can be offered than his elaboration of the divisional organization. Some stages in the development of the Peninsular divisions have already been separately noticed. They were first formed of the old brigades of the Douro campaign with a staff from each of the two military departments and the commissariat. Later a brigade of Portuguese was attached. Then a field brigade of artillery. Then an engineer officer was attached to its staff; later still representatives from the medical department. The divisional mules were added, and the stock-bullocks allotted on a divisional basis. Then the Waggon Train at the end of 1812 was broken up and divided between the divisions to act as an ambulance corps. A proportion of the Corps of Guides and the Royal Staff Corps was attached to each. There was an assistant-provost-marshal in each division and later a detachment of the Staff Corps of Cavalry (1813). And finally, for a brief month in 1814, a signalling section was formed, to manage the telegraph. Except for cavalry, Wellington's division was that which took the field in 1914.

In the last months of the war he was tending towards a corps organization, no doubt in order to secure some further degree of delegation. Although the staff of the divisional commanders who commanded corps was strengthened (in talent rather than numbers), the Corps never came to possess the individuality and personality that the divisions had, and Wellington continued to direct the divisions as if this embryonic corps organization had never existed. Its existence, however, is worth observing as indicating the systematic trend towards delegation, of which one of the principal effects was to ease the burden borne by the Headquarters staff. In the Austrian service, whose staff enjoyed a high reputation at one time, even brigades were organized as loosely as Wellington's two or three Corps, and the necessity of repeating orders down to regimental level involved a crippling amount of secretarial work that made the Austrian army a byword for slowness.[1] The French owed their rapidity of movement largely to the extent to which command was delegated to corps commanders. In Wellington's Army delegation was not carried so far. But it was sufficient to allow the Commander a close control over his divisions and at the same time to reduce the purely mechanical and very lengthy process of copying and abstracting orders.

The division has a tactical significance which it is out of place to touch upon here. But even as an administrative device it cannot be regarded as an innovation. It was new to the British army—so new that in 1807, although it had already been used in active operations, the word was not in general currency[2]—but it was not unheard of.[3] It was certainly no invention of Wellington's. In fact, we look in vain to Wellington's administration of his Army to discover innovations. He used essentially the traditional methods of subsisting his troops. His topographical and secret intelligence services, while adapted to the peculiarities of Peninsular warfare, were, fundamentally, those his predecessors had employed. While deviating on occasion from standard eighteenth-century practice and, like those who had broken the rules before, paying the penalty, he quartered his Army as his military ancestors had quartered theirs; and, as has been remarked, his reversion to encampments might, in an historical sense, be even regarded as reactionary. To issue movement orders through the Q.M.G.'s Department, though his doing so proclaimed him an adherent of the new school, had become

---

[1] Col. F. N. Maude, *The Campaign of Ulm* (London, 1909), p. 40 (cit. hereafter as 'Maude'); see also *Mollinary*, i. 106–7, and ii. 53–55, for the same defect in the Austrian Staff in 1849 and 1859.

[2] See *Bunbury*, p. 457 n., where Moore asks Bunbury what a division is.

[3] *v. sup.*, pp. 51–52.

customary in the British service generally since the resuscita-
tion of the Department in 1803.

'The Wellingtonian system', 'Wellington's staff'—how
often have such phrases been used without drawing the
distinction, which is vital, between what was customary or
obligatory in Wellington's time and what was peculiar to the
Army that fought under Wellington's orders. As often as
not the innovation came from elsewhere than from Wellington. Yet everything that he touched—and he touched everything—bore the mark of his own personality. The divisions
of Cathcart and Moore were not the individual organisms—
individual at once in temperament and in self-sufficiency—
that Wellington led across Spain into France in 1813. His
commissariat was not the mixture of country bumpkins, rapa-
cious contractors, and 'Black Guard Blues' that dragged
behind the Duke of York's Army in Flanders in the bad
old days of '94. It not only supplied his own Army but out-
played the French. And to his intelligence service he brought
his own peculiar faculty of informing himself. Quite apart
from outposts and 'observing officers', he carried resources
within his mind. When he was sent to India his library was
stocked with books on India. When he had been Castlereagh's military oracle he had turned his reading to Mexico,
to Nicaragua, to Venezuela, Chile, Denmark, and Sweden,
in response to the chimerical projects of the times. So, when
he was sent to the Peninsula he carried not only a Spanish
prayer-book from which to learn the language, but Sir Charles
Stuart's old Portuguese letter-books of 1797 and General
Richard Stewart's of 1803, amongst other sources from which
he made his first appreciation of the form a war in Portugal
would assume. Murray afterwards observed that this appreciation, written in August 1808, contained all the principles
on which Wellington's conduct for the next six years was
founded.[1] There was another science, Wellington discovered,
could be learned from Stuart's papers: 'how an officer at
the head of an army can treat the Secretary of State like a
dog'.[2] Few generals have devoted their spare hours so

---

[1] In an article in the *Edinburgh Review* (1839), lxix. 301. The dispatch referred
to is that dated *H.M.S. Donegal*, 1 Aug. 1808 (*Disp.* iii. 46–47).
[2] Wellesley to Murray, Zambujal, 13 Sept. 1808 (*Murray Papers*, 22, fos. 101–4).

advantageously to utilitarian scholarship. Perhaps the new
Military Depot gave some assistance, but it would be mistaken to suppose that Wellington's extraordinary fund of
general information came from anywhere but his own resources and his own retentive memory.

Similarly his control of troop movements was strict and
personal. Orders for the movement of formations were either
written in his own hand or dictated or verbally communicated
to the Q.M.G. and by him issued in Wellington's name. Was
his command over-centralized? It might possibly be argued
that his method of issuing orders, and the dependence of his
generals upon those orders, somewhat handicapped the vigour
of a pursuit after victory. But there were other reasons that
could account for failures on those occasions when this criticism might be offered, and in the ordinary circumstances of
offensive and defensive warfare his method of command may
be said without hesitation to have been always equal to the
demands made upon it. It may be compared with that of
Mack, the general who had the effective command of the
Austrian forces at Ulm in 1805, who afterwards acknowledged that at one vital moment his mind was so absorbed
in drafting an operation order of eight folios, 'in which not
one word was superfluous', that he was incapable of addressing himself to the more urgent crisis that awaited his attention.[1] What would be said of Wellington if he had been
defeated on 28 July 1813 and he had excused himself on the
ground that the French had disturbed him as he was writing
his famous order on the coping of the bridge at Sorauren?

A very considerable degree of centralization is unavoidable
if command is to be effective, and the extent to which a
general delegates or retains control must be reflected in the
size of his staff. An attempt has already been made[2] to give
some idea of the numbers employed at Wellington's Headquarters, but there should be added, in strict accuracy, the
staff of the Portuguese Army, whose exact composition is not
known, and also that of the Spanish Army. Even so, since
Wellington was Commander-in-Chief of the whole Spanish
army, and Portuguese Headquarters was the ambulant headquarters of the whole military force of Portugal, the mere

[1] *Maude*, pp. 40–41.   [2] *v. sup.*, pp. 56–58, and Appx. II.

sum of these components would not produce a satisfactory result. For comparative purposes it would be interesting to obtain precise figures of the composition of Napoleon's Headquarters or of Marlborough's. But Napoleon not only commanded a much larger army than ever Wellington had but also managed the affairs of the French nation and much else besides from wherever in Europe he might pitch his camp; and the staff officers of Marlborough listed in the Establishments[1] were clearly supplemented by officers drawn from the regiments as assistants; of their numbers we are not, unfortunately, informed. A more just comparison may be made from the table at Appendix IX, in which the military staffs of the British, Russian, and Austrian contingents, each 30,000 strong,[2] of the Army occupying France, 1815–18, are enumerated. It will be seen that, as a matter merely of digits, the British Headquarters were stronger than the others. The British Q.M.G.'s Department was perhaps unduly overweighted because it was also the office of the Chief-of-Staff of the whole Allied Army of Occupation.[3] But whatever importance may be attached to the figures one fact emerges from the table: that Wellington's staff was composed of officers of much higher rank and greater standing than those of the Allied Contingents. Murray was a lieutenant-general: his opposite number in the Austrian Army was a major. This fact gives some colour to an otherwise unconfirmed impression that Wellington's Peninsular staff contained more officers of field rank than those of his contemporaries in other European armies. It may account for the efficiency of Wellington's staff as compared with Napoleon's, which has been described on good grounds as the weak spot of the French Imperial army.[4]

Whatever its effect or its cause, it is nevertheless somewhat surprising, as it is fairly plain that commanders of

[1] e.g. *Calendar of Treasury Books, 1708* . . . xxii, part i (London, H.M.S.O., 1952), cdxx–cdxxi.

[2] The Prussian contingent, which also numbered 30,000, did not render its returns in a form that would enable a similar table to be drawn up (*Murray Papers*, 131, fos. 97–98; 132, fos. 121–4; 134, fos. 186–90). The civil staffs defy all attempts at a tabular comparison of this kind.

[3] One officer from each contingent was attached to Wellington in his capacity as Commander-in-Chief of the whole force, but these have been deducted in the table.

[4] *Vachée*, p. 99.

continental armies allowed themselves to be managed by their staff officers to an extent which Wellington never permitted and to which, indeed, he was wholly opposed in principle. To Wellington command was indivisible: abroad, particularly in the Prussian and Austrian services, command and direction were a composition of two separate elements, allowing a partnership between a 'general' and a relatively junior 'expert'—Coburg and Mack, the Duke of Brunswick and Massenbach, Schwarzenberg and Radetzky, Blücher and Gneisenau, Radetzky and Hess—which became accentuated during the nineteenth century by the growing ascendancy of the *Generalstab* until eventually it becomes scarcely possible to speak of Hindenburg without his Ludendorff. How much the British, or Wellington's, attitude to the position of a staff officer had already diverged from that prevailing in the Austrian service is shown in a correspondence that took place between Murray and Major Hauer, the chief-of-staff of the Austrian contingent during the Occupation. Hauer, wishing to make some movement order not approved of by his chief, asked Murray to intervene by persuading him to act according to Hauer's advice. 'The general', he said, 'looks upon himself as the sole repository of the whole executive power, of which giving orders is a part; and if the chief-of-staff makes any counterproposal or remonstrance, no matter how respectful, the general thinks his jurisdiction is being trenched upon.' Murray, very properly in the British view, declined to interfere and Hauer acknowledged that his zeal had carried him too far.[1] It is clear from Müffling's conduct at Waterloo that sentiments similar to Hauer's were already deeply embedded in the Prussian service. Müffling, Blücher's liaison officer at Wellington's Headquarters, had had considerable experience on the staff, but it was hardly a fraction of the experience many of Wellington's staff had received in the Peninsula. In his estimation it entitled him, however, on the morning of Waterloo to express to the Duke his anxieties about the strength and weakness of the British line of battle, and, during the battle, to take upon himself to suggest to Vivian and Vandeleur that their cavalry brigades

[1] Hauer to Murray, Colmar, 13 and 29 Oct. 1818 (*Murray Papers*, 150, fos. 90–92, 272).

should fall upon some broken French infantry. Vivian and Vandeleur very properly declined to act on this proposal, and later Wellington told Müffling how rightly they had acted. If they had attacked without his permission he would have had them court martialled, he said, and he explained why a commander, situated as he was at Waterloo, should never for a moment deprive himself of the free disposition of all his troops. He meant, in effect, the general alone should oversee the whole battle from a commanding point with his glass in his hand, and that he did not look to staff officers or subordinate commanders to conduct his business for him.[1]

The centralization of the initiative, the close control he maintained over his Army has, despite his providing it with the means to act independently, and despite the steps he took towards the delegation of certain business, been held against Wellington as preventing the emergence of a school of general and staff officers capable of acting on their own when in independent command. It has become almost a commonplace of modern historians to speak of generals brought up in 'Wellington's rigid and unimaginative school'. No one who has studied the *Dispatches*, where each subordinate commander is supplied with instructions on how to act in every conceivable contingency, will describe Wellington as unimaginative; and if by rigidity is meant a strict obedience to orders, it must be said at once that that was a quality which was regarded as the highest military virtue not only in his time but for several generations after his death. 'Initiative' is a very modern slogan: 'zealous discharge of the duty towards the public service' was the common phrase of the day. Independence was presumption. It has been said that Moore, by favouring officers who could act on their own, made a more valuable contribution to the British army. Even if this were true (and it is a very doubtful hypothesis), it is not the kind of achievement that would have recommended itself to Wellington (or Moore). Wellington was sent to defeat the French in the Peninsula, and he succeeded. And he beat Napoleon. A country does not look to a general to do more in wartime than defeat its enemies, use his subordinates how he will. It

[1] Gen. Friedrich Karl Ferdinand, Freiherr von Müffling, *Aus meinem Leben* (Berlin, 1851), pp. 242–6.

would not be grateful to a general if he appealed to posterity (as poor Moore's apologists make him appeal) by saying, 'I admit I have not been very successful with my Army, but it contains some excellent officers who will do very well for you one day'.

Visitors to Wellington's Headquarters looked in vain for the outward and visible signs of his autocratic temper. A young commissary fresh from England, coming one summer afternoon into Fuenteguinaldo when Headquarters lay there, imagined all the flower of the Army 'would be collected around the hero who commands it, gallant men on stately steeds, in short, all the pomp and circumstance of war within the precincts of a circle'. But instead, he found 'the village presented the veriest piece of still-life, not to be quite dead, that I ever saw. In the market place were some half-dozen Spanish women sitting in a row, selling eggs and cabbages, and half-a-dozen soldiers in their undress were their buyers. Now and then an officer in a plain blue coat would cross the plaza, on foot or horseback. And this was all which met the eye'.[1] When, after the armistice in April 1814, Clausel came over the line of demarcation to pay his respects at Wellington's Headquarters, he searched without success for an a.d.c. to introduce him, and it was fortunate that his own a.d.c. fell in with Larpent, the Deputy-Judge-Advocate. 'I told them', says Larpent, 'that there was no chance of finding an aide-de-camp, but perhaps we might find a sergeant.' There was no one, however, but 'an ignorant sentinel', and, after trying a door or two, they blundered on Lord Wellington himself, to whom Larpent introduced Clausel. Clausel's astonished a.d.c. confessed that Soult and Suchet would have had about six aides-de-camp in the first room and a general officer in waiting in the second.[2] Moore, no autocrat, had a Headquarters run on strictly 'regimental' lines: Wellington, who ruled his Headquarters when there was business to be done as no man had before him, paid little attention to outward form.

Without the presence of Wellington the whole complex

[1] *Buckham*, pp. 43–44.
[2] *Larpent*, pp. 508–9 (24 Apr. 1814). See also Edward Hawke Locker, *Views in Spain* (London, 1824), pl. xxii.

fabric of administration would have broken down. The absence of a commander cannot but lead to some dislocation; but Wellington and his decisions were so essential a part of the command that his absence, had it lasted for no more than a few weeks, and, on occasion, even a few minutes, must almost inevitably have led to failure. It was not the type of command that anyone could wield. No one knew better than Raglan the physical and intellectual labour involved in such a command, yet when, in spite of his age, he attempted it he failed and died under the strain.[1] All depended on Wellington's presence, and the remarkable fact is that he was always there. He had a cold or two, occasionally a touch of lumbago, and once (at Orthez) he was slightly *ofendido* by a spent bullet. But during those five years in the Peninsula he never missed a day's work. In 1809, he said long after,

I went abroad and took command of the Army, and never returned, or even quitted the field, till the nations of the Peninsula . . . were delivered from the French armies; till I had invaded France, won the battle of Toulouse; established the British Army within French territory; of which I governed several departments; till the general peace was signed at Paris; and the British cavalry, sent by sea to Portugal, Spain and the south of France, marched home across France, and embarked for England in the ports of France in the British Channel![2]

[1] '[Hardinge] said that, though under the Duke's eye and management the arrangement [of the Ordnance Department] answered perfectly, yet, whenever it came to be superintended by a less extraordinary mind, that it would be found that too much business devolved on each person.' Conversation of 10 Aug. 1824 (*Mrs. Arbuthnot's Journal*, i. 333).
[2] Wellington to Croker, Strathfield Saye, 19 Dec. 1846 (*Croker Papers*, iii. 124).

APPENDIX I

LIST OF OFFICERS SERVING IN THE ADJUTANT-GENERAL'S AND QUARTERMASTER-GENERAL'S DEPARTMENTS IN THE PENINSULA, 1 APRIL 1809 TO 25 JUNE 1814

Note. These lists are compiled from the General Orders of the Army and the monthly returns and Instruction Books in the *Murray Papers*, and give details of the officers' services only during the period of their appointments in the above departments. Certain other particulars have been added to illustrate points raised in the text, drawn from a variety of different sources: *Philippart*, obituaries in C.U.S.M., *Ann. Reg.*, the records of service in the P.R.O., school-lists, *Burke, Cokayne, D.N.B.*, county histories, monumental inscriptions, and others.

Adjutant-General's Department

AINSLIE, MAJOR CHARLES PHILIP (?–1812). As Major, 4th Dragoons, *app.* A.A.G. and attached to the Cavalry Div., 12 May 1810.

AUCHMUTY, GENERAL SIR SAMUEL BENJAMIN (1781–1868). 2nd s. of Samuel Auchmuty, of Brianstown, by Frances (*née* Savage), of Bally-gawley, co. Sligo.

As Captain, 7th Fusiliers, *app.* D.A.A.G., and attached to 6th Div. on its formation, 6 October 1810. Attached to Pack's Brigade, 26 April 1811, and in May 1811 reattached to 6th Div. A witness at Colonel Hon. Basil Cochrane's trial; then on leave, he returned to the Peninsula, February 1813, as extra-a.d.c. to Cole.

AYLMER, GENERAL MATTHEW, 5TH BARON (1775–1850). E. s. of Henry, 4th Baron. R.M. College, 1805.

As Lieut.-Colonel, Coldstream Guards, *app.* A.A.G., 1 April 1809. Attached to Sherbrooke's Column, 8 May 1809. Attached to 1st Div. (Sherbrooke), 18 June 1809. *App.* D.A.G. (*vice* E. M. Pakenham), 1 January 1812, which *app.* he held till 2 July 1813 though absent during the second half of 1812.

BAYLEY, LIEUTENANT CHARLES. As Lieutenant, 31st, *app.* D.A.A.G. and attached to 2nd Div., 23 January 1810.

BERKELEY, GENERAL SIR GEORGE HENRY FREDERICK (1785–1857). E. s. of Admiral Hon. Sir George Cranfield Berkeley. Educ. Harrow, 1798–1800.

As Major, 35th, *app.* A.A.G., 1 April 1809. Attached to 5th Div., (?) from its formation, 8 August 1810, until 5 March 1811, when he went to 7th Div. on its formation. He returned to 5th Div., 7 December 1811.

BOUVERIE, GENERAL SIR HENRY FREDERICK (1783–1852). 3rd s. of Hon. Edward Bouverie, of Delapré Abbey, Northants. Educ. Eton.
As Captain and Lieut.-Colonel, Coldstream Guards, *app.* A.A.G., 18 April 1812. Attached to 1st Div., July 1812. Acted at A.A.G. to the Right Column (Hill's), October 1813 onwards.

BRADFORD, LIEUT.-COL. SIR HENRY HOLLES (1781–1816). Y. s. of Thomas Bradford, of Woodlands, near Doncaster, and Ashdown Park, Sussex.
As Lieut.-Colonel, 2/11th, *app.* A.A.G. and attached to 6th Div., 20 November 1811 until 30 July 1812, when he was attached to 4th Div.
Died of the effects of wounds received at Waterloo at La Vacherie, near Lillers.

BROWNE, LIEUT.-GEN. SIR THOMAS HENRY (?–1855). Commandant of the Depot at Belém, 9 August 1811. As Lieutenant, 23rd, *app.* D.A.A.G., 12 April 1812, and thenceforward acted in the field in the A.G.'s office.

CAMPBELL, MAJOR ALLAN WILLIAM (1786–1813). 2nd s. of Lieut.-Gen. Sir Alexander Campbell by his 1st wife, Olympia Elizabeth, d. of William Morehead, of Cartuther, near Liskeard.
As Captain, 74th, *app.* D.A.A.G., 1 July 1809. Resigned voluntarily to rejoin his regiment and transferred to the Portuguese service, 15 March 1810. Wounded at Sorauren, 28 July 1813, and died at Bilbao in October.

CAMPBELL, GENERAL SIR COLIN (1776–1847). 5th s. of John Campbell of Melfort (1730–90).
As Major, 70th, *app.* A.A.G., 1 April 1809. *App.* Commandant at Headquarters, 4 May 1809, which situation he retained throughout the war. Lieut.-Colonel, 25 September 1811.

CAPEL, GENERAL HON. THOMAS EDWARD (1770–1855). 2nd s. of 4th Earl of Essex by his 2nd wife, Harriet, d. of Colonel Bladen.
As Lieut.-Colonel, 1st Guards, *app.* A.A.G., 3 September 1811, to act at the head of the Department at Cadiz. (See Macdonald, General Sir John.)

CHURCHILL, COLONEL CHATHAM HORACE (1791–1843). s. of Maj.-Gen. Horace Churchill (died 1817), greatnephew and godson of Horace Walpole.

As Lieutenant and Captain, 1st Guards, *app.* D.A.A.G., 24 October 1812, and attached to 2nd Div., and acted as Hill's Military Secretary. Bvt.-major, *app.* A.A.G., 22 November 1813.

CLARGES, LIEUT.-GEN. RICHARD GODDARD HARE (?–1857). 2nd s. of Rev. J. Hare, of Stratton, Wilts. Educ. Rugby.

As Captain Hare, 23rd, *app.* D.A.A.G. at Cadiz, 21 February 1810. Attached to 1st Div. (Graham's) in Portugal, 1 December 1811. Acting-A.A.G. to 6th Div., 30 July 1812. Promoted Major, 12th, 1 July 1813, and *app.* A.A.G., 3 July 1813, and attached to Graham's Corps. Acting-A.A.G. to 6th Div. in October 1813.

(He took the additional name of Clarges in 1834.)

COCKBURN, GENERAL SIR FRANCIS (?–1868). 4th s. of Sir James Cockburn of Langton, co. Berwick, 7th Bart.

As Captain, 60th, *app.* D.A.A.G., 1 April 1809, acting occasionally as D.J.A.G. Attached to 4th Div., 30 July 1809, and to 3rd Div., 22 February 1810. He left the Peninsula in that year.

Afterwards Governor of the British Honduras and the Bahamas.

COOKE, MAJ.-GEN. SIR HENRY FREDERICK (1784–1837). s. of Colonel George John Cooke, of Harefield, Mx. (known as 'Kangaroo' or 'Kang' Cooke).

As Lieutenant and Captain, Coldstream Guards, *app.* D.A.A.G., 3 May 1809. Attached to 4th Div., 18 June 1809, but was detained sick at Lisbon, 30 July 1809. He was attached to 4th Div. from 29 April till 13 October 1810, and was then attached to 1st Div. Exchanged to the North American Staff, 23 July 1812.

COTTON, GENERAL SIR WILLOUGHBY (1783–1860). s. of Admiral Rowland Cotton by his wife, Elizabeth, d. of Sir Willoughby Aston, Bart., of Aston, Salop.

As Lieutenant and Captain, 3rd Guards, *app.* D.A.A.G., 1 April 1809. Attached to Payne, 8 May 1809; attached to Headquarters, 16 June 1809; to 2nd Div., 18 June 1809; to 2nd Div. again, 10 March 1810; to Light Div., 29 June 1810; to 2nd Div., 11 May 1811. Returned home on promotion, 8 August 1811, but rejoined the regiment in the Peninsula in 1813.

CRAIG, COLONEL HENRY (?–1846). As Captain, 30th, *app.* D.A.A.G., 14 October 1810, and attached to 4th Div. Attached to the Corps of Marines at Alhandra, 14 November 1810, and to 5th Div., 5 March 1811. Later D.A.A.G. at Lisbon, and in 1814 at Pasajes.

DARLING, GENERAL WILLIAM LINDSAY (?–1864). As Major, 2nd Garrison Battalion, *app.* A.A.G., 19 April 1814.

DARROCH, GENERAL DUNCAN (1776–1847). s. of Duncan Darroch, who purchased the barony of Gourock from the Stewarts of Castlemilk.

As Lieut-Colonel, 36th, was at the head of the Department under Cradock's command. *Re-app.* A.A.G., 1 April 1809, and remained as such, mostly acting at Lisbon, until the end of 1811.

DASHWOOD, LIEUT.-COL. CHARLES (1787–1832). 3rd s. of Sir Henry Watkin Dashwood, 3rd Bart., of Kirtlington Park. Educ. Harrow.

As Lieutenant and Captain, 3rd Guards, *app.* D.A.A.G., 1 April 1809. Attached to 4th Div., 23 February until 29 April 1810, and to 1st Div. from 29 April to 13 October 1810. Attached to 6th Div. early in 1813. Bvt.-major, *app.* A.A.G., 4 September 1813, and attached to 1st Div.

D'OYLY, LIEUT.-COL. SIR FRANCIS (?1777–1815). E. s. of Rev. Matthias D'Oyly, Prebendary of Ely, Rector of Uckfield; nephew of General Francis D'Oyly and e. bro. of General Henry D'Oyly (1780–1855).

As Bvt.-major, 1st Guards, *app.* A.A.G., 30 November 1811, and attached to 1st Div., 1 December 1811. Attached to 7th Div., 7 December 1811, with which he remained at the end of the war.

Killed at Waterloo.

DÜRING, LIEUT.-GEN. GEORG VON (?–1872). As Lieutenant, 1st Line Battalion, K.G.L., attached as D.A.A.G., 1 April 1809. Bvt.-major, *app.* A.A.G., 21 June 1813. Served mostly in the Adjutant-General's Office.

ECKERSLEY, LIEUT.-COL. NATHANIEL (?–1837). Quartermaster, Royal Dragoons, and Adjutant, 1800–9.

As Captain, Royals, *app.* D.A.A.G., 3 October 1812, and attached to 2nd Cavalry Div. (Erskine's), and after its break-up, spring 1813, to the A.G.'s Office.

EGERTON, LIEUT.-GEN. RICHARD (1783–1854). 9th s. of Philip Egerton, of Oulton, Cheshire, y. bro. of Sir John and Sir Philip, the 8th and 9th baronets.

As Captain, 34th, *app.* D.A.A.G., 11 August 1810, and attached to Hill's Corps. Attached to 4th Div., 11 May 1811. Wounded at Albuera and returned home. Rejoined as extra-a.d.c. to Hill, 28 March 1813.

ELLEY, LIEUT.-GEN. SIR JOHN (?–1839). As Lieut.-Colonel, Royal Horse Guards, *app.* A.A.G., 1 April 1809, and attached to the Cavalry, with which he remained for the rest of the war.

ELLIOTT, CAPTAIN GEORGE. As Captain, 48th, *app.* D.A.A.G., 1 April 1809. Transferred to the Q.M.G.'s Department, 30 May 1809, q.v.

FITZCLARENCE, LIEUTENANT GEORGE: see Munster, Maj.-Gen. George Augustus Frederick, 1st Earl.

FITZROY, LIEUT.-COL. LORD CHARLES (1791–1865). 2nd s. of 4th Duke of Grafton. Educ. Harrow.
 As Ensign, 1st Guards, *app.* D.A.A.G., 26 March 1812, and attached to 2nd Div. Acting-A.A.G. to 2nd Div. after Rooke was wounded, 10 November 1813.

FORDYCE, CAPTAIN ALEXANDER (?–1809). As Captain, 81st, Brigade-major to Hill's Brigade and acting-D.A.A.G., 2nd Div. (Hill's), from 26 June 1809. Killed at Talavera, 27 July 1809.

GOODMAN, MAJ.-GEN. STEPHEN ARTHUR (?–1844). As Captain, 48th, *app.* D.J.A.G., 25 August 1809. Major, 1812. Acting D.A.G. and in charge of the Department, September to October 1812.
 Afterwards Vendue-Master of Demarara and Essequibo.

GRAHAM, CAPTAIN HENRY CHARLES EDWARD VERNON: see Vernon, General Henry Charles Edward.

HARE, CAPTAIN RICHARD GODDARD: see Clarges, Lieut.-Gen. Richard Goddard Hare.

HARRIS, LIEUT.-COL. SIR THOMAS NOEL (1785–1860). s. of Rev. Hamlyn Harris, Rector of Whitwell, Rutl., and Campden, Glos.
 Having retired as Captain, Royal Dragoons, in 1809, he returned to the army as Cornet, 13th Light Dragoons, March 1811, and was attached as D.A.A.G. in the Peninsula, 4 May 1811 until 14 December 1811.

HEISE, LIEUT.-COL. AUGUST (?–1819). As Captain, 2nd Light Battalion, K.G.L., *app.* D.A.A.G., 3 April 1812, and attached to 2nd Div. Promoted Bvt.-major and A.A.G., 21 June 1813.

HINÜBER, LIEUT.-GEN. HEINRICH VON (?–1833). As Bvt.-lieut.-colonel, 68th, *app.* A.A.G., 1 April 1809, and attached to Hon. Edward Paget's Brigade, 8 May 1809.
 Promoted Major-General, 4 June 1811, he later commanded a brigade in 1st Div.

HOEY, LIEUTENANT W. R. (?–1810). As Lieutenant, 18th Hussars, attached as D.A.A.G., 16 May 1810, having previously served as Hon. Charles Stewart's a.d.c. Mortally wounded in front of Buçaco, 25 September 1810.

HOOD, LIEUT.-COL. HON. FRANCIS WHELER (?1785–1814). E. s. of Henry, 2nd Viscount Hood. Educ. Eton.

As Captain and Lieut.-Colonel, 3rd Guards, *app.* A.A.G., 12 December 1813, and attached to 2nd Div. Killed at Aire-sur-l'Adour, 2 March 1814.

HOPE, GENERAL SIR JAMES ARCHIBALD (1785–1871). s. of Lieut.-Col. Erskine Hope, 26th, related to the Hopes of Craighall.

As Major, 90th, *app.* A.A.G., 25 February 1813, acting with Graham's Column. Attached to Beresford's Column, autumn 1813.

HURFORD, LIEUTENANT JOHN (1777–1839). Enlisted in the 3rd Guards, 1 April 1794.

As a sergeant in the 3rd Guards he served in the A.G.'s Office in the Peninsula, and was given an ensigncy without purchase in the 48th, 20 August 1812, and a lieutenancy in the 13th Veteran Battalion, 25 January 1813. Attached to the Department, 14 September 1812. *App.* 'sub-deputy-A.A.G.', 15 May 1814.

Afterwards Deputy Ordnance Barrackmaster, Island Bridge, Dublin.

JAMES, CAPTAIN FRANCIS (?–1812). As Captain, 81st, *app.* D.A.A.G., 5 August 1811, and attached to 5th Div., till 7 December 1811, when he was attached to 4th Div. Severely wounded at Badajoz, 7 April 1812, he died later that year.

LONDONDERRY, GENERAL CHARLES WILLIAM, 3RD MARQUESS (1778–1854). O. s. of Robert, 1st Marquess, by his 2nd wife.

As Brig.-Gen. Hon. Charles Stewart, *app.* A.G., 1 April 1809. Absent from the Army: December 1809 to January 1810; 15 December 1810 to 5 January 1811; 9 January to 24 May 1811. Left the Peninsula about 8 April 1812, but did not resign his *app.* till 10 May 1813.

MACDONALD, LIEUT.-COL. ARCHIBALD (?–1828). As Captain, 45th, *app.* D.A.A.G., 11 May 1811, and attached to the cavalry on the south bank of the Tagus. Promoted Major, 1st West India Regiment, and *app.* A.A.G., 27 June 1811.

MACDONALD, LIEUT.-GEN. SIR JOHN (?–1850). Related to the family of Flora Macdonald.

As Major, half-pay, 1st Garrison Battalion, *app.* A.A.G., 24 February 1810, to act at the head of the Department at Cadiz, which he left at about the same time as Graham (*v. sup. sb.* Capel), though his *app.* was continued till 25 December 1812. After acting as M.S. to Sir John Hope in Ireland, March 1812 to September 1813, he returned to the Peninsula with Sir John, with whose Column he acted as A.A.G. nominally from 25 September 1813.

Afterwards A.G. to the Forces, 1830–50.

MACGREGOR, MAJ.-GEN. SIR EVAN JOHN MURRAY (1785–1841). E. s. of Sir John MacGregor Murray of Lanrick, Bart.

As Major MacGregor Murray, 103rd, *app.* A.A.G. at Cadiz, where he remained until his *app.* as A.Q.M.G. East Indies, 29 August 1812. (He took the name of Murray MacGregor in 1822.)

M'MULLIN, ENSIGN. As Ensign, 63rd, attached as D.A.A.G., 11 May 1811. Died 4 August 1811.

MARLAY, LIEUT.-COL. GEORGE (1791–1830). O. s. of Major George Marlay (s. of George Marlay, Bishop of Dromore), by his wife, Lady Catherine, d. of the Earl of Lanesborough.

As Captain, 14th, *app.* D.A.A.G., 23 November 1812, serving first at Lisbon and, in 1813, attached to Light Div. Promoted Bvt.-major, 14th, 21 June 1813, attached as A.A.G. to Light Div.

MELLISH, LIEUT.-COL. HENRY FRANCIS (1780–1817). s. of Henry Mellish, of Blythe, near Bawtry.

As Captain, 87th, *app.* D.A.A.G., 1 April 1809, and attached to 4th Div., 21 June 1809 till Cooke's return (q.v.). Attached to Light Div., 11 March 1811. Promoted Major, Sicilian Regiment, and *app.* A.A.G., 11 May 1811.

MUNSTER, MAJ.-GEN. GEORGE AUGUSTUS FREDERICK, 1ST EARL (1794–1842). s. of the Duke of Clarence (William IV) by Mrs. Jordan.

As Captain George FitzClarence, 10th Hussars, *app.* D.A.A.G., 25 April 1813, having served as a.d.c. to Hon. Charles Stewart, 1809 to 1811.

MURRAY, MAJOR EVAN JOHN MACGREGOR: see MacGregor, Maj.-Gen. Sir Evan John Murray.

NAPIER, GENERAL SIR GEORGE THOMAS (1784–1855). 2nd s. of Colonel Hon. George Napier by his wife, Lady Sarah (*née* Lennox).

As Bvt.-lieut.-colonel, 52nd, *app.* A.A.G., 29 January 1814, and attached to 6th Div. *App.* cancelled, 3 February 1814.

OBINS, LIEUT.-COL. HAMLET (?–1848). Perhaps of the family of Obins, of Portadown.

As Captain, 20th, Brigade-major to Stirling's Brigade and was acting-A.A.G. to 6th Div. at Toulouse, where he was severely wounded.

OSBORNE, CAPTAIN KEANE (?–1812). As Captain, 5th Dragoon

Guards, *app.* D.A.A.G., 20 November 1811. Transferred to Q.M.G.'s Department, 30 November 1811 (q.v.).

PAKENHAM, MAJ.-GEN. HON. SIR EDWARD MICHAEL (1778–1815). 2nd s. of Edward Michael, 2nd Baron and 1st Earl Longford.

As Colonel, *app.* A.A.G., 15 November 1809, and D.A.G., 3 March 1810. Acted as A.G. during Stewart's absences: December 1809 to January 1810; December 1810 to May 1811. He had commanded troops in the field previously, and did so uninterruptedly from his resignation as D.A.G., 1 January 1812, until 22 June 1813. *App.* A.G., 10 May 1813. Killed at New Orleans, 8 January 1815.

PAKENHAM, LIEUT.-GEN. HON. SIR HERCULES (1781–1850). 3rd s. of Edward Michael, 2nd Baron and 1st Earl Longford.

As Captain, 95th, *app.* D.A.A.G., 1 September 1809, and attached to 3rd Div. Promoted Major, 7th West India Regiment, 30 August 1810, and *app.* A.A.G., 1 October 1810, remaining attached to 3rd Div. until being severely wounded at Badajoz, 7 April 1812.

PONSONBY, MAJ.-GEN. HON. SIR FREDERICK CAVENDISH (1783–1837). 2nd s. of Frederick, 3rd Earl of Bessborough. Educ. Harrow.

As Major, 23rd Light Dragoons, *app.* A.A.G., 2 January 1810. Attached to Fane's Cavalry Brigade, 8 October 1810.

REYNELL, LIEUT.-GEN. SIR THOMAS, BART. (1777–1848). Y. but o. surviving s. of Lieutenant Thomas Reynell, 2nd s. of the 3rd baronet.

As Lieut.-Colonel, 71st, *app.* A.A.G., 14 November 1810, and attached to 4th Div. Returned to England with dispatches, April 1811, and accompanied Cradock to the Cape as his M.S.

ROOKE, LIEUT.-COL. JOHN CHARLES (?–1813). As Captain and Lieut.-Colonel, 3rd Guards, *app.* A.A.G., 10 April 1810, and attached as A.A.G. to 2nd Div., with which he remained until being mortally wounded at the Nivelle, 10 November, and dying on 19 December 1813.

ROWAN, LIEUT.-COL. SIR CHARLES (1782–1852). 5th s. of Robert Rowan, of Mullans, co. Antrim.

As Captain, 52nd, *app.* D.A.A.G., 15 March 1811. Attached to Headquarters until 18 June, when, having been promoted Major (9 May 1811), he acted as A.A.G. to Light Div., from 29 July 1811. Bvt.-lieut.-colonel, 27 April 1812.

Chief Commissioner of the Metropolitan Police Force on its formation, 1829, until 1850.

STEWART, BRIG.-GEN. HON. CHARLES: see Londonderry, General Charles William, 3rd Marquess.

STEWART, LIEUT.-COL. HON. JAMES HENRY KEITH (1783–1836). As Bvt.-major, 95th, *app.* A.A.G., 10 November 1812, and attached to Hon. Edward Paget's Div. (1st). *App.* cancelled, 28 November 1812 (see Q.M.G.'s List).

STOVIN, GENERAL SIR FREDERICK (1783–1865). s. of James Stovin, of Whitgift, Yorks.

As Captain, 28th, *app.* D.A.A.G., 3 May 1812, and attached to 3rd Div. Promoted Bvt.-major and A.A.G., 12 July 1812, he remained with 3rd Div. Bvt.-lieut.-colonel, 26 August 1813.

TIDY, COLONEL FRANCIS SKELLY (1775–1835). As Major, 14th, *app.* A.A.G., 1 April 1809, but returned to England with dispatches in bad health the following June.

TRIP VAN ZOUDTLANT, LIEUT.-COL. JONKHEER OTTO ERNST GELDER (1774–1816). As Captain, 11th, *app.* D.A.A.G., 10 January 1810. Attached to Payne's Cavalry, 10 March 1810, and to Fane's Cavalry, 16 May 1810. Promoted Major, Royal African Corps, 1 April 1813, and A.A.G., 30 August 1813, he remained attached to Cavalry.

TRYON, LIEUT.-COL. CHARLES (?–1826). Perhaps s. of Thomas Tryon, of Bulwick, Northants.

As Captain, 88th, *app.* D.A.A.G., 11 April 1812, and attached to 4th Div. Bvt.-major and A.A.G., 17 August 1812, and Bvt.-lieut.-colonel, 26 August 1813.

VERNON, GENERAL HENRY CHARLES EDWARD (1779–1861). s. of Henry Vernon, of Hilton Park, Staffs. Assumed the name of Graham.

As Captain Graham, 26th, *app.* D.A.A.G., 1 April 1809. Attached to 3rd Div., 6 August 1809. Attached to Light Div. till 29 June 1810. On promotion to Major, 66th, 13 June 1811, he joined his regiment. (He resumed the name of Vernon in 1838.)

WATERS, LIEUT.-GEN. SIR JOHN (1774–1842). Grandson of Edward Waters, High Sheriff of Glamorganshire in 1754.

As Captain, 1st, and Lieut.-Colonel, Portuguese service, *app.* A.A.G., 15 April 1811. Acting-A.G. during the autumn of 1812.

WHITE, CAPTAIN CHARLES. As Lieutenant and Captain, Coldstream Guards, *app.* D.A.A.G., 11 April 1812.

WILLIAMSON, LIEUT.-COL. THOMAS (?–1828). As Bvt.-major, 30th, *app.* A.A.G., 1 April 1809. Attached to Mackenzie's Brigade, 3 May 1809, and to 3rd Div. (Mackenzie's), 18 June 1809. Attached to 2nd Div., 6 August 1809, until being *app.* A.A.G. at Coimbra, 24 January 1810, a situation he resigned, 24 August 1810.

WOOD, LIEUT.-COL. CHARLES (1790–1877). 8th s. of Thomas Wood, of Littleton, Mx. His e. bro. Thomas, mar., 1800, Caroline, 2nd d. of the 1st Marquess of Londonderry.

As Lieutenant, 52nd, *app.* D.A.A.G., 25 February 1812. Promoted Captain, 68th, 17 September 1812. Left the Peninsula in spring 1813 to accompany Hon. Charles Stewart on the continent.

WYNYARD, CAPTAIN WILLIAM CLINTON (1789–1814). E. s. of Lieut.-Gen. William Wynyard, D.A.G. (1759–1819), and bro. of Lieut.-Gen. R. H. Wynyard (1802–64).

As Lieutenant and Captain, Coldstream Guards, *app.* D.A.A.G. at Cadiz, 16 September 1811.

Quartermaster-General's Department

ABERCROMBY, COLONEL HON. ALEXANDER (1784–1853). 4th s. of Lieut.-Gen. Sir Ralph Abercromby (1738–1801). R.M. College, 1801–2.

As Lieut.-Colonel, 28th, *app.* A.Q.M.G., 4 February 1813, and attached to 6th Div. Attached to 2nd Div. in Jackson's absence, April to October 1813. On leave, October 1813 to 16 January 1814, and then attached as A.Q.M.G., 7th Div.

ANDERDON, CAPTAIN THOMAS OLIVER (1786–1856). s. of John Proctor Anderdon, of Farley Hall, Berks., by his wife, Anne, d. of Thomas Oliver (1733–1815), the last Lieut.-Governor of Massachusetts. R.M. College, 1808.

As Captain, 7th Fusiliers, *app.* D.A.Q.M.G., 19 February 1810, and attached to 4th Div., but was transferred to 3rd Div., March 1810. Resigned from the Department and left the Peninsula without leave, February 1811. Resigned his commission, but with permission to sell, 8 August 1811.

Afterwards called to the Bar, November 1822; Q.C. and Bencher, Lincoln's Inn.

ARBUTHNOT, LIEUT.-GEN. SIR THOMAS (1776–1849). 5th s. of Thomas Arbuthnot, of Rockfleet, co. Mayo, by his 3rd wife.

As Bvt.-lieut.-colonel, 5th West India Regiment, *app.* A.Q.M.G., 25 June 1813, and attached to 3rd Div., 5 July 1813. Remained with the Department till May 1814.

BAINBRIGGE, LIEUT.-GEN. SIR PHILIP (1786–1862). s. of Lieut.-Col. Philip Bainbrigge (of a Derbyshire family), killed at Egmond-aan-Zee when commanding the 20th, 1799. R.M. College, 1810.

As Captain, 93rd, *app.* D.A.Q.M.G., 18 September 1810. Engaged mainly in sketching but was temporarily attached to 4th

Div., April 1812, and to 6th Div., summer of 1812. Promoted Major and A.Q.M.G., Permanent Staff, 20 October 1812.

BALCK, LIEUTENANT GEORG (?–1815). N.C.O., 7th Line Battalion, K.G.L., September 1806.

As Lieutenant, 7th Line Battalion, K.G.L., *app.* D.A.Q.M.G., 1 April 1809. Employed exclusively in sketching and reconnoitring. Remained on the strength of the Department until the end of the war.

BATHURST, LIEUT.-GEN. SIR JAMES (1782–1850). 2nd s. of Henry Bathurst, Bishop of Norwich (1744–1837), and bro. of Benjamin Bathurst. R.M. College, 1802.

As Lieut.-Colonel, 60th, *app.* A.Q.M.G., 1 April 1809, but acted only as M.S. to Wellington, 1809–10. Promoted Lieut.-Colonel, Permanent Staff, 1810, and returned home, December 1810, his mind having become deranged.

BECKWITH, MAJ.-GEN. JOHN CHARLES (1789–1862). s. of Captain John Beckwith, 23rd Light Dragoons, and a nephew of Sir Sydney and Sir George Beckwith.

As Captain, 95th, *app.* D.A.Q.M.G., 16 (or 3) August 1812, and attached to Light Div. Attached for a short time at the end of 1812 to 7th Div. Promoted Bvt.-major and A.Q.M.G., 3 March 1814, continuing to serve with Light Div. Lost a leg at Waterloo.

Retired, 1820, and interested himself in the Waldenses, among whom he died, at Torre Pellice.

BELL, GENERAL SIR JOHN (1782–1876). s. of David Bell, a wealthy merchant, of Bonytoun, Fifeshire.

As Lieutenant, 52nd, *app.* D.A.Q.M.G., 6 August 1810. Remained attached to Light Div. until 19 May 1813, when he became acting-A.Q.M.G., 4th Div. Promoted Major, 4th, and A.Q.M.G., 21 June 1813. As A.Q.M.G., 4th Div., he was also A.Q.M.G. to Beresford's Column, 1813, 1814.

BERESFORD, LIEUT.-COL. WILLIAM (?1777–?). ?4th and 3rd surviving s. of Richard Beresford, of Ashbourne and Bentley, Derby. R.M. College, 1808.

As Captain, 8th Garrison Battalion, *app.* D.A.Q.M.G., 1 April 1809, and employed, first at Lisbon and, after July, at Elvas and on various missions. On leave, April to September 1810; exchanged to 31st, 9 August 1810; attached to 6th Div., October 1810 to August 1811; on leave, August 1811 to February 1812. Promoted Bvt.-major, 31st, and A.Q.M.G., 18 August 1812, he was removed to the Home Staff, 25 October 1812.

Retired on half-pay, 1832; resigned 1835.

BLAQUIERE, MAJOR HON. GEORGE (1782–1826). 3rd s. of Sir John Blaquiere, Bart., and 1st Baron De Blaquiere (1732–1822).

As Major, Permanent Staff, *app.* A.Q.M.G., 1 April 1809, but does not appear to have returned to the Peninsula after the Corunna campaign, and his name ceases to appear after July 1809.

BOURKE, GENERAL SIR RICHARD (1777–1855). s. of John Bourke, of Dromsally, co. Limerick, a relation of Edmund Burke. Educ. Westminster, and Oriel and Exeter, Oxford. B.A., 1798. R.M. College, 1801–2.

As Lieut.-Colonel, Permanent Staff, *app.* A.Q.M.G., 1 April 1809. Attached to Cuesta's Headquarters, 30 May to 28 June 1809. He returned home in November and ceases to appear in the returns.

Governor, New South Wales, 1831–7.

BRISTOW, MAJ.-GEN. HENRY (1785–1874). R.M. College, 1809.

As Captain, 11th, *app.* D.A.Q.M.G., 25 February 1812. Attached to 7th Div. Promoted Major, 11th, and A.Q.M.G., 20 January 1814, and stationed at Pasajes, where he remained till the end of the war.

BROKE, MAJOR CHARLES: see Vere, Maj.-Gen. Sir Charles Broke.

BROWNRIGG, LIEUT.-COL. ROBERT JAMES (1790–1822). E. s. of General Sir Robert Brownrigg, Q.M.G. to the Forces, 1803–11. Educ. Eton.

As Captain, 52nd, *app.* D.A.Q.M.G., 18 July 1810, and attached to 1st Div. Returned home on leave, July 1811, and accompanied his father to Ceylon.

BRYANT, CAPTAIN J. V. (?–1814). As Lieutenant, 44th, *app.* D.A.Q.M.G., 18 August 1810, and served as such at Cadiz. Struck off the return, 24 September 1810. Later promoted Captain, 91st.

CAMPBELL, MAJ.-GEN. WILLIAM (1783–1852). 2nd s. of William Campbell, Commissioner of the Navy Board, and bro. of Lieut.-Col. Sir John Campbell. Educ. Harrow (1792–7), and Pembroke and Emmanuel, Cambridge.

As Captain, 23rd, *app.* D.A.Q.M.G., 19 November 1809, and attached to 3rd Div. (Craufurd's) till the formation of Light Div., when he was attached to that. For a short time (January to April 1811) he acted as A.Q.M.G. to the Cavalry; and in September 1811 he was attached to Cavalry, with which he remained to the end. Bvt.-major, 12 April 1814.

CATHCART, GENERAL CHARLES MURRAY, 2ND EARL (1783–1859). E. surviving s. of General William, 1st Earl Cathcart. Educ. Eton. R.M. College, 1800–3.

As Major Hon. C. Cathcart, Permanent Staff, *app.*, 23 February 1810, A.Q.M.G. at Cadiz, where (though he did not arrive till June) he remained at the head of the Department till June 1811, being *app.* Lieut.-Colonel and Deputy-Q.M.G. there, 31 August 1810. Returned to the Peninsula, *app.* A.Q.M.G., 25 December 1812, and acted as 'first Assistant' with the Cavalry until accompanying Graham to the Netherlands as D.Q.M.G., January 1814. He was struck off the Peninsula returns, 24 February 1814.

COOKE, MAJ.-GEN. SIR HENRY FREDERICK (1784–1837). s. of Colonel George John Cooke, of Harefield, Mx.

As Lieutenant and Captain, Coldstream Guards, *app.* D.A.Q.M.G., 1 April 1809, but transferred to the A.G.'s Department, 3 May 1809 (q.v.).

COTTON, MAJ.-GEN. EDWIN ROLAND JOSEPH (1777–1844). E. s. of Joseph Green, of Hall Green, Worcs., and Portugal House, Birmingham, by his wife, Elizabeth, d. and h. William Cotton, of Etwall, Derby.

As Major E. R. J. Green, 10th, *app.* A.Q.M.G., 25 April 1809, but he never joined Wellington's Army and he does not appear in the returns after November 1809. He served on the east coast of Spain: at Tarragona, Medas Islands, Belpuig, in reconnaissance, &c., and was taken prisoner, 1813.

(He assumed the name of Cotton in 1833.)

CUTCLIFFE, LIEUT.-COL. JOHN MERVYN (1778–1822). s. of Charles Newell Cutcliffe, of Dammage, Devon (1746–1813). Educ. Eton.

As Captain, 23rd Light Dragoons, *app.* D.A.Q.M.G., 17 July 1809. Employed on various small missions and with the Cavalry, and fell sick in September, never returning.

DE LANCEY, COLONEL SIR WILLIAM HOWE (1781–1815). s. of Stephen De Lancey, a Loyalist American, later Governor of Tobago; nephew of General Oliver De Lancey, Barrackmaster-General. R.M. College, 1801–2.

As Lieut.-Colonel, Permanent Staff, *app.* Deputy-Q.M.G., 1 April 1809, and served continuously as such throughout the war. Acting-Q.M.G., December 1811 to August 1812 and December 1812 to March 1813. Acted at the head of the Department with the Left Column of the Army, May 1813 to April 1814.

Q.M.G. in the Netherlands under Wellington, May to June 1815, he was mortally wounded at Waterloo.

DICKSON, LIEUT.-GEN. SIR JEREMIAH (1777–1848). E. s. of William Dickson, Bishop of Down. Educ. Eton, 1789–93. R.M. College, 1802.

As Major, Permanent Staff, *app.* A.Q.M.G., 15 September 1812, and attached as A.Q.M.G., 7th Div., 20 November 1812, until being transferred to the Cavalry, 27 January 1814.

DOYLE, MAJ.-GEN. CARLO JOSEPH (1787–1848). 2nd s. of Maj.-Gen. Welbore Ellis Doyle.

As Captain, 87th, *app.* D.A.Q.M.G., 9 May 1809, and attached to Sherbrooke's Column and, later, to the Cavalry, January to June 1810. Attached to Fane's Cavalry Brigade, 24 July 1810; and to 3rd Div., 24 June 1811 until about 1 December. Promoted Major, 1st Garrison Battalion, 23 January 1812, he left the Peninsula to join it in Jersey.

DRAKE, COLONEL THOMAS (1782–1851). 3rd s. of Rev. John Drake, Fellow of All Souls, Rector of Amersham and Vicar of Deptford. Educ. Westminster (K.S.), and Christ Church, Oxford; B.A., 1803; M.A., 1806. R.M. College, 1807 and 1810 (twice).

As Captain, 95th, *app.* D.A.Q.M.G., 16 May 1811, but went home on leave in July. *Re-app.* 20 March 1813, and attached as D.A.Q.M.G. to 7th Div. Promoted Bvt.-major, 95th, 22 April 1813, and *app.* Deputy-Q.M.G. in the Ionian Islands, 27 April 1813, he left the Peninsula in July 1813.

DUMARESQ, LIEUT.-COL. HENRY (1792–1838). s. of Colonel Dumaresq, of a Jersey family.

As Captain, 3rd Garrison Battalion, *app.* D.A.Q.M.G., 29 April 1813, and was shortly after attached to 4th Div., with which he served until the end of the war.

(Afterwards private secretary to his brother-in-law, General Sir Ralph Darling, when Governor of New South Wales.)

D'URBAN, LIEUT.-GEN. SIR BENJAMIN (1777–1849). s. of John D'Urban, surgeon. R.M. College, 1803.

As Lieut.-Colonel, 2nd West Indian Regiment, *app.* A.Q.M.G., 1 April 1809, and was *app.* Q.M.G. of the Portuguese army, 20 April 1809, which situation he retained until January 1817.

ELLIOTT, CAPTAIN GEORGE. As Captain, 48th, transferred from the A.G.'s Department, 8 May 1809. He obtained leave to return to England in August 1809 for his health and was struck off, 24 January 1810. Having exchanged to the 5th Garrison Battalion, he was sent to the Peninsula to avoid financial embarrassments at home, and was *app.* D.A.Q.M.G., 14 April (or 27 May) 1823, and remained with the Department.

EVANS, GENERAL SIR GEORGE DE LACY (1787–1870). s. of John Evans, magistrate of Moig, co. Limerick. R.M.A. Woolwich.

As Lieutenant, 3rd Dragoons, *app.* D.A.Q.M.G., 13 March 1814, and was struck off, 25 May.

He commanded the British Legion in Spain, 1837, and the 2nd Div. of the Expeditionary Force sent to the Crimea, 1854.

FORREST, LIEUT.-COL. RAMUS (1786–1827). s. of — Forrest, a Poor Knight of Windsor. Educ. Eton.

As Captain, 3rd (Buffs), *app.* D.A.Q.M.G., 6 August 1813, and attached to 7th Div. He was placed at Pauillac for the embarkation of the Army at the end of the war. Promoted Major, 34th, 2 June 1814.

He died in the Lunatic Asylum at Fort Pitt, Chatham, 'labouring under mental hallucination and a chronic disease of the lungs'.

GEDDES, LIEUT.-COL. WILLIAM. Town-Major of Lisbon, 25 October 1809, and as Bvt.-major, 83rd, *app.* A.Q.M.G., 3 August 1812, and acted as such in charge of the office at Lisbon *vice* Mackenzie. Promoted Bvt.-lieut.-colonel, 83rd, 4 June 1814, he remained at Lisbon until the end of the war.

GLEDSTANES, MAJOR NATHANIEL (?–1830). Nephew of General Sir Albert Gledstanes. R.M. College, 1809.

As Captain, 68th, *app.* D.A.Q.M.G., 6 December 1811, taking over the office at Coimbra *vice* Marston, and in July 1812 acting as the Assistant with 6th Div. until December 1812, when he was advised to resign by Gordon, on account of some neglect of duty which occurred during the retreat from Burgos. Resigned, 25 January 1813.

GOMM, FIELD MARSHAL SIR WILLIAM MAYNARD (1784–1875). E. s. of Lieut.-Col. William Gomm, 85th, who was killed at Pointe-à-Pitre, Guadeloupe. R.M. College, 1806.

As Captain, 9th, *app.* D.A.Q.M.G., 1 September 1810, and attached to 5th Div., with which he remained until the end of the war. Promoted Major, 9th, 10 October 1811, A.Q.M.G., 6 December 1811, and Captain and Lieut.-Colonel, Coldstream Guards, 17 August 1812.

Commander-in-Chief, India, 1850–6.

GORDON, GENERAL SIR JAMES WILLOUGHBY, Bart. (1773–1851). s. of Captain Francis Grant, R.N. (who took the name of Gordon, 1768), by his wife, Mary, y. d. of Sir Willoughby Aston, Bart., of Aston, Salop.

As Colonel, Royal African Corps, and when Quartermaster-General of the Forces, *app.* Q.M.G., 8 May 1812, joining Headquarters on 2 August. Left Headquarters about 11 December, and was struck off, 25 December 1812.

Quartermaster-General of the Forces until 1851.

GRANT, LIEUT.-COL. COLQUHOUN (1780–1829). s. of Duncan Grant, of Lingieston, co. Moray.

As Major, 11th, *app*. A.Q.M.G., 20 March 1814, and placed in charge of the Guides and the Post Office *vice* Sturgeon. Bvt.-lieut.-colonel, 19 May 1814.

GREEN, MAJOR EDWIN ROLAND JOSEPH: see Cotton, Maj.-Gen. Edwin Roland Joseph.

GRIFFITHS, MAJOR JOHN CHARLES (1790–1845). As Lieutenant, 94th, *app*. D.A.Q.M.G., 19 December 1813, and attached to 2nd Div., with which he remained until the end of the war.

GUANTER, CAPTAIN JACQUES DE (1781–?1864). 2nd s. of don Mariano de Guanter (of a Catalan family resident in France) by his wife, Madeleine de Banyuls.

As Lieutenant, Chasseurs Britanniques, *app*. D.A.Q.M.G., 12 October 1811, at Cadiz. He was severely wounded at Tarifa, 29 December 1811, losing his right eye and undergoing a trepanning. Struck off the returns, November 1812.

HAMILTON, COLONEL JOHN (1776–1858). As Lieutenant and Captain, Coldstream Guards, *app*. D.A.Q.M.G. at Cadiz, 2 May 1810, 'by Lieut.-General Graham'. He acted at the head of the Department there after Graham's departure, June 1811. Promoted Captain and Lieut.-Colonel, 30 January 1812. Struck off the returns, 25 April 1812.

HARVEY, GENERAL SIR ROBERT JOHN (1785–1860). s. of John Harvey, of Thorpe Lodge, Norfolk, by his wife, Frances, d. of Sir Roger Kerrison. R.M. College, 1809.

As Captain, 53rd, *app*. D.A.Q.M.G., 1 April 1809. Attached to the Portuguese army, 12 June 1809. Employed in intelligence duties and on various missions until January 1811, when he went on leave. He returned in June 1811, was promoted Major, 53rd, and A.Q.M.G., 25 June 1811, and until the end of the war 'was the organ of communication between the Duke of Wellington and the Portuguese troops'. Bvt.-lieut.-colonel, 21 June 1813.

HAVERFIELD, LIEUT.-COL. JOHN (1780–1830). s. of John Haverfield, of Kew Green, Surrey, J.P. Educ. Rugby. R.M. College, 1804–6.

As Captain, 48th, *app*. D.A.Q.M.G., 1 April 1809, but was never employed in the Peninsula in that capacity after the Vimeiro campaign, and ceases to appear in the returns after June 1809.

HEATHCOTE, CAPTAIN RALPH (1782–1854). O. s. of Ralph Heathcote, Minister Plenipotentiary at the Court of the Archbishop Elector of Cologne, by his wife, Antoinette (*née* de Wolter).

As Captain, Royal Dragoons, *app.* D.A.Q.M.G., 12 August 1810, and attached to Hill's Corps and the cavalry employed with it. He was taken into the Q.M.G.'s office, 5 June 1811, probably when Reynett was taken ill, and remained in it until rejoining his regiment, 25 February 1812.

HERRIES, LIEUT.-GEN. SIR WILLIAM LEWIS (1785–1857). 2nd s. of Colonel Charles Herries, of Herries' Bank, and bro. of John Charles Herries, Commissary-in-Chief, &c. Educ. Eton. R.M. College, 1806.

As Captain, Meuron's, *app.* D.A.Q.M.G., 28 November 1812, and attached to 5th Div., with which he remained until losing his leg in the sortie from Bayonne, 14 April 1814.

HUMPHREY, LIEUT.-COL. GEORGE. As Captain, 27th, *app.* D.A.Q.M.G., 25 May 1809. Employed on various missions before obtaining leave, September 1809. He rejoined his regiment, 8 May 1810, after returning to the Army, 18 February 1810, and having been stationed as D.A.Q.M.G. at Abrantes.

HUTCHINS, LIEUT.-COL. THOMAS (1779–1823). Of a family owning considerable property in Kensington. R.M. College, 1809.

As Captain, 3rd Dragoons, *app.* D.A.Q.M.G., 19 September 1812. Promoted Major, 3rd Dragoons, and A.Q.M.G., 10 December 1812, but returned to his regiment, 25 March 1813.

JACKSON, LIEUT.-GEN. SIR RICHARD DOWNES (1776–1845). s. of Christopher Jackson, of Petersfield, Hants. R.M. College, 1800–2.

As Captain and Lieut.-Colonel, Coldstream Guards, *app.* A.Q.M.G., 31 March 1811, and attached to 1st Div. on his arrival from Cadiz, April 1811. Attached to 2nd Div., ?18 October, until returning home on leave, April 1813, he was, on his return in October, re-attached to 2nd Div. and Hill's Corps, in succession to Abercromby. He remained as Hill's A.Q.M.G. until the end of the war.

KELLY, COLONEL DAWSON (?1782–1837). 5th s. of Thomas Kelly, of Dawson's Grove, co. Armagh. His sister Alicia was sub-governess to Princess Charlotte, 1805–8.

Having, as Captain, 27th, served in the Department during the winter of 1808–9, he was *re-app.* D.A.Q.M.G., 1 April 1809. Attached to Cotton's Cavalry Brigade, 6 May 1809, he became afterwards the D.A.Q.M.G. at Headquarters. Promoted Major, 73rd, 31 October 1811, and A.Q.M.G., 6 December 1811, he was struck off, 25 February 1812.

KELLY, LIEUT.-COL. EDWARD (?1771–1828). s. of Captain Edward Kelly, of a family long resident in Queen's County and the Curragh.

As Captain, Royal Dragoons, *app.* D.A.Q.M.G., 31 October 1809, and attached to Payne's Cavalry, December 1809. He returned to England on leave and was struck off the returns, 24 April 1810, having taken up an appointment at the R.M. College. He came back to the Peninsula at Murray's request and, as Captain, 1st Life Guards, *app.* D.A.Q.M.G., 14 April 1813. He fell sick in the autumn, went home, and was struck off 'supposed dead', but was *re-app.* on his return, 25 December 1813.

KIRCHBERGER, CAPTAIN FRIEDRICH (1778–1829). Of one of the Bernese patrician families.

As Captain, de Watteville's, *app.* D.A.Q.M.G. at Cadiz, 25 August 1812, and stationed at Cartagena. Struck off, 24 November 1813.

LANGTON, MAJOR ALGERNON (1781–1829). 3rd s. of Bennet Langton, of Langton Hall, Lincs. (Dr. Johnson's 'Lanky') by his wife, afterwards Dowager Countess of Rothes. R.M. College, 1806.

Having served in the Department during the winter of 1808–9, he was, as Captain, 61st, *re-app.* D.A.Q.M.G., 1 April 1809. Attached to Mackenzie's Corps, 3 May 1809, he was absent, sick, November 1809 to January 1810. He was sent with the force that was detached to Cadiz, February 1810, and acted at the head of the Department there until 25 May 1810, when he returned home. He fought a duel with Northey (q.v.) at Cheltenham, 26 August 1810, and returned to Cadiz in July 1811. He accompanied the Cadiz garrison to Madrid in September 1812, and remained with the Department to the end.

(He afterwards took Holy Orders.)

LIGHT, COLONEL WILLIAM (?1786–1839). s. of Captain Francis Light, R.N., by his wife, Martina Rozells, perhaps d. of the Rajah of Kedah.

As Lieutenant, 4th Dragoons, *app.* D.A.Q.M.G., 5 November 1812, and attached to the Cavalry, accompanying Ponsonby's Brigade in 1813. After Vitoria he was sent by Cotton to act with Mina, and he was reattached to the Cavalry when it came out of winter-quarters in 1814.

(Afterwards Surveyor-General of South Australia.)

MACKENZIE, CAPTAIN WILLIAM (?–1814). As Captain, 42nd, *app.* D.A.Q.M.G., 1 April 1809, and after several assignments was put in charge of the Department's office at Lisbon, 7 July 1809 (*vice* Beresford) until February 1812, when he fell sick and 'lost his senses'. He returned to England to recover in July 1812, and was struck off, 24 November 1813, without having come back to the Peninsula.

MARSTON, LIEUT.-COL. MOLYNEUX (?–1834). E. s. of Daniel Marston, merchant, of Dublin, by his wife, Dorothea, sister of Hon. Isaac Corry, Chancellor of the Irish Exchequer.

As Major, 48th, *app.* A.Q.M.G., 8 May 1810, and stationed at Coimbra until after the battle of Buçaco; A.Q.M.G. to the proposed Naval Detachment, November 1810; resumed his duties at Coimbra on its reoccupation, March 1811, until December 1811. Promoted Bvt.-lieut.-colonel, 1 January 1812, and attached to 6th Div., ?May to November 1812. A.Q.M.G. at Coimbra, December 1812 to May 1813; at Bilbao, 27 July 1813 to January 1814; and at Saint-Jean-de Luz until the end.

MAW, CAPTAIN JOHN HENRY (?–1812). As Captain, 23rd, *app.* D.A.Q.M.G., 1 April 1809, and was attached to J. Murray's Brigade and others during the Oporto campaign. But, 'as they derived little aid from him', he was allowed to return home to rejoin his regiment (June 1809), with which he was later killed at Badajoz, 6 April 1812.

MERCER, LIEUT.-COL. ROBERT (1782–1814). 2nd s. of Lieut.-Col. Robert Mercer, of a family owning considerable property in Marylebone, by his wife, Jean, d. of Sir Robert Henderson of Fordell, 5th Bart. Educ. Westminster. R.M. College, 1803–4.

As Lieutenant and Captain, 3rd Guards, *app.* D.A.Q.M.G., 7 May 1809, and was attached to Sherbrooke's Column and to 1st Div. on its formation, with which he remained until April 1811, when he was transferred to 7th Div., newly formed. Promoted Captain and Lieut.-Colonel, 3rd Guards, and A.Q.M.G., 10 March 1812, he remained with 7th Div. until obtaining leave home, June 1812. (He was killed at Bergen-op-Zoom, 8 March 1814.)

MONTGOMERY, MAJOR HENRY (?–1819). R.M. College, 1811.

As Captain, 50th, *app.* D.A.Q.M.G., 28 October 1812, and attached to 2nd Div. Promoted Major, 50th, and A.Q.M.G., 6 January 1814, he continued to serve with Hill's Corps.

MORGENTHAL, LIEUTENANT WILLIAM (?–1821). As Ensign, 60th, attached as D.A.Q.M.G., 1 April 1809, and served in the office at Lisbon, in charge of 'the financial part of the business', until ill health compelled him to ask for leave, October 1812. Promoted Lieutenant, 2nd Royal Veteran Battalion, 1 November 1809. Struck off, 25 October 1812.

(He was declared incapable of managing his own affairs in 1817.)

MURRAY, GENERAL SIR GEORGE (1772–1846). 2nd s. of Sir William Murray of Ochtertyre, Bart., by his wife, Lady Augusta Mackenzie, d. of George, 3rd Earl of Cromarty. Educ. Royal High School and Edinburgh University. R.M. College, 1802.

As Colonel, *app.* Q.M.G., 1 April 1809. He remained in charge of the Department until 24 December 1811, and was struck off, 7 May 1812, having received promotion to Brigadier-General, 4 June 1811, and to Major-General, 1 January 1812. He returned to the Peninsula, 17 March 1813, and was *re-app.* Q.M.G. from 26 December 1812, retaining the situation until the end.

Secretary of State for War and Colonies, 1828–30; Master-General of the Ordnance, 1834–5 and 1841–6.

NORTHEY, LIEUT.-COL. LEWIS AUGUSTUS (?1777–1868). s. of Major Thomas Northey by his wife, Margaret, d. of J. L. Hancorne, of Gower, Glam.; a relation of Sir Herbert Taylor, and nephew of William Northey, Groom of the Bedchamber to George III. R.M. College, 1802–3.

Having been in charge of the Department at Lisbon, November 1808, and under Donkin during the winter 1808–9, he was *re-app.* A.Q.M.G., 1 April 1809, as Major, Permanent Staff. He had already returned home on leave and never served after 1809. He challenged Langton (q.v.) to a duel at Cheltenham, 26 August 1810, and was found guilty at a court martial, but was allowed to retain his rank. He returned to the Peninsula, April 1813, but he remained unemployed at Lisbon until coming home, April 1814.

OFFENEY, LIEUT.-COL. OTTO WILLIAM (?1763–1812). Of a Prussian family, he was an officer in the old Hanoverian army, one of the first to join the K.G.L.

As Lieut.-Colonel, 7th Line Battalion, K.G.L., *app.* A.Q.M.G., 31 March 1811, and was attached as 'first Assistant' to Hill's Corps. Taken ill during the Almaraz campaign, May 1812, he returned to Lisbon and died at Belém, 12 August.

OSBORNE, CAPTAIN KEANE (?–1812). He had married, 1805, Theodosia Ward, grand-d. of the 1st Viscount Bangor. R.M. College, 1808.

Transferred from the A.G.'s Department, and, as Captain, 5th Dragoon Guards, *app.* D.A.Q.M.G., 30 November 1811, and was attached to 3rd Div. He was killed at Salamanca, 22 July 1812.

PERCY, CAPTAIN HON. FRANCIS JOHN (1790–1812). 7th s. of Algernon, 1st Earl of Beverley (i.e. a relation by marriage of Col. Willoughby Gordon's).

As Captain, 23rd, *app.* D.A.Q.M.G., 3rd August 1812. He died 21 August.

PIERREPONT, MAJOR C. A. (?–1812). As Captain, 20th, *app.* D.A.Q.M.G., 10 April 1811. Promoted Major, Permanent Staff, and A.Q.M.G., July 1811. Mainly employed sketching. Killed in the attack of the hornwork at Burgos, 19 September 1812.

PORTEOUS, CAPTAIN ALEXANDER (1783–1860). bro. of David Porteous, brewer and distiller of Crieff.

As Lieutenant, 61st, *app.* D.A.Q.M.G., 24 July 1811. Worked in the office of the Department at Lisbon, and deputized for Mackenzie (q.v.) from February 1812 until the *app.* of Geddes in August. Afterwards joined the Army, and was struck off, 24 February 1814.

READ, LIEUTENANT RICHARD (?–1812). As Lieutenant, 82nd, *app.* D.A.Q.M.G., 25 February 1811, and served at Cadiz. He died, 9 November 1812.

READ, LIEUT.-COL. WILLIAM (?–1827). As Major, Permanent Staff, *app.* A.Q.M.G., 14 December 1813.

REYNETT, GENERAL SIR JAMES HENRY (1786–1864). s. of Rev. Henry James Reynett, D.D.

As Captain, 52nd, *app.* D.A.Q.M.G., 1 April 1809, and was employed in the Q.M.G.'s office at Headquarters until about 20 June 1811. Removed to the Home Staff, 25 October 1812, he afterwards became Military Secretary to the Duke of Cambridge in Hanover.

SCOVELL, GENERAL SIR GEORGE (1774–1861). s. of George Scovell, of Circencester. R.M. College, 1808.

As Captain, 57th, *app.* D.A.Q.M.G., 1 April 1809. First attached to Cotton's Cavalry Brigade, he was placed in charge of the Corps of Staff Guides on their re-formation, 23 May 1809. Promoted Bvt.-major, 57th, and A.Q.M.G., 30 May 1811, he was also given the superintendence of 'all military communications', 14 August 1811. He devised the cavalry forge adapted for transport on mules. *App.* Major Commandant of the Staff Corps of Cavalry on its formation (more properly under the A.G.), 13 March 1813, he was struck off, 25 June 1813.

(Afterwards Lieut.-Governor and Governor of the R.M. College, Sandhurst.)

STANHOPE, LIEUT.-COL. HON. JAMES HAMILTON (1788–1825). 3rd s. of the 3rd Earl Stanhope (the inventor of the iron printing-press named after him) by his 2nd wife.

As Lieutenant and Captain, 1st Guards, *app.* D.A.Q.M.G., 11 October 1812, and attached to 1st Div. and Graham's Column. Severely wounded at S. Sebastian, 25 July 1813, he came home and was struck off, 24 November 1813.

STAVELEY, LIEUT.-GEN. WILLIAM (1783–1854). Of a Yorkshire family.

As Captain, Royal African Corps, *app.* D.A.Q.M.G., 11 June

1813. Employed throughout the war upon reconnaissance and sketching.

STEWART, LIEUT.-COL. HON. JAMES HENRY KEITH (1783–1836). 6th s. of 7th Earl of Galloway, and y. bro. of Lieut.-Gen. Hon. Sir William Stewart.

As Captain, 95th, *app.* D.A.Q.M.G., 10 August 1811, and attached to 6th Div., and in January 1812 to Light Div. Promoted Major, 95th, and A.Q.M.G., 27 April 1812, he was attached to 7th Div. *vice* Mercer, June 1812, and to 1st Div. as A.A.G. for about two months in November. Reattached to Light Div., March 1813, promoted Lieut.-Colonel, 7th West India Regiment, 3 June 1813, he returned home in September. He rejoined the Army, serving with the Cavalry as A.Q.M.G., in April 1814.

STILL, CAPTAIN NATHANIEL TRYON (1779–1862). O. s. of Robert Still, of East Knoyle and Mere, Dorset, by his wife, Sarah, d. of John Tryon of Collyweston, Northants. R.M. College, 1809.

As Captain, 3rd (Buffs), *app.* D.A.Q.M.G., 15 January 1810, and attached temporarily to Headquarters on his arrival, April 1810. Attached temporarily to 4th Div., September 1810, and to 3rd Div., March 1811 (*vice* Anderdon), he obtained leave home, 24 June 1811. Without returning to the Peninsula, he was struck off, 24 October 1811.

He later obtained a commission in the militia and the 5th Regiment, and was J.P. in Devon and Dorset, and Fellow of New College.

STURGEON, LIEUT.-COL. RICHARD HENRY (?1781–1814). R.M.A. Woolwich. Mar. Susan Curran, Robert Emmet's fiancée (who died at Hythe, 1808).

As Lieut.-Colonel, Royal Staff Corps, *app.* A.Q.M.G., 25 April 1813, and placed in charge of the Corps of Staff Guides and the Post Office *vice* Scovell. Incurring Wellington's displeasure for the failure of his office after Orthez, he is said to have got himself deliberately killed at the outposts near Vic-en-Bigorre, 19 March 1814.

SUTTON, MAJOR MATTHEW (?–1823). Having been employed in the Q.M.G.'s office at Lisbon during the winter of 1808–9, he was *re-app.* D.A.Q.M.G., 1 April 1809, as Captain, 97th, and attached to Mackenzie's Corps, 3 May 1809. Absent, sick, from November until the summer of 1810, he was attached to Leith's Corps (later 5th Div.), 17 July 1810, but was forced to resign through ill health, 31 August 1810, and returned home totally blind.

TAMM, CAPTAIN JOÃO CARLOS DE. As Lieutenant, Portuguese Royal Engineers, he was attached to the Department for the Oporto campaign and *app.* D.A.Q.M.G., 25 May 1809. Promoted Captain, Portuguese Engineers, June 1809, he was employed in various mapping tasks with the Staff Corps, until 24 June 1810, when, 'becoming negligent', he was dismissed.

THORN, LIEUT.-GEN. SIR NATHANIEL (?–1857). R.M. College, 1807.

As Captain, 3rd (Buffs), *app.* D.A.Q.M.G., 3 March 1810, and attached to 2nd Div. and Hill's Corps until the end of the war. Promoted Bvt.-major, Buffs, and A.Q.M.G., 3 March 1814.

TORRENS, COLONEL ROBERT (1784–1840). A cousin of Maj.-Gen. Sir Henry Torrens, the Military Secretary at the Horse Guards.

As Major, 1st West India Regiment, taken by Hope to the Army and *app.* A.Q.M.G., 28 September 1813, and attached to Hope's Corps. Returned home, November 1813, he was offered by Graham a staff situation in his force in Flanders. He came back to the Peninsula, and was attached as A.Q.M.G. to 1st Div., *vice* Upton, 30 April 1814.

TWEEDDALE, FIELD MARSHAL GEORGE, 8TH MARQUESS OF (1787–1876). E. s. of the 7th Marquess.

As Lieutenant and Captain, 1st Guards, *app.* D.A.Q.M.G., 31 October 1809, and attached to the Cavalry. On leave from January to April 1810, and again from January to April 1811, he was attached to the Cavalry acting with Hill's Corps. Promoted Major, 41st, and A.Q.M.G., 14 May 1812, and wounded at Vitoria, 21 June 1813, he was invalided home and was struck off, 25 May 1814, without, however, returning to the Army.

UPTON, GENERAL HON. ARTHUR PERCY (1777–1855). 3rd s. of 1st Baron Templetown. Educ. Westminster.

As Captain and Lieut.-Colonel, 1st Guards, *app.* A.Q.M.G., 28 October 1812, and attached to 1st Div., with which he remained until returning home on leave, 30 April 1814.

VERE, MAJ.-GEN. SIR CHARLES BROKE (1779–1843). 2nd s. of Philip Broke, of Nacton, Suffolk, y. bro. of Rear-Admiral Sir Philip Bowes Vere Broke, commanding *H.M.S. Shannon* in the fight with the *Chesapeake.* R.M. College, 1799–1803.

As Major Charles Broke, 5th, *app.* A.Q.M.G., 18 December 1809. Engaged on reconnaissance until February 1810, he was then attached to 4th Div., *vice* Anderdon, with which he remained until 18 May 1813. Major, Permanent Staff, 7 February 1811, and Bvt.-lieut.-colonel, 24 April 1812. From 19 May 1813 until the end of the war he was employed in the Q.M.G.'s office at Headquarters.

VINCENT, LIEUT.-COL. WILLIAM (1786–1834). E. s. of Arthur Vincent, of Summerhill, co. Clare, by his wife, d. of Colonel Berkeley Westropp; nephew of Lieut.-Gen. J. Vincent. R.M. College, 1809.

As Captain, 82nd, *app.* D.A.Q.M.G., 29 August 1812; attached to 6th Div. from April 1813 until being promoted Major, 82nd, 13 November, and rejoining his regiment, 24 November 1813.

WALKER, CAPTAIN ISAAC (1786–1844). As Lieutenant, 88th, *app.* acting-D.A.Q.M.G. at Cadiz, 20 March 1810, and served there until 18 August 1810, when he joined his regiment in Portugal.

WALLER, COLONEL ROBERT (?–1836). R.M. College, 1802–4. As Captain, 103rd, *app.* D.A.Q.M.G., 1 April 1809, and attached to 2nd Div. on its formation, with which he served until being severely wounded and losing the use of his right arm at Albuera, 16 May 1811. Returned home, promoted Major, 103rd, and A.Q.M.G., 23 July 1811, he was, on rejoining the Army, attached to 3rd Div., with which he remained until 5 July 1813. A.Q.M.G. at Santander, 12 August 1813; promoted Lieut.-Colonel, 103rd, 26 August.

WHITE, CAPTAIN WILLIAM (1784–1812). Of a family resident near High Wycombe, twin bro. of Lieutenant Gillespie White, 13th Light Dragoons, who died at Damietta, 15 October 1801. R.M. College, 1802–5.

As Captain, 13th Light Dragoons, *app.* D.A.Q.M.G., 12 November 1810. Attached to Cavalry: first Anson's Brigade, and, 1811, Le Marchant's Brigade, he was mortally wounded at Salamanca, and died, 23 July 1812.

WHITTINGHAM, LIEUT.-GEN. SIR SAMUEL FORD (1772–1841). E. s. of William Whittingham, a wealthy wholesale merchant of Bristol; brother-in-law of Richard Hart-Davies, M.P. R.M. College, 1806.

As Captain, 13th Light Dragoons, *app.* D.A.Q.M.G., 25 April 1809, but he was already a brigadier in the Spanish service, and although he retained his staff-appointment until the end of the war, he never served in Wellington's Army.

WOODFORD, MAJ.-GEN. SIR JOHN GEORGE (1785–1879). 2nd s. of Lieut.-Col. James Woodford by his wife, Lady Susan, d. of Cosmo, 3rd Duke of Gordon.

As Lieutenant and Captain, 1st Guards, *app.* D.A.Q.M.G., 25 June 1813, and when promoted Captain and Lieut.-Colonel, *app.* A.Q.M.G., 6 July 1813. Attached to 6th Div., with which he served until the end of the war.

APPENDIX II

The Marquess of Wellington
    Bonduc
    Smily
    3 footmen
    2 grooms
    3 cooks
    3 assistants
    1 Italian
    1 goatboy
    3 carmen
    2 huntsmen
    6 bâtmen
    3 orderly sergeants
    12 Portuguese dragoons
    Domingo Alves and 19 muleteers
    2 orderly dragoons
    Sergeant Smithroe
    3 women
    3 farriers
Colonel Colin Campbell, A.A.G. and Commandant
    4 servants
Lieut.-Col. Lord FitzRoy Somerset, Military Secretary
    4 servants
Lieut.-Col. Prince William of Orange, a.d.c.
    8 servants
Lieut.-Col. U. Burgh, a.d.c.
    4 servants
Lieut.-Col. Hon. Alexander Gordon, chief a.d.c.
    4 servants
Lieut.-Col. Charles Fox Canning, a.d.c.
    4 servants
Major Georg Krauchenberg
    3 servants
Major John Fremantle, a.d.c.
Lieutenant the Marquess of Worcester, a.d.c.
    3 servants

Captain the Earl of March, a.d.c.
    4 servants
Maj.-Gen. D. José O'Lawlor, Spanish Liaison Officer
    4 servants
Maj.-Gen. D. Miguel Ricardo de Álava, Spanish Liaison Officer
    4 servants
Senhor Sodré, Interpreter
    4 servants

Adjutant-General's Department:
    Maj.-Gen. Sir Edward Pakenham, A.G.
     John Duval, William Read, servants
    Captain A. C. Wylly, a.d.c.
    Lieut.-Col. John Waters, A.A.G.
    Major Georg von Düring, A.A.G.
    Captain Nathaniel Eckersley, D.A.A.G.
    Captain Thomas Henry Browne, D.A.A.G.
    Lieutenant John Hurford, attached
    Sergeant Bryant, 3rd Guards
           " Heaton, 34th
           " Swanson, 79th
    Corporal Endle, 83rd
           " Buchan, 3rd Guards (printer)
    Private James Daniels, Mounted Staff Corps
           " John Rowley, 1st Royal Dragoons
           " Lewis Pettit, 7th
           " John Sutcliffe, 7th
           " Edward Thomas, 66th
           " John Courtney, 97th
           " Friedrich Ishuil, 5th Line Bn., K.G.L.
           " Christian Bielefeld, 1st Line Bn., K.G.L.
           " John Roberts, 2nd (Queen's)

Quartermaster-General's Department:
    Maj.-Gen. Sir George Murray, Q.M.G.
     6 private servants
     4 bâtmen
    Lieutenant Charles Moray, a.d.c.
     1 private servant
    Lieut.-Col. Charles Broke, A.Q.M.G.
     Private Robert Biggs, 40th
          " Richard Finch, 48th
          " Luís Gonçalves, 11th Port. Inf.

Lieutenant James Freeth, R. Staff Corps
  1 servant
Sergeant J. Williams, 3rd Guards
   „   Charles Hockey, 3rd (Buffs)
Corporal William Hatton, 1st Guards
Private S. Draycott, 3rd Guards
   „   Samuel Frost, 16th L.D.
   „   J. McCaffrey, 27th
   „   John Shotton, R. Staff Corps
   „   William Dunn,   „   „
   „   James Speedy, R. Waggon Train
   „   Daniel Fitzpatrick, Mounted Staff Corps
Spanish Officers attached to the Department:
  Major Pierre Baradiu
  Captain Tomás Connolly
  Captain Ange Auberge
Office of the Military Communications of the Army:
  Lieut.-Col. Richard Henry Sturgeon, Director of the Military
    Post
                   ?   Sub-Director of the Military Post
  Postmaster Sergeant
  Assistant Postmaster Sergeant
  Clerk to Director
  8 messengers
  2 servants
Office of the Director of Telegraphs attached to Headquarters:
  Director of Telegraphs
  1 sergeant
  2 servants

Medical Department:
  Dr. James McGrigor, Inspector-General of Hospitals
  William James, Purveyor to the Forces
    4 servants
  Edward Hodges, Purveyor to the Forces
    3 servants
  Dr. James Forbes, Physician
    3 servants
  Jonathan Croft, Deputy-Purveyor
    2 servants
  George Keys, Deputy-Purveyor
    2 servants
  James Wallington, Deputy-Purveyor
    2 servants

Lachlan McPherson, Deputy-Purveyor
  2 servants
William Lyons, Apothecary
  2 servants
Messrs. Barney, Purveyor's Clerk, and 1 servant
      Warner,   ,,   ,,
      Cornish   ,,   ,,
      Nicholls   ,,   ,,
      St. John   ,,   ,,
      Catherwood ,,   ,,

Paymaster's Department:
  Stanhope Hunter, Deputy-Paymaster-General
    5 servants
  J. R. Whitter, Assistant-Paymaster-General
    4 servants
  R. Jones, Assistant-Paymaster-General
    2 servants
  R. D. Cooke, clerk
  J. A. Woolryche, clerk
  J. Walter, clerk
  J. Fasson, clerk
  S. Cumberland, clerk
  J. Feital, clerk
    7 servants

              Total (at least)   277
                   say   300

Add: Commissary-General's Department, say   50
    Commanding Officer Royal Artillery and Inspector-
      General, Field Train, say   40
    Commanding Royal Engineer, say   12
    Provost-Marshal and assistants, say   8
    Deputy-Judge-Advocate-General F. S. Larpent, say   3
    Quartermaster to Headquarters, Lieutenant W. B.
      Hook, Mounted Staff Corps, say   4
                        417

APPENDIX III

Maj.-Gen. Charles Alten, G.O.C.
  Captain Georg von Baring, a.d.c.
Lieut.-Col. Charles Rowan, A.A.G.
Major Hon. James Stewart, A.Q.M.G.
Captain Charles Beckwith, D.A.Q.M.G.
Mr. Filder, Assistant-Commissary-General.
  Clerk to Mr. Filder.
Assistant-Provost-Marshal.
Maj.-Gen. Vandeleur, commanding 2nd Brigade.
  Brigade-major Smith.
  Assistant-Commissary-General attached to 2nd Brigade.
Lieut.-Col. Barnard, commanding 1st Brigade.
  Brigade-major Eeles.
  Lieutenant Hon. Charles Gore, acting a.d.c.
  Assistant-Commissary-General attached to 1st Brigade.

APPENDIX IV

LIST OF STORES FOR A HOSPITAL OF 500 MEN

2 Hospital Tents and Marquees, Poles, &c.
500 Palliasses.
500 Blankets.
500 pr. of Sheets.
500 Coverlids.
500 Bolster-cases.
2 cwt. Rice.
1 cwt. Oatmeal.
56 lb. Sago.
1 45-gal. Copper and Trevet.
50 Camp-kettles.
200 Pint-pots.
100 Quart-pots.
200 Trenchers.
500 Spoons.
1 cwt. Portable Soup.
2 Round Tents, complete.
200 Linen Shirts.
200 Nightcaps.
1 Jar of Oil with wick.
1 large Tea-kettle.
1 Flesh-fork and Soup-ladle.
1 pr. Scales and Weights.
1 Steelyard.
2 Brass Cocks.
2 Spades.
2 Shovels.
2 Saws.
2 Hatchets.
500 Nails.

2 Hammers.
2 doz. Knives and Forks with carvers.
10 gal. Vinegar.
2 cwt. Salt.
60 Biers for wounded men.
200 yards Flannel.
10 lb. Tea.
1 cwt. Sugar.
$\frac{1}{4}$ cask Port Wine.
100 Bowls.
Birch-brooms, Sweeping-brushes, Mops, and Scrubbing-brushes.
6 Water-buckets.
6 Bedpans.
6 Stool-pans.
200 Chamberpots.
10 Basins.
3 Urinals.
12 Saucepans.
10 Lamps.
3 gal. British spirit and Cask.
2 cwt. Hard soap.
1 cwt. Soft soap.
10 Baggage water-decks.
1 Box of Stationery and Books.
Candles.
Flour.
Raisins.
1 Bathing Tub.

APPENDIX V

ARTICLES OF CAMP EQUIPMENT AND THE SCALE OF ISSUE IN THE PENINSULA

	Per Cavalry Regt. of 8 troops[1]	Per Infantry Battn. of 10 companies
Tent, with pole and iron collar . .	..	3 per coy.[2]
„ Mallets	..	2 per tent[2]
„ Pins	..	40 per tent[2']
Powder-bags	1 per troop[3]	1 per coy.[3]
Drum-cases	..	2 per coy.[3]
Canteens and straps	1 per man	1 per man
Haversacks	1 per man	1 per man
Blankets	1 per man	1 per man[4]
Bill-hooks	1 per 10 men	1 per 10 men
Camp-kettles	1 per 10 men	1 per 10 men[5]
Sets of forage-cords (4 per set) . . .	½ set per horse	..
Picquet ropes	1 per 9 horses	..
Water buckets	1 per 12 horses	..
Nosebags (hair)	1 per horse	..
Cornsacks	1 per horse	..
Saddle water-decks (not issued to Hussars) .	1 per horse	..
Reaping-hooks	10 per troop	..
Spades	1 per troop	5 per battn.
Shovels	1 per squadron	5 per battn.
Pickaxes	1 per squadron	5 per battn.
Felling-axes	1 per squadron	5 per battn.
Public mules	14 per regiment	13[6] per battn.
Packsaddles { crooked haucums[7] / straight haucums / boarded haucums[8] } . .	14 per regiment	13 per battn.
Bridles and collars (with winkers) . .	14 per regiment	13 per battn.
Medicine panniers	4 per regiment	2 per battn.
Sergeant-armourer's panniers . .	2 per regiment	..
Sergeant-saddler's panniers . .	2 per regiment	..
Baggage-straps for the Paymaster . .	1 set per regt.	2 per battn.
Camp Colours, poles, and cases . .	1 per troop[3]	1 per coy.[3]

[1] In the autumn of 1811 the establishment of cavalry regiments was reduced from 4 squadrons of 2 troops each to 3 squadrons of 2 troops each.

[2] Tents were not issued to infantry battalions until 1 March 1813. They were carried on the mule hitherto used for the camp-kettles. See n. 5 below.

[3] This was the home scale of issue. They do not appear to have been a normal issue in the Peninsula.

[4] Blankets were issued to infantry in lieu of greatcoats.

[5] This was the heavy 'Flanders' kettle weighing between 30 and 38 oz. It was

replaced on 1 March 1813 by the light tin camp-kettle weighing 22 oz. distributed to infantry battalions on a scale of 1 to every 6 men, and carried by the men. The home scale for the Flanders kettle was 1 per 5 men.

6 One to each company for the carriage of the camp-kettles, one for the surgeon's panniers, one for intrenching tools, and one for the paymaster's books. The 15 mules per battalion stipulated in G.O. dated Abrantes, 19 June 1809, appears to be a misprint for 13.

7 Otherwise called 'Devonshire crooks' and used for the carriage of the camp-kettles and the surgeon's and veterinary surgeon's panniers.

8 Used for the carriage of intrenching tools.

APPENDIX VI

1. 'MEMORANDUM' IN WELLINGTON'S HAND, HEADED 'MOVEMENT, 6TH AUGUST'

(*Murray Papers*, vol. 38, fos. 118–19)

3d, 7th, Bradford's Brigade, and Don Carlos's Infantry and Ponsonby's Cavalry to move by their right on Aldea Real and cross the River Pirón and encamp.

The 1st Battn. 5th Regiment must move to Cuéllar.

The Regt. of Infantry at Cuéllar must move to join its Division at Aldea Real.

The 4th, 5th Divisions and Pack's Brigade of Infantry and Alten's Cavalry to move by their right towards the Pirón River and encamp between Mudrián and Tremerose.

> Query: whether there are roads leading from Tremerose on Abades and thence on Otero de Herreros so as to get this column on the Guardarrama Road without difficulty.

The Heavy Artillery and Reserve to move from Mata de Cuéllar to Mudrián.

The 1st Division to move from Megeces and Cogeces to move by the left of the Pirón to Remondo, where they will cross the river and encamp.

The Light Division to move from Aldeamayor to Cogeces and Megeces and encamp.

> Query: respecting the shortest road and whether they can come further.

The Dragoons belonging to Anson's Brigade now with the 1st and Light Divisions to be placed on the road between Cuéllar and Tudela to keep up the communication between the troops at Cuéllar and General Anson's Brigade, which must remain at Villabáñez.

The 6th Division, the 1st Battn. 5th, the 1st Battn. 38th, 1st Battn. 82nd, 2nd Battn. 4th, 1st Battn. 42nd, are to move to Cuéllar. These Regiments to be quartered in the Convent, which they must clear out for that purpose.

Their hospitals, which must be for slight cases only, must be in the Castle.

The Comy-Genl. must take measures to supply these troops with provisions.

2 (*a*). 'MOVEMENTS OF THE TROOPS ON THE
6TH OF AUGUST, 1812'

dated Headquarters, Cuéllar, 5 August 1812 (*Murray Papers*, vol. 88,
pp. 44–47)

Colonel Ponsonby's Brigade of Cavalry to move at 3 o'clock tomorrow morning by its right to the River Pirón, cross that river and
encamp on its left bank near to the village of Mozoncillo. The Brigade
is to proceed by the villages of Zarzuela del Pinar and Fuentepelayo.

The regiment of Light Infantry of the K.G.L. stationed near
Cuéllar to move at 3 o'clock tomorrow morning by its right through
the village of Sanchonuño to Navalmanzano, where the regiment is to
remain until further orders.

Major-General Victor Baron Alten's Brigade of Cavalry to move
by its right at 3 o'clock tomorrow morning by Sanchonuño, Pinarejos
and S. Martín Mudrián to the River Pirón, near to Mudrián, and encamp on its right bank between Mudrián and the mill of Tremerose,
as near to the latter place as can be done without fatiguing the horses.

The 3rd Division, 7th Division, Brig. General Bradford's Brigade
and the troops under Major-General D. Carlos de España to move at
3 o'clock tomorrow morning by the right and proceed by the village of
Zarzuela del Pinar and Fuentepelayo, and, crossing the River Pirón,
encamp on its left bank near to the village of Mozoncillo.

Brig.-General Pack's Brigade, the 4th and 5th Divisions, to move
at 3 o'clock tomorrow morning by the right and proceed by the village
of Gomezserracin to the River Pirón and encamp on its right bank near
to the village of Mudrián between that village and the Puente del
Roble.

The following battalions to march to Cuéllar and report their
arrival to Major-General Clinton:

2/4th
1/38th
1/82nd

The Heavy artillery and Reserve Ammunition under the command
of Lieut.-Colonel Dickson to move tomorrow morning at 3 o'clock
from El Pino by Fresneda de Cuéllar to Mudrián and encamp on the
Pirón River near to that village and between the 4th and 5th Divisions.

The 1st Division to move tomorrow morning at 3 o'clock by its
right from its present encamping ground and, crossing the River
Pirón, proceed by the left bank of that river to Remondo, where it will
recross that river and encamp.

The undermentioned battalion of the 1st Division to proceed to Cuéllar and report its arrival to Major-General Clinton:

1/42nd.

The Light Division to move at 3 o'clock tomorrow morning by its right from Aldeamayor by Arrabal and Cogeces del Rio Cega to El Pino and encamp on the Rio Cega near to the Puente el Pino.

The Dragoons attached to the Light Division to move (when the Light Division marches) to Montemayor, and to remain there to keep up the communication between Major-General Anson's Brigade of Cavalry at Villabáñez and Viloria, where the detachment of dragoons with the 1st Division is to proceed at 3 o'clock tomorrow morning and to be stationed for the purpose of keeping up the communication between Viloria and Cuéllar.

The Baggage to follow the columns.

Headquarters 6th of August at Aldea Real or Mozoncillo.

J. W. GORDON, Q.M.G.

2 (b). 'MEMORANDUM FOR THE COMMISSARY-GENERAL'

dated Cuéllar, 5 August 1812 (*Murray Papers*, vol. 88, p. 48)

The undermentioned troops having been ordered to march into Cuéllar on the 6th inst., and to remain in quarters there until further orders, the Commissary-General will take the necessary measures to supply the troops with provisions:

the whole of the 6th Division
1/5th
1/38th
2/4th
1/42nd
1/82nd

making in the whole, about 6,000 men. The troops will be quartered in the Convent and the sick in the Castle.

J. W. GORDON, Q.M.G.

APPENDIX VII

DRAFT IN MURRAY'S HAND HEADED 'FORMATION AGAINST THE ENEMY'S REARGUARD AT FOZ-DO-AROUCE, MARCH 15TH, 1811'

(*Murray Papers*, vol. 33, fo. 165)

THE Light Division (left in front) will move along the slopes to the left of the Great Road *slanting up so as to gain the heights from which the ground falls towards Foz-do-Arouce.*

Col. Hawker's Brigade of Cavalry will move out for the present as a reserve upon the open ground to the right of the Great Road.

One troop Horse Artillery will move with || Sir W. Erskine || *the Light Division.* The other will remain with Colonel Hawker's Brigade.

The 3rd Division *(right in front) will continue* to move along the Great Road.

The 5th Division to ascend the Serra to the left above the Light Division *leading out to the left of the hill seen after passing through Miranda-do-Corvo.*

The 1st Division will follow the 3rd Division.

The 6th Division will follow the Light Division.

Major-General Anson's Brigade of Cavalry || when it comes up || will follow so as to support the Light Division. || Geo. Murray, Q.M.G.||

The intention is to throw the Army into a diagonal position, the right refused and the left pushed forward so as to gain the heights that over-hang the village of Foz-do-Arouce and command the bridge.

Br. Gl. Pack's Brigade will move down the heights further to the left, directing itself upon Foz-do-Arouce to co-operate with the Light Division and observing the banks of the Ceira on its left bank.

G.M.

Note. Passages between these lines || are crossed through.

APPENDIX VIII

1. PENCIL NOTES IN MURRAY'S HAND ON THE BACK OF A COPY OF A MOVEMENT ORDER DATED MELGAR DE FERNAMENTAL, 10 JUNE 1813

(*Murray Papers*, vol. 41, fo. 146)

GENERAL Fane upon Celada supported by all General Hill's Infantry except two brigades.

The Hussars upon Hornillos supported by two brigades of General Hill's Infantry.

The Light Division to follow the Hussars preceded by Br. Genl. Ponsonby's Brigade.

2. DRAFT 'ARRANGEMENT' FOR 12 JUNE 1813

(*Murray Papers*, vol. 41, fo. 151)

The Right Column of the Army with the exception of two brigades of the infantry of that column will march upon Celada del Camino, the cavalry in front. This column will move forward from the vicinity of Castrojériz at 5 a.m.

Two Brigades of the Infantry of the Right Column of the Army, preceded by M.Gl. Alten's Brigade of Cavalry, will move from Castrojériz upon Hornillos del Camino. M.Gl. Alten will put his Brigade in march from its cantonments in sufficient time to move forward from Castrojériz at 5 a.m.

The Hussar Brigade, followed by M.Gl. [*sic*] Ponsonby's Brigade of Cavalry will move by Castrillo de Murcia to Isar.

The Light Division will move from Villasandino and follow Br.Gl. Ponsonby's Brigade. This Column will form near Castrillo de Murcia and move forward from there at $\frac{1}{2}$ past 5 a.m.

Each of these columns will halt near the places on which their march is above directed and will receive further orders.

The Baggage of each of the above columns is to follow in the rear of the column in the order of the troops of which the columns is composed.

The Baggage of Headquarters will follow in rear of the column which marches upon Hornillos and will halt at the village of Iglesias.

The Civil Departments of Headquarters will remain at Castrojériz.

APPENDIX IX

COMPARATIVE TABLE OF THE MILITARY STAFF COMPOSING THE HEADQUARTERS OF THE BRITISH, RUSSIAN, AND AUSTRIAN CONTINGENTS IN FRANCE EACH OF 30,000 MEN, AT MARCH 1816

	British			Russian			Austrian		
	Officers	*O.R.s*	*Total*	*Officers*	*O.R.s*	*Total*	*Offiers*	*O.R.s*	*Total*
General Commanding-in-Chief	1	..	..	1	..	..	1	..	..
a.d.c.'s	6	..	7	5	..	6	2	..	3
Chief of Staff	..	..	..	1	..	..	..	..	..
a.d.c.'s	..	..	..	2	..	3	..	..	..
Adjutant-General	1	..	.	1	..	..	1	..	..
a.d.c.'s	2	..	..	..	..	..	..	..	..
Assistants:									
lieut.-cols. and majors	5	..	..	1	..	..	2	..	..
captains	1	..	..	3	..	..	3	..	..
lieuts. and ensigns	2	..	..	2	..	..	15	..	..
clerks and orderlies	..	11	22	..	?	7	..	10	31
Quartermaster-General	1	..	..	1	..	..	1	..	..
a.d.c.'s	2	..	..	..	..	..	..	..	..
Assistants:									
lieut.-cols. and majors	4	..	..	..	..	..	..	..	..
captains	4	..	..	2	..	..	3	..	..
lieuts. and ensigns	1	..	..	5	..	..	2	..	..
clerks and orderlies	..	15	27	..	?	8	..	3	9
Military Secretary	1	..	..	1	..	..	..	..	..
Assistants	3	..	4	1	..	2	..	..	..
Commandant of H.Q.	1	..	1	1	..	1	..	..	..
Officer Commanding Artillery	1	..	..	1	..	..	..	..	..
Assistants	6	..	7	3	..	4	..	..	..
Officer Commanding Engineers	1	..	..	1	..	..	1	..	..
Assistants	9	..	10	4	..	5	4	..	5
Total	52	26	78	36	?	36	35	13	48

BIBLIOGRAPHICAL NOTE

[*Note.* All books published in London unless otherwise stated]

I. CONTEMPORARY MANUSCRIPT AND PRINTED SOURCES

(*a*) The central administration of the army:

MS. Papers in the Public Record Office (W.O. series), classed under the heads of the various departments: e.g. W.O. 6, Secretary of State; W.O. 4, Secretary-at-War; W.O. 3, Commander-in-Chief's Office, &c.

Reports of the Commissioners of Military Enquiry appointed by Act of 45 Geo. III, c. 47 (1806–12).

(*b*) The Army in the Peninsula:

(i) Papers of the Commander of the Forces:

Dispatches of F.M. the Duke of Wellington, K.G., from 1799 to 1818, ed. Lieut.-Col. John Gurwood, 1834–9, and later enlarged editions (1848, 1852, easier to handle).

Supplementary Dispatches and Memoranda of F.M. the Duke of Wellington . . ., ed. 2nd Duke of Wellington, 1858–72.

(ii) Papers of the Adjutant-General:

A good many are printed both in the later editions of *Disp.* and in *Suppl. Disp.*

(iii) Papers of the Quartermaster-General:

MS. Correspondence of Sir George Murray in the National Library of Scotland, Edinburgh, of which some are printed in *Suppl. Disp.* and *Memoir annexed to an Atlas containing the principal Battles, Sieges and Affairs . . .* 1841, from which they were incorporated into the later editions of *Disp.* Neither of the two latter can be relied on for true transcripts of the original MS. Some papers were published in articles by Sir George Murray in the *Quarterly Review*, 1836–8 (Vols. 56, 57, 61).

(iv) Papers of the Commissary-General:

MS. Correspondence of Sir Robert Hugh Kennedy, in the author's hands, by no means complete over the years 1810–14.

(v) Ordnance Department:

The Dickson Manuscripts, ed. Colonel J. H. Leslie, 1908–9 (though not properly a departmental correspondence).

2. GENERAL ORDERS, COURTS MARTIAL, ETC.

(*a*) *Collected General Regulations and Orders* for the army at large (various editions).

Instructions for the Q.M.G.'s Department, 1814.

The Portuguese *Ordens do Dia* (1809–14).

(*b*) Thomas Reide, *Treatise on Military Finance* (1795, 1810).
Major Charles James, *Regimental Companion* (1811).
Selected General Orders in Spain and Portugal, ed. Lieut.-Col. John Gurwood, 1837, with a useful introduction.

(*c*) *General Whitelocke's Trial* (1809).
Sir John Murray's Trial (1815).
Willoughby Gordon's evidence in *The Investigation of the Charges brought against the Duke of York* (1809).
Proceedings upon the Inquiry relative to the Armistice and Convention [of Sintra] (1809).

3. CONTEMPORARY LETTERS AND DIARIES

(*a*) Adjutant-General's Department:
The Pakenham Letters, 1800–1815, ed. Lord Longford, 1913.

(*b*) Quartermaster-General's Department:
The Peninsular Journal of Major-General Sir Benjamin D'Urban, 1808–1817, ed. I. J. Rousseau, 1930.
The Letters and Journals of F.M. Sir W. M. Gomm, 1799–1815, ed. F. C. Carr-Gomm, 1881.
Ralph Heathcote: letters of a young diplomatist, ed. Countess Günther-Gröben, 1907 (uninformative).
MS. Journal of Sir George Scovell in the Public Record Office (W.O. 37/4–7B).
MS. letters of Lieut.-Col. Robert Mercer in the Scottish Record Office (Fordell MSS.).

(*c*) Ordnance Department:
The Dickson Manuscripts, ed. Colonel J. H. Leslie, 1908–9.
The Letters of Colonel Sir Augustus Simon Frazer, 1859.
Burgoyne's Diary in the *Life and Correspondence of F.M. Sir J. F. Burgoyne*, ed. Lieut.-Col. Hon. George Wrottesley, 1873.

(*d*) Commissariat Department:
[J. E. Daniel], *The Journal of an Officer in the Commissariat Department*, 1820.
A. L. F. Schaumann's Journal, ed. and trs. as *On the Road with Wellington*, by A. M. Ludovici, 1924.
[P. W. Buckham], *Personal Narrative of Adventures in the Peninsula*, 1827.

(*e*) Other departments:
The Private Journal of Judge-Advocate [F. S.] Larpent, 1853, though indifferently edited, a source of first-class importance.

(*f*) General Officers and a.d.c.'s:
General R. B. Long's letters, ed. as *Peninsular Cavalry General, 1811–1813*, by T. H. McGuffie, 1951.
MS. Journals and letters of General John, 4th Earl of Hopetoun, at Hopetoun House.

Sir William Warre's *Letters from the Peninsula, 1808–1812*, ed. Rev. Edmond Warre, 1909.
Sir T. Shaw-Kennedy's Diary, published in Lord FitzClarence, *Manual of Outpost Duties*, 1849.
Captain Roverea's letters printed in Colonel F. de Roverea, *Mémoires*, Berne, 1848.

4. AUTOBIOGRAPHIES, ETC.

(*a*) Those written before the appearance of Napier's *History*:

Sir James McGrigor, *Autobiography and Services*, 1861.
Sir George Napier, *Passages in the Early Military Life of Sir G. T. Napier*, 1864.
Sir Harry Smith, *Autobiography*, ed. G. Moore Smith, 1901.
The autobiographical portions of Lord Londonderry's *Narrative of the Peninsular War*, 1828.

(*b*) Those written after Napier's *History*:

Sir Andrew Leith Hay, *Narrative of the Peninsular War*, 1831 (little affected by Napier).
Colonel Sir J. Stepney Cowell-Stepney, *Sketches of Campaigning Life*.
Sir R. D. Henegan, *Seven Years Campaigning in the Peninsula and the Netherlands*, 1846.
Sir R. I. Routh, *Observations on Commissariat Field Service*, 1852, contains Peninsular experiences.

5. BIOGRAPHICAL MATERIAL

Philippart's *Royal Military Calendar*, 1815, 1820, based upon memoirs furnished by the officer himself or on his record of service (W.O. 25/747).
The articles in *D.N.B.*, which, however, should be used with caution.
A. M. Delavoye, *Life of Lord Lynedoch*, Devonport, 1881.
The Memoirs of Sir G. Lowry Cole, ed. Maud Lowry Cole and Stephen Gwynn, 1934.
Lord Stanhope, *Notes of Conversations with the Duke of Wellington, 1831–1851*, 1881, contains many interesting sidelights, if used with care.

6. REGIMENTAL HISTORIES

Those histories which embody unpublished diaries, chronicles, and records compiled during service in the Peninsula often contain valuable reflections of the performance of the staff; e.g. Colonel H. C. Wylly's of the Sherwood Foresters, Lieut.-Col. Neil Bannatyne's of the 30th, Colonel Willoughby Verner's and Colonel Cope's of the Rifle Brigade, Colonel Lewis Butler's of the 60th, Captain Smythie's of the 40th, C. T. Atkinson's of the Royals, the 24th and the 39th.

7. PERIODICALS

(*a*) Reminiscences and controversial material are to be found in the early military periodicals, e.g.
Military Panorama (1812–14), the *Royal Military Chronicle* (1810–17), and Colburn's *United Service Magazine* (1829–1930).

(*b*) Documents and articles published in current periodicals, e.g. the Journal of the *Royal United Service Institution* (1858), the *Cavalry Journal* (1906), the Proceedings of the *Royal Artillery Institution* and its successor the *Royal Artillery Journal* (1858), the Journal of the Society for *Army Historical Research* (1921), and occasionally the *Army Quarterly* and the *English Historical Review*.

8. MODERN WORKS

C. M. CLODE, the *Military Forces of the Crown*, 1869 (quite indispensable).
COLONEL CLIFFORD WALTON, *History of the British Standing Army, 1680–1700*, 1894 (not immediately relevant).
MAJ.-GEN. A. FORBES, *History of the Ordnance Services*, 1929 (a valuable study of the army supply system).
HON. SIR JOHN FORTESCUE, *History of the British Army* (caps. xxx and xxxvi are perfunctory and unsympathetic).
HAMPDEN GORDON, *The War Office*, 1935 (little historical material).
SIR CHARLES OMAN, *Wellington's Army*, 1913.

9. CONTINENTAL SOURCES

COLONEL VACHÉE, *Napoléon en Campagne*, Paris, 1913.
WALTER GÖRLITZ, *Der deutsche Generalstab: Geschichte und Gestalt*, Frankfort, 1953.
BRONSART VON SCHELLENDORFF, *Der Dienst des Generalstabes* (Eng. trs. W. A. Hare, 1877–80).
Benedeks Nachgelassene Papiere, ed. H. Friedjung, Dresden, 1904.
FZM. ANTON VON MOLLINARY, *Quarante-six ans dans l'Armée austro-hongroise, 1833–1879* (Fr. trs.), Paris, 1913.
MAX LEHMANN, *Scharnhorst*, Leipzig, 1886–7.
GENERAL F. K. F. VON MÜFFLING, *Aus meinem Leben*, Berlin, 1851.

10. BIBLIOGRAPHIES

There is a very useful list of officers' autobiographies, letters, &c., in Sir Charles Oman's *Wellington's Army*, 1913 (Appendix). In Spanish there is the *Diccionario Bibliográfico de la Guerra de la Independencia española*, Madrid, 1944–52 (compendious but uncritical). In Portuguese there is the *Relação das Espécies bibliográficas e iconográficas relativas à Revolução francesa e Império*, ed. Adolpho Loureiro, Lisbon, 1909 (not confined to the Peninsular War).

INDEX

M'Mullin, Ens., 176.
Magazines, 66–67, 82–83, 96, 99, 100;
  Magazinssystem, 69–70, 90, 97–98,
  99 n.; *see also* Commissariat Line.
Maitland, Gen. Frederick, 53.
Maps, 103–7; map-making, 108–12.
Marlay, Lieut.-Col. George, 176.
Marlborough, John, 1st Duke of, 133,
  156, 165.
Marston, Lieut.-Col. Molyneux, 187–8.
Masséna, Marshal André, Prince of
  Essling, 112, 154.
Massenbach, Col. Christian K. A. L.
  von, 152, 166.
Maw, Capt. John Henry, 188.
Medical Board, 13–14, 34, 46.
Medical Department (in the Peninsula),
  see Inspector-General of Hospitals (in
  the Peninsula).
Mellish, Lieut.-Col. Henry Francis, 63,
  176.
Mentelle, Edme, and F.-S., 104, 106.
Mercer, Lieut.-Col. Robert, 188.
Military Chest, 74, 93, 95.
Military Depot, *see* Repository for
  Military Knowledge.
Military Secretary (Horse Guards), 17,
  43–44, 47, 50, 64, 158.
Military Secretary (in the Peninsula),
  34, 39, 43–44, 60–62, 118, 119.
Mitchell, Sir Thomas Livingston, 110,
  111.
Moira, Lieut.-Gen. Lord, *see* Hastings,
  Gen. Francis, 1st Marquess of.
Moncrieff, Col. James, 20.
Mondego, R., 87.
Montgomery, F.M. B. L., 1st Vis-
  count, 102, 158.
Montgomery, Maj. Henry, 49, 188.
Moore, Lieut.-Gen. Sir John, 44, 106,
  155, 156, 163, 167, 168.
Moray, Capt. Charles, 140 n., 195.
Mordaunt, Gen. Sir John, 20.
Morgenthal, Lieut. William, 188.
Morrison, Gen. George, 20 & n.
Müffling, Gen. F. K. F., Frhr. von,
  166–7.
Mules: Regimental, 84–86, 200 & n.;
  Division mules, 86–87, 90, 91–92, 97,
  161; Mule brigades, 88.
Munster, Maj.-Gen. George A. F., 1st
  Earl, 63, 176.
Murray, Maj. Evan John MacGregor,

see MacGregor, Maj.-Gen. Sir E.
  John Murray.
Murray, Gen. Sir George, 25, 29, 41 n.,
  42, 43–45, 46, 47, 48–49, 52–53, 54,
  55, 57, 59–60, 61, 62, 64, 106, 109
  & n., 110, 111, 118, 120, 121, 125,
  140 & n., 145–52, 155–6, 157–8, 163,
  165, 166, 188–9; *see also* Quartermaster-General (in the Peninsula).
Murray, Com.-Gen. John, 47, 74; *see
  also* Commissary-General (in the Peninsula).
Murray, Gen. Sir John, 41, 119.
Murray Pulteney, Gen. Sir James, 45,
  130.

Nantiat, Jasper, 106.
Napier, Gen. Sir Charles, 26 & n.
Napier, Gen. Sir George Thomas, 176.
Napier, Lieut.-Gen. Sir William F. P.,
  149–50.
Napoleon, 58, 154, 165.
Necessaries, *see* Clothing.
Neves Costa, Col. José Maria das,
  105 & n.
Nivelle Operation, 147.
Northey, Lieut.-Col. Lewis Augustus,
  48, 189.

Obins, Lieut.-Col. Hamlet, 176.
Offeney, Lieut.-Col. Otto William, 20,
  48 n., 189.
Off-Reckonings, 78.
Ordinaries, 5–6, 74.
Ordnance, the Board of, 6–9, 15, 16, 17,
  18 n., 26, 34.
Ordnance corps, the two, 8–9, 75 & n.
Ordnance Department (in the Penin-
  sula), 75–76, 77.
O'Ryan, Capt. José, 117.
Osborne, Capt. Keane, 176–7, 189.

Pakenham, Maj.-Gen. Hon. Sir Edward
  M., 49, 59, 62, 158, 177; *see also*
  Adjutant-General (in the Peninsula).
Pakenham, Lieut.-Gen. Hon. Sir Her-
  cules, 177.
Pass Order, 141–2.
Paterson, Lieut.-Col. Daniel, 12, 13 n.,
  30.
Patronage (in Staff-Appointments), 20,
  26, 46–50, 53–54, 62–65, 158–60.
Paymaster-General of the Forces, 6, 30.

Paymaster-General, Deputy (in the Peninsula), 34, 74.
Peacocke, Gen. Sir M. Warren, 55.
Percy, Capt. Hon. Francis John, 189.
Pereira, Lieut.-Col. José Clemente, 117.
Physician-General, 14.
Picton, Lieut.-Gen. Sir Thomas, 37, 53.
Pierrepont, Maj. C. A., 110 n., 189–90.
Ponsonby, Maj.-Gen. Hon. Sir Frederick C., 177.
Popham, Rear-Adm. Sir Home R., 127, 128.
Porteous, Capt. Alexander, 190.
Portuguese Headquarters, 58 n., 164.
Postal Service: Civil, 122–4, 125; Military, 124–6, 196.
Printing-Press, 89 & n., 195.
Provisions, 79–80, 94.
Provost-Marshal, 153, 161.
Purveyor-General, 13, 34.
Purveyor's Department (in the Peninsula), 76, 77–78.

Quartering, 131–7; see also Bivouac; Cantonments; Tents.
Quartermaster-General of the Forces, 10, 11, 12–13, 18, 19–31, 47, 121 n.; Permanent Assistants, 28; Assistants, Deputy-Assistants, &c., 30 n.
Quartermaster-General (in the Peninsula), 34, 36, 39, 41, 42, 47–49, 51–54, 57, 59–60, 62, 63–64, 78, 84, 90, 106, 108–11, 113, 118, 119–22, 124, 125, 130–1, 134–52, 153, 155, 156, 157–8, 162, 164, 165, 166.
Quartermaster-General's Stores, see Camp Equipage.
Quinta das Longas, 40.
Quinta de Gramicha, 40.
Quinta de S. João, 40.
Quinta de S. José, 40.

Radetzky von Radetz, Fm. Josef, Graf, 45, 166.
Raglan, F.M. FitzRoy J. H., 1st Baron, 61–62, 169.
Read, Capt. F. M., 57, 110 n.
Read, Lieut. Richard, 190.
Read, Lieut.-Col. William, 190.
Repository for Military Knowledge, 29–30, 42, 110, 164.
Requisition, 68–69, 81–82, 89, 90; Requisitionssystem, 69, 98–100.

Reynell, Lieut.-Gen. Sir Thomas, 177.
Reynett, Gen. Sir James Henry, 48 n., 57, 190.
Robe, Lieut.-Col. William, 75 n.
Rooke, Lieut.-Col. John Charles, 177.
Routes, 137–9.
Roverea, Maj. Alexandre de, 114.
Rowan, Lieut.-Col. Sir Charles, 63, 177.
Roy, Maj.-Gen. William, 20, 109.
Royal Staff Corps, 28–29, 108, 110 n., 136, 161.
Royal Military College: Senior Department (High Wycombe), 24–26, 63, 159; Junior Department (Marlow), 25 & n.
Royal Waggon Train, 89–90, 161.
Rumann, Lieut.-Col. Lewis, 117, 118.

St. Vincent, Adm. John, 1st Earl, 3 n.
Sampaio, H. T. de, Conde da Póvoa, 81.
Scharnhorst, Gen. Gerh. Joh. D. von, 21, 25, 152.
Schwarzenberg, Fm. Karl Philipp, Fürst, 166.
Scovell, Gen. Sir George, 108, 116, 120, 124, 125, 126 n., 135, 136, 151, 190.
Secretary-at-War, 5, 6, 9, 12, 13, 14, 15, 16, 17, 31.
Secretary of State, 4–5; for War and Colonies, 9–10, 16, 17, 31–32, 163.
Smith, Lieut.-Gen. Sir Harry G. W., 36, 37–38, 147.
Somerset, Lieut.-Col. Lord FitzRoy, see Raglan, F.M. FitzRoy J. H., 1st Baron.
Sontag, Lieut.-Gen. John, 20.
Sorauren, 145 & n., 164.
Spanish Headquarters, 58 n., 164.
Spencer, Gen. Sir Brent, 157.
Staff College, see Royal Military College.
Staff Corps, see Royal Staff Corps.
Staff Corps of Cavalry, 154, 161.
Staff Guides, see Guides, Corps of Mounted.
Stanhope, Lieut.-Col. Hon. James H., 190.
Staveley, Lieut.-Gen. William, 110 n., 190–1.
Stewart, Brig.-Gen. Hon. Charles, see Londonderry, Gen. Charles William, 3rd Marquess.
Stewart, Lieut.-Col. Hon. James H. K., 178, 191.

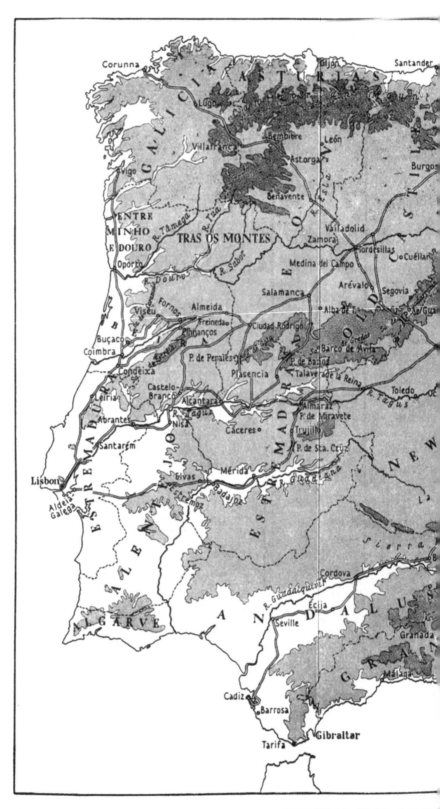

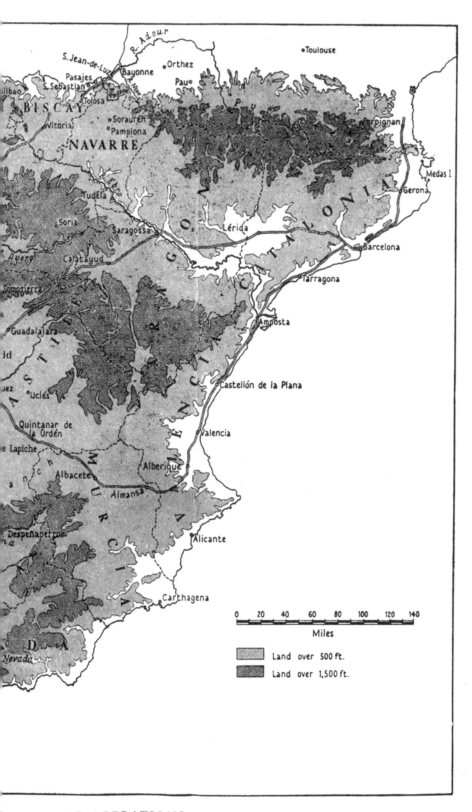